Real Estate Investing: A Complete Guide to Wealth-Building Secrets

Charles Klotsche

Prentice-Hall, Inc.
Englewood Cliffs, New Jersey

Prentice-Hall International, Inc., *London*
Prentice-Hall of Australia, Pty. Ltd., *Sydney*
Prentice-Hall of Canada, Ltd., *Toronto*
Prentice-Hall of India Private Ltd., *New Delhi*
Prentice-Hall of Japan, Inc., *Tokyo*
Prentice-Hall of Southeast Asia Pte. Ltd., *Singapore*
Whitehall Books, Ltd., *Wellington, New Zealand*

Library of Congress Cataloging in Publication Data

Klotsche, Charles
  Real estate investing.

  Includes index.
  1. Real estate investment.   I. Title.
HD1382.5.K57   332.63'24   81-19245
0-13-762948-6   AACR2

Printed in the United States of America

Dedication

To the entrepreneurs of this world, who so often discover what is worthwhile pursuing, inspiring others to join in the pursuit ... and in the process perpetuate the tradition of free enterprise. For two of the most generous masters of this fine art, Roberta and J.M. Klotsche, my special thanks.

Introduction

Why This Book Was Written

Thirty million people or 15% of the population in the United States relocate annually, creating a wide range of opportunities for the knowledgeable and aggressive real estate professional. It is also a fact that an individual can acquire money-making properties that few major corporations have the time, inclination, or flexibility to recognize and profit from. This book has been written in order to expand on these concepts, stressing the successful investment strategies I have developed and implemented over the years. These carefully tested strategies will cover the entire spectrum of real estate acquisition, syndication and development.

Proven Methods for Acquisition and Development

With this book you will profit from the interrelationships that enable many professionals to pyramid small amounts of equity into sizable fortunes. Most of us realize that real estate requires more knowledge, skill and judgment to achieve success than many other investment fields, and this book will be your guide to developing, pricing, acquiring, financing, and syndicating a multitude of worthwhile ventures.

I will provide proof that *no* other investment vehicle commands a higher loan to value ratio than real estate. You will be given time-tested methods that will show you how to control sizable assets, utilizing little *if any* of your own money—and how to develop a strategy to financially leverage these assets so they will appreciate at an inflationary rate equal to or *exceeding* the costs of holding them.

"How To" Techniques Found in This Book

With this book you will be able to master all the major factors involved in sophisticated real estate analysis and deal effectively with the important demands and requirements of the acquisition and development process. This book presents the total picture on why real estate is the soundest and most lucrative investment vehicle today. (This is even more relevant since President Reagan's Tax Act of 1981.) These concepts will be supported by over 100 case histories and actual examples. To illustrate, this book will show you:

- How to determine the maximum upside potential on *any* investment property.
- How to utilize the proven techniques for pyramiding and leveraging to infinity.
- How to obtain a lender's maximum commitment on all major categories of investment properties.
- How to quickly and successfully raise equity funds through limited partnerships.
- When to profitably dispose of a property after the tax sheltered benefits have diminished.
- How to analyze risk, values and management capabilities on *all* major investment properties.
- How to master the development process; interrelationships between architects, contractors, brokers and lenders.
- How to determine and apply the most favorable tax angles, including many found in the 1981 Tax Act.
- How to structure a quick return on your equity by principally utilizing other people's money.

Formulas for Successful Investment

This book will show you how population shifts relate to predictable purchasing power and changing property values, and through proper analysis and leverage how property values can readily be increased by hundreds of thousands of dollars. You will establish yourself as an expert knowing that every project, for example, reverts in some way to square footage analysis, as every apartment building or office complex has a predictable square-foot rental, and all shopping centers have a certain calculable retail sales volume per square foot. Almost all raw land is purchased in acres and subdivided and resold on a per-square-foot basis. Included in this book are proven methods for understanding the comparative analysis process, enabling you to categorize rent and expense figures into appropriate units, demonstrating to you how to arrive at a realistic value by balancing the cash returns against the potential risk and burdensome management factors.

This book will show you extraordinary opportunities (many will exceed your most optimistic imagination) to explore alternative strategies for negotiating and securing investment real estate. We will probe the changing concepts and lucrative alternatives that are separating the mediocre investors from the truly successful new breed of real estate entrepreneurs, who in many instances achieve as much as a 500% annual return on their investments.

Proven Strategies and Practical Examples

This book will enable you to successfully compete, where you will be able to select from a multitude of practical experiences, in order to fully understand the entire acquisition and development process. I will provide over 100 convincing examples, all drawn from my professional career. Here are just a few:

- An example of how a subordinated land lease combined with a deferred payment schedule required *no equity* on a $5,000,000 condominium project.

- An example of a 576-unit apartment complex purchased out of bankruptcy by syndicating 25 limited partners with $20,000 each to invest, showing an eventual profit of $2,300,000 for an overall return on equity of 750%.

- An example of acquiring and subdividing raw acreage where the owner's subordination, combined with leveraged bank financing, required *no equity* on a 32-lot $1,500,000 subdivision.

- An example of acquiring a distressed 50-unit condominium project; how it was located and purchased for 30¢ on the dollar, requiring no equity, and resulting in a $550,000 profit in 9 months.

- An example of developing two major office complexes where the accurate prediction of income and operating expenses combined with subordinated ground leases achieved 110% financing on this $2,500,000 complex.

Many of these examples involve sizable projects; however, the concepts can be scaled down and applied to any type of real estate investment.

How This Book is Organized

This book is arranged in a fashion that will help you logically progress through the analysis and acquisition process. Collectively, the 16 chapters serve as a complete guide for the lucrative acquisition and development of any investment real estate property. They provide an invaluable overview of the real estate industry. Each chapter assists you in developing a sharp focus on every relevant method of evaluating the major categories of real property.

The first two chapters on techniques of investment analysis provide you with the most updated and proven methods of valuing investment real estate. Chapters 3 and 4 detail the interrelationship between leverage and tax-deferred benefits, providing an important insight into the intricate ramifications to you as an investor. Chapter 5 outlines the proven techniques for raising equity. Chapter 6 details successful methods for understanding the development and construction process. Chapters 7 through 9 show you how to profitably acquire, develop or convert apartment buildings and condominiums. Chapters 10 through 13 provide the *proven* formulas that I have used, supported by relevant case studies, to successfully acquire, manage and resell raw land, shopping centers, office, commercial and industrial complexes. Chapters 14 and 15 detail the special benefits found in distressed properties, resort developments and time-shared ventures. The final chapter provides a sophisticated game plan of the lucrative trends and properties to be capitalized on in the 1980's.

Who Will Profit from This Book

Real property is a resource whose success ultimately depends on the ingenuity of the entrepreneur. This book will enable you to capitalize on a multitude of local and regional trends and spot growth patterns and fully comprehend the ramifications of the timing, management and financing that are so vital to surviving in this rapidly changing and rewarding industry. By understanding these successfully proven formulas, you will readily adjust, as I have done, to any regional or local market providing rewarding and exciting opportunities.

This book will help you to logically understand and project the future streams of income on rental properties, permitting you to apply the appropriate amount of financial leverage. Real estate with its potential for high percentage debt financing to value, provides the ultimate hedge against inflation as today's debt is repaid with tomorrow's worthless dollars.

These winning analytical formulas and successful methods of acquisition have worked for me, and these concepts when properly applied, will enable you to become the prime beneficiary from the upward-spiraling values of real estate. This book will be on the desk of every successful real estate developer, broker, counselor, investor, architect, planner, syndicator, and all those involved in the creative process of construction, syndication, selling, management and financing of investment real estate.

Charles Klotsche

Acknowledgments

Editing: *Ms. Joan M. Krager*
              Omaha, Nebraska

Graphics: *Mr. Ralph Johnson*
              Albuquerque, New Mexico

Manuscript: *Ms. Virginia Cox*
              Santa Fe, New Mexico

Contents

Chapter 5 Limited Partnerships: A Simple Vehicle for Raising Equity Capital 99

Chapter 6 Understanding the Development Process 117

Chapter 7 Dollars and Sense of Apartment Investments 137

Chapter 8 Lucrative Opportunities in Residential Condominiums   157

Chapter 9 Cashing in on Apartment Conversions   177

Chapter 10 Successful Techniques of Land Acquisition and Development 195

Chapter 11 Building Equity Through Shopping Center Developments 215

Chapter 15 Creating Quick Value In Resort Developments And Time-Sharing Markets   287

Chapter 16 An Overview for Investment Real Estate In the 1980's   309

1

Proven Techniques Of Investment Analysis

The first six chapters of this book will provide you with the most updated and proven techniques of investment analysis, syndication, acquisition and development techniques in all major areas of commercial and residential real estate ventures. This chapter will outline, step by step, the important interrelationships for evaluating, leveraging, predicting income and expenses, and preserving income and profits through major tax vehicles that will enable you to pyramid sizable fortunes in relatively short periods of time.

The various types of real estate investments often display considerable differences. This chapter stresses the proven methods of comparative analysis which accurately separate rental income and expense figures into the appropriate units for the various categories of real estate investments, permitting you to arrive at realistic values by balancing the cash returns against the potential risk and management factors.

Today's new breed of successful real estate entrepreneurs realizes that the often changing rules and formulas of investment analysis are valid only insofar as they take into account the exceptions, which are detailed both in number and complexity. You will learn many of them here and, even more important, you will learn how to apply the many rules of thumb to specific local and temporal conditions.

This chapter will demonstrate to you how consistency of income is based upon the unfulfilled demands in the marketplace and how the stability and long-term profitability is totally contingent upon proper investment analysis. Some of the terms advanced in these chapters might not be completely familiar to you, and a brief explanation is offered in the Glossary for the more complicated ones.

The Importance of Anticipating the Market

In determining the cash flow from any given real estate investment, one must correctly analyze both the rental income and the operating expenses. A true picture of the anticipated gross income for the entire holding period of an asset is the key factor in the analysis, since an initial small error in determining the rental income will have large ramifications when you eventually get to the bottom line. Consistency of income must be projected based on the unfulfilled rental demands in the marketplace. Potential increase in rentals will depend on the flexibility and stability of the project and the creativity of its management. For instance, two of the most common mistakes found in managing apartment complexes are to underestimate expenses and to incorporate a vacancy factor that is unrealistic for the area which does not allow for wide seasonal fluctuations, such as found near universities or resorts. I have seen several instances where the owners of large complexes were not successful in either passing through the additional cost of the utilities or absorbing large seasonal vacancies. Eventually, the entire cash flow from these projects was consumed by these analytical deficiencies.

Analyzing the Key Factors in Real Estate Acquisition and Development

When you develop or acquire investment real estate, you must emphasize in your analysis the areas that will most affect your gross income. For instance, the key factors in a shopping center are the retail traffic generated within the marketing area and the potential sales per square foot of occupied space in that location, since rental increases based on sales volume are built into most leases. Office complexes must be looked at in relation to the demand for professional services in close proximity to the area or within commuting distance of it. Apartments must be analyzed for conveniences and amenities provided to potential tenants after a careful demographic study of the population of the area. The less predictable the income for any given project, the higher the yield the project will have to command. This is especially true of single-purpose structures such as hotels, theaters and restaurants in which high fixed operating expenses limit the viability to a given type of commercial occupancy.

Over the years I have, on many occasions, acted as broker for free-standing, fast food franchise buildings. These are extremely risky investments as the shell, and especially the interior improvements and equipment, are so single-purposed that if the market absorption doesn't materialize or excessive competition surfaces, the prospects for rerenting at comparable rates are extremely difficult. This is also true for convenient mini-supermarket operations.

High yields should also be prevalent in low-income housing developments with unstable tenancy. In such situations, the strength of the occupants' leases and the demand for the services they desire are obviously critical factors that can change over relatively short periods of time.

The object of analysis of any income-producing property is to determine the true long-term "economic rent" as opposed to the shorter run "contract rent" and to assess the potential for improving the economic rent and the long-term desirability of the project over a period of potential diminished occupancy. Most operating statements provided by owners or real estate brokers are either pro forma or optimistically promotional. Only a document provided by a certified public accountant extending back three to five years can reflect the income and operating expenses accurately.

How to Avoid Manipulated Financial Statements

Cash accounting—actual receipt and disbursement only— cannot be attested to by a certified public accountant and is subject to misleading manipulation, especially at year end. Owners can distort financial statements by ballooning rents and deferring expenses; as on the cash basis, only what is coming in and going out can be recorded. Maintenance costs, anticipated tax and utility increases, and normal capital replacement obligations can be deferred into another calendar year. Income figures are particularly subject to distortion at various advantageous times of the year, especially where percentage-of-gross-income leases are prevalent.

A cash-accounted project is particularly suspect if the seller has been attempting to dispose of the property for some time. In such a situation an intelligent purchaser should ask to see the seller's filed federal tax returns on the investment for the previous five years of operation. No sensible businessman overestimates his income and underestimates his expenses in reporting taxable income to the Internal Revenue Service. However, a clever owner, especially if he is anticipating a sale, will commingle many properties in the same statement in order to disguise what income and expenses relate to that particular investment holding.

Understanding the Predictable Operating Expenses

Operating expenses can vary from zero, where the leases are structured in such a fashion that the tenants pay all the current operating expenses and contractually agree to absorb all future increases, to extremes such as found in prestigious office complexes, where daily janitorial services, secretarial services, and even telephone answering is provided. In some cases these expenses can be upwards of 40% of the gross income.

I have from time to time owned office complexes that incorporated executive suites. In one particular building I offered a complete package, including telephone answering, secretarial, telex, and duplicating services. In this complex with about twenty tenants, the expenses were 45% of the gross income; however, this was not an alarming figure, as the services offered were very much in demand and could easily be absorbed by the tenants.

High expense ratios must be analyzed for their realism in the current marketplace and for the feasibility of passing along the unforeseen increases to the tenants through rent escalation clauses, in order to stabilize the operating income after expenses over the economic life of the structure. The expenses that can normally be predicted with a high degree of certainty are:

- taxes
- insurance
- maintenance
- utilities
- janitorial services
- parking assessments

The attentive owner usually passes these direct costs on to the tenants in the form of rent escalation clauses calculated through or tied to various government cost-of-living indexes, or by annual increases through a prorated calculation of the operating expenses. I have successfully used both methods, and in several of my office complexes I am currently using a combination of cost-of-living and direct pass-through prorations. The more sophisticated tenants in these structures usually adjust only for actual out-of-pocket expense increases. The real moneymakers in these particular buildings are the occupants who are tied to actual cost-of-living. Since the utilities are prorated separately and passed on directly to the tenants, the annual cost-of-living increase goes right down to the bottom line in terms of income, making these leases extremely lucrative during inflationary periods.

Normal operating statements also contain reserves for replacement of such major items as heating and air conditioning units, water heaters, roofs, window coverings, furniture and appliances, since eventual replacement involves a large immediate capital expenditure, which should be budgeted for and escrowed in advance.

The Importance of the Appraisal Process

Even though the value of any given income property depends upon many factors outside the scope of an appraisal done under current market conditions, the need for one generally arises at some point in the development or acquisition process. A qualified independent appraiser can often add assurance of objectivity of the local situation. Most of these individuals balance the replacement cost, the area's comparative sales, and the capitalized income methods in order to arrive at an equitable value. In spite of this, one must remember that an appraisal is only one opinion of the current market value *without* concern for:

- the financing techniques involved,
- the tax bracket of the investor,
- the future yield in the marketplace after holding the asset, and
- the creative management abilities required of the potential owner.

An appraisal is of little merit to the more sophisticated investor, except as it relates to first-mortgage financing. Capitalization rates on income assigned to appraisals are normally capricious in that they do not take the tax bracket of the purchaser into consideration, nor do they attempt to reflect any creative or unusual leverage.

To the extent that they generally establish replacement value for a given property, appraisals can be beneficial. I rely almost exclusively on them when it comes to selling residential projects. I recently received a considerably higher appraisal on a 50-unit $2,500,000 condominium project that I developed, having had the initial appraisal done prior to construction and an updated one after the units were completed. It is extremely important to update appraisals, as the market is ever changing, and in certain areas, particularly the residential sector, moving upward very rapidly. In this particular condominium project, the reappraisals were approximately 10% or $5,000 per unit higher when the project was ready to be marketed.

Well-documented and creative appraisals can have an astronomical effect on selling prices of investment real estate. In one particular office complex I owned, the appraisal reflected the potential future rental increases projected over the remaining economic life of the structure, which were then discounted back to represent their present value. The current leases were low in relation to the existing market rents, and this technique raised the value of the property well over $100,000.

Determining the maximum amount required to duplicate an existing structure by having an appraisal also sets a ceiling on its value. The more important requirement for successful investment— the stabilized income stream as reflected in the value of the leases— can often exceed the replacement value of an investment property. Obviously, the replacement cost approach to real estate valuation has more validity in the residential than in the commercial sector.

The Implication of Income Capitalization Rates and Stabilized Cash Flow

Having established the true economic rent on a project and anticipated operating expenses as accurately as possible, you then reduce the income by the actual or estimated operating expenses in order to determine the amount of income the project will generate before debt service, depreciation, and other tax-related factors. In other words, your next step is to project the cash flow and the appropriate or corresponding value of the property free and clear of any mortgage encumbrances, since this is the basis on which you, the owner, your lending institution, and the marketplace will capitalize the value of your investment. Anticipating this, you can quite accurately predetermine the financial leverage you will obtain from a lending institution, a concept that we will discuss later.

Establishing the capitalization rate (the easiest approach to valuation and arriving at an equitable yield on a given project) can be approached simply by figuring the value of a given investment property based upon the average or comparable yield found in the marketplace for a similar property. The reciprocal of the desired yield, or that yield divided by 100, is what is known as the "capitalization rate." This capitalization rate, or the reciprocal of the yield, should be multiplied by the annual income generated from the project after deducting operating expenses to arrive at a fair market value on which the appropriate debt service can be structured. In other words, if you as an investor wish to receive a 12% return on a property, after operating expenses but before debt service, you divide 12 into 100 to obtain the capitalization rate of 8.83. If the property has an annual cash flow of $100,000 after operating expenses, you multiply the cash flow by 8.83, which places a value of $883,000 on the free and clear property, before you structure the debt service. Said differently, an investment with a $100,000 cash flow that must command a 12% return in the marketplace will have a fair market value of $883,000. I have seen yields drop considerably in the last four or five years, creating astronomical values on properties that I or my associates have acquired. This is especially prevalent in quality shopping centers, apartments, and office buildings, as foreign money is currently attracted to these large prestigious complexes.

If you intend to place a high degree of leverage on your investment, your capitalization rate and yield will be governed by the amount of that financing. For instance, if a project is carrying a 10.5%, 25-year first mortgage, the overall yield on that portion of the project that is leveraged will have to be approximately 3/4 of 1 percentage point over the 10.5% simple interest in order to fully amortize the interest and principal of that mortgage. Obviously, the larger the equity yield or spread in relation to the fixed mortgage obligation, the more lucrative and potentially leveraged your transaction becomes.

How to Structure a Lender's Presentation

I recently took an office complex package to a lender and we discussed capitalization rates, among other things. The lender was impressed by the fact that I had not only totally analyzed the free and clear return on the property, which is in effect his protection for his first mortgage, but that I had also thought out the return on equity and the debt service coverage ratios. In this way, the cash flow not only provided an ample cushion for me as the investor, but also reassured the lender of the stability of his first mortgage position. I was successful in obtaining a $1,200,000 first mortgage on my building within a matter of weeks after the presentation. A recapitulation of that presentation follows.

CHART 1-1

PRO FORMA

Lessee	Annual Term	*SFNRA	% Area	*Rate Per SFNRA	Annual Rate
Tenant #1	3	20,650	81.6%	$ 9.71	$200,508
Tenant #2	5	3,819	15.0%	8.00	30,552
Tenant #3	5	850	3.4%	9.75	8,288
Gross Rental Income		25,319			$239,348
Vacancy & Collection Loss @ 4%					9,574
Adjusted Gross Income					229,774
Other Income: Parking 128 spaces @ $6.90/month					10,598
Total Effective Gross Income					$240,372

Expenses:		*$/SFNRA
Management	$ 5,150	$ .203
Maintenance	3,300	.130
Janitor	8,800	.348
Utilities	4,669	.184
Insurance	1,121	.044
Operating Expenses	$23,040	$ .910
Real Estate Taxes	6,000	.237
Total Adjusted Expenses	$29,040	$ 1.15
Parking Lease	13,662	
Total Expense	$42,702	

Net Operating Income $197,670

CAPITALIZATION

Assumptions:	Mortgage	75%
	Interest Rate	12.5%
	Term	30 years
	Mortgage Constant	.12807
	Equity Dividend	9%

An equity dividend rate of 9% before depreciation and debt service is sufficient to attract equity capital for the subject development. Financing at the term and rate noted are readily available in the current commercial mortgage market.

Mortgage Equity Band of Investment:

	Value Ratio	Applicable Rate		Weighted Average
Mortgage Component	(.75)	(.12807)	=	.0961
Equity Component	(.25)	(.09)	=	.0225
Property	1.00 Overall Rate		=	.1185
			Called:	.119

Valuation:

Stabilized Net Income	$\dfrac{\$197,670}{.119}$ = $1,661,092	
Overall Rate		
Value via income capitalization approach	$1,660,000	

*SFNRA = Square foot net rentable area

How Depreciation Affects Yield and Eventual Capital Gains on Investments

As an example of the full effect of cash flow, physical appreciation and/or depreciation, and accounting depreciation, let us analyze a hypothetical situation in which a property is purchased for $125,000 and sold ten years later for $150,000.

$125,000 = purchase price
 −25,000 = cash equity of purchaser
$100,000 = first-mortgage loan
 − 20,000 = loan reduction at the time of sale
$ 80,000 = outstanding loan balance at time of sale
$150,000 = sale price at end of ten years
 − 80,000 = loan balance at end of ten years
$ 70,000 = cash proceeds from sale after repayment of loan.

During the ten-year term of ownership, our investor used the straight-line method of depreciation, allowing a 15-year useful life permitted under the Economic Recovery Tax Act of 1981:

15 years = 100% depreciation
1 year = 6.67% depreciation
10 years = 67% depreciation

From the purchase price of $125,000, $25,000 was allocated to land value, which is not a depreciable asset by Internal Revenue Service standards:

$125,000 purchase price
 - 25,000 land value

$100,000 total depreciable value
 × 6.67% total depreciation

$ 6,667 × 10 years = $66,667 total depreciation

No accelerated depreciation was used, and the depreciated book value at time of sale was:

$125,000 purchase price
  -66,667 total depreciation

or $ 58,333 depreciated book value

The Effect of Cash Flow and Leverage on Yield

The average annual cash flow generated from this hypothetical investment after operating expenses was $15,000, which represents a 12% cash return on the sales price of $125,000. However, from this must be deducted the cost of financially carrying the property. Let's assume that over 25 years the mortgage interest rate averaged 9.75% on the outstanding loan balance, showing a constant total interest and amortization factor of approximately 10.5%. This constant factor, readily available in most investment real estate tables, combines the simple interest rate and the additional amount of money necessary to fully amortize the principal on the mortgage over the 25-year period. The longer the mortgage is held, the larger percentage of funds is applied to the reduction of principal. I personally attempt to obtain at least a 75% to 80% loan-to-value ratio on any income property I develop or acquire. This is normally accomplished through new financing or a combination of existing owner-carried mortgages and short-term bank notes. Without this leverage and offsetting deductions for interest and depreciation, my project yields would not be adequate. Suffice it to say that in our example, during the first year, $9,500 applied toward interest, and in the remaining years the average interest payment was $8,500 per year. In the first year, mortgage amortization was about 1%, but the average over ten years was 2% of the total value of the initial mortgage of $100,000, or approximately $2,000 per year.

Remembering that we are dealing with averages and percentiles precisely calculated and best derived from professionally prepared tables, we subtract a debt service constant of 10.5%, or

$10,500, from the income after expenses, and find that the cash return on our investor's equity averaged $4,500 per year. We can itemize this as follows, again depending upon the mortgage tables for precise sums:

$ 15,000 annual income after operating expenses
×   10 years

$150,000 total income over ten years
−85,000 mortgage interest, ten-year average

$ 65,000
−20,000 mortgage amortization, ten-year average

$ 45,000 total cash return on equity ÷ 10 years =
       $4,500 net annual return after debt service.

Our investor's equity was $25,000, which we divide into the annual cash return of $4,500:

$$\frac{\$ 4,500}{\$25,000} = 18\% \text{ cash return on equity}$$

How to Analyze Yield to Include Potential Appreciation

Next we must build in a "reversionary factor" representing the difference between the purchase and sales prices:

$150,000 sales price after 10 years of holding
−125,000 initial cost of acquisition

$ 25,000 total gain or appreciation over 10-year holding
       period ÷ 10 years = $2,500 annual appreciation.

We then add the annual cash return to the annual gain through appreciation:

$4,500 annual cash return
 2,500 annual gain through appreciation
$7,000 total annual benefits.

We divide this figure by the original equity:

$$\frac{\$ 7,000}{\$25,000} = 28\% \text{ yield reflecting the effects of the reversionary factor.}$$

By any investment standard, 28% is an attractive return. Achieving it is possible when you can predict with any degree of certainty the projected income and the appreciation or the reversionary effect. This concept is not difficult for a potential investor to understand, especially in an inflationary period when the cost of replacing current real estate assets is spiraling.

The replacement value of a property normally strikes a kind of middle ground between its "economic" value and its "book" value, the latter being determined by depreciation allowances taken during the period of holding. The book value is artificially low by comparison with either the economic or the replacement value; the replacement value can be high in terms of inflated dollars, but low in terms of income or consumer demand. The attraction of stories about the Gold Rush lies in the exaggerated discrepancy between the simple human needs and the supporting facilities to accommodate them. But we are straying off the subject of depreciation, which has more exciting and complex ramifications in the analysis of your financial objectives.

The Positive Effect of Depreciation and Equity Buildup Upon Yield

We previously discussed the 6.67% yearly depreciation allowance taken on the $100,000 asset, or $6,667 per year. This sum is allowable annually to offset the cash flow before debt service of $15,000 derived by the owner of our hypothetical property. The depreciation deduction is recognized as a tax liability only when the property is sold. It is then considered a long-term capital gain and taxed at a more favorable rate. In other words, you, as the owner of a property, have the offsetting use of funds, in this case an annual allowance of $6,667 per year for depreciation, on which the tax is deferred and ultimately reduced to a rate far less than you would pay on ordinary income.

I, like many other investors, balance my investment portfolio with a combination of cash-flow and tax-sheltered investments. In many of my cash-generating projects, such as condominium ventures and land subdivisions, I shelter the income with office complexes or other investment-oriented real property. This is not difficult to achieve if you acquire or develop a few selected, well-thought-out projects each year.

With a cash flow after debt service of $4,500 a year, the $6,667 annual depreciation deduction completely shelters our hypothetical project's cash flow from any immediate tax liability, while the equity buildup on the first mortgage is an additional $2,000 per year, averaged over the ten-year holding period. Under an accelerated schedule of depreciation, the deductions could be potentially increased up to $10,000 per year to shelter both the cash flow and the full principal amortization of the first mortgage, and provide shelter for other income as well.

To return to the more conservative straight-line method of depreciation currently applicable to the majority of real estate investments, let us assume that our investor is in a 50% individual tax bracket. He receives $6,667 worth of income from his project with no immediate tax consequences or has, in effect, an after-tax saving of $3,333 per year. The tax-deferred income that he receives has the following effect on his return from the project:

$ 4,500 cash income per year from the project

2,000 annual mortgage amortization (equity buildup)

2,500 annual gain on the sale of the asset
    (25,000 ÷ 10 years)

3,333 annual after-tax benefits from depreciation

$12,333 total yearly economic benefits derived from the
        project.

If we divide the $25,000 equity investment into the $12,333 in annual benefits, we find that the project shows an annual return of 49%.

$$\frac{\$12,333}{\$25,000} = 49\% \text{ return on equity.}$$

I have found on projects I have owned or developed with leveraged mortgages of approximately 75%, that appreciation adds a minimum of 10% to the return on equity per year. The norm is closer to 15% or 20%, especially on office buildings and apartment complexes.

Eliminating Capital Gains Taxes on Your Investment

We have been playing with percentages, admittedly, but herein lies the challenge of the analytical process. The day of reckoning comes with the sale of the asset, as a substantial portion of the return on our equity calculations above is based on the increased value of the project plus the decreased outstanding balance on the first mortgage. Even then, postponement of your taxes is possible if the project is restructured and refinanced. As an example, I have acquired sizable equities in properties I have owned over the years because of the increased cash flow generated by the inflationary process. Instead of selling many of these properties in order to retrieve my equity, I have refinanced them, and, in many cases, taken part of my equity out tax-free due to the large amount of leverage achieved on the refinancing.

An investor may decide to refinance rather than sell our hypothetical property at the end of ten years. If he is fortunate enough to obtain a 75% loan to value (and for this purpose we will consider the $150,000 sales price as the appraised value), he will be in a position to obtain a mortgage of $112,500. At the end of ten years, you will recall, the first mortgage is reduced to $80,000. Subtracting this from the amount of the new or refinanced mortgage leaves him with the sum of $32,500 tax-free after he pays off the existing mortgage.

> $112,500 refinanced mortgage amount
> $\underline{-80,000}$ old mortgage balance
> $ 32,500

The only disadvantage to this approach is that you cannot start a new depreciation schedule at the higher appraised value. Even though you refinance, depreciation continues on the basis of the initial acquisition price. You obtain higher interest deductions, since they are greater in the initial years of the mortgage, and you increase the overall amount of your first-mortgage financing, pocketing the difference tax-free.

Calculating the Depreciated Book Value and Capital Gains Obligations

To complete the financial analysis, let's pursue the tax effects of the sale as they affect the overall yield on our investor's equity. We start with the $150,000 sales price of the asset at the end of the ten-year holding period in order to arrive at the tax obligation incurred by the sale. From the original purchase price, we deduct the 6.67% depreciation per year for the ten-year holding:

> $125,000 original purchase price
> $\underline{-66,667}$ depreciation deduction (6.67% of $100,000 per
>   year × 10 years)
> $ 58,333 depreciated book value.

From the sales price of $150,000 we subtract the $58,333 depreciated book value, leaving our investor with a long-term capital gain of $91,667. Since that long-term gain is taxed at 50%, $45,833 is declared taxable income by our investor at the time of the sale. Assuming that he is in the 50% individual tax bracket, he will have a federal taxable obligation of $22,916 at the time he disposes of the property. For purposes of presentation we will not include our investor's obligation for state taxes.

Calculating the Capital Gains Tax

If we analyze this $22,916 federal tax over the ten-year holding period of the asset, the capital gain would amount to $2,291 per year. This federal income tax must be incorporated into the calculations, reducing our overall yield:

$ 4,500 annual cash flow
 2,500 annual gain on the sale of the asset
 2,000 annual amortization of the first mortgage
                                    (equity buildup)
 3,333 annual tax benefits from depreciation
$12,333 total annual benefits
 –2,291 annual tax liability for capital gains upon sale
$10,042 total annual economic benefits

The total annual economic benefits are now $10,042 with future capital gains taxes deducted, as compared to the initial $25,000 equity investment, showing an approximate return of 40% per year.

$$\frac{\$10,042}{\$25,000} = 40\% \text{ return on equity.}$$

If our investor had struck a market boom, which many of us have lately, and realized an even greater resale profit on this investment, he would have had a further cushion of protection under a new ceiling on capital gains tax established in 1981. Regardless of your tax bracket, now a maximum of 50%, you would have had to pay federal capital gains tax on no more than 20% of the total profit from this particular investment.

The eventual value of a given investment is subject to two conditions, the resale market and the tax situation of the individual investor. As we mentioned previously, even a qualified appraiser has no knowledge of the latter, and the position of the investor on the tax ladder also explains the assertion that each participant in any real estate venture can have a different objective in selecting that investment. In deciding whether to sell or hold property, you must analyze not only the market, but also your individual tax situation.

Timing of the Resale: Its Effect on Cash Flow and Declining Writeoffs

The propitious moment for resale depends upon how the depreciation schedules are structured, combined with the long-term predictability of a project's income. It is normally safe to generalize that the income from a properly leveraged project is almost completely tax-sheltered for the first seven to ten years. After that, interest deductions decrease and mortgage amortization, which is not tax-deductible, increases. Of all the properties I have owned, very few have exhausted their depreciation benefits before the sixth or seventh year. This is especially true after enactment of the Tax Recovery Act of 1981. Since then I have established a policy of utilizing the most conservative method of depreciation on most of my investments to avoid the stiff recapture provisions of that legislation. A more detailed discussion of this act appears in Chapter 4. The one exception was a 181-space mobile home park where many of the deductions were taken in the first two years. This, combined with a nondepreciable high land cost and the fact that many of the utility systems were deeded to the appropriate utility companies, exhausted the depreciable base quite rapidly.

If you decide to retain a property after depreciation, and interest deductions no longer shelter the full income generated from it, appreciation and mortgage amortization will have to increase considerably faster than they did early in the life of the investment in order to permit you to retain a comparable yield due to the declining tax benefits. While amortization tables will show a larger equity buildup during the latter part of the holding period of the investment, appreciation is considerably more difficult to analyze or achieve. Rents can normally not be raised as expeditiously on older properties as they can on newer ones, and aging properties require larger maintenance, operating expenses, and greater reserves for capital improvements.

How to Analyze Yield to Include Present-Value Techniques

The most sophisticated of calculations in real estate investments is determining the present value of all cash and related benefits flowing into a project. In real estate, income generated early in the life of an investment is tax-deferred until the end of the holding period, at which time a long-term capital gains tax is normally paid on the difference between the depreciated book value and the proceeds of the sale. The project's cash flow, in many cases entirely tax-free during the holding period of the investment, can be analyzed and these tax-deferred benefits can be incorporated into the effective yield generated by the investment. This is called the "present value theory," or "internal rate of return." In addition to the yield on a project's cash flow, this approach calculates both the method and amount of depreciation, the individual's tax bracket, and the appropriate amortization reduction on the debt service encumbrances.

I do an internal rate of return presentation on all properties I am either acquiring or selling, and I recently completed a presentation on a $3,000,000 office complex which I owned and offered for sale. By utilizing internal rate of return and projecting this into a hypothetical buyer's 50% tax bracket, I increased the overall yield on this particular office complex by 6%. The general parameters of the presentation included:

- projected inflationary rents and income,
- projected rates of appreciation,
- creative tax benefits,
- long-term fixed mortgages rates, and
- refinancing or exchange provisions for deferring taxation.

What one is accomplishing through the internal rate of return method is calculating the effect of utilizing the government's money through established methods of tax deferral until eventual sale through the use of depreciation and a high degree of mortgage financing. The theory behind the internal rate of return is that money generally doubles in value every ten years at a compounded interest rate of 8%. If you as an investor have the use of these tax-free funds for a long period, the overall effect substantially increases your return on equity, as the value of the income stream in any given investment is based strictly on the time value of money. Using the

FIGURE 1-1

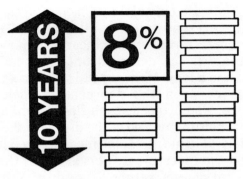

MONEY DOUBLES EVERY TEN YEARS
COMPOUNDED AT AN 8% INTEREST RATE.

deferred time value of money approach, an investor achieves an additional return by generating tax-free dollars, consequently raising the overall yield.

You as a sophisticated investor, using the present-value theory, can work backwards from the rate of return you wish to achieve in selecting a property for investment. By calculating the annual cash flow generated from an investment and the additional benefits you will receive after calculating all tax ramifications for your specific tax bracket, you thus can measure your investment in terms of present values.

How to Use the Payback Analysis Method

The payback analysis method is a less sophisticated approach than the present-value theory, in which the amount of risk and yield is calculated against the period of time it takes to repay your equity from the future income stream of an investment. In analyzing a return strictly on the amount of time it takes to repay your equity investment, you must also calculate the potential risk of any liability on a recourse mortgage. I use this method, for instance, when analyzing subdivisions, especially where outside investors are used. I structured this type of presentation on a 100-plus lot subdivision where the land contract payment was a non-recourse obligation, and it showed a very lucrative and quick return on equity to the investors in the project. In this projection the initial sales indicated a return of equity within 18 months, due to the highly leveraged owner financing and favorable release provisons. This was feasible even after considering the 6 to 8 month period of time required for construction of the improvements.

The weakness of the payback analysis method is that an investment in a development consists not only of an equity contribution, but also the additional amount of the total obligation, which includes a first-mortgage commitment. This factor should also be accounted for in your calculations.

Proven Methods of Deferring Taxation Through Installment Sales

However wholeheartedly you may explore the advantages of depreciation in your own particular tax situation, you should be interested in "book" or "accounting" depreciation only, more commonly referred to as the cost recovery system under the Economic Recovery Tax Act of 1981. This is another way of saying you anticipate that your investment holdings will appreciate in value. Not only can you deduct the artificial depreciation, but the corresponding appreciated value is taxed at the favorable rate appropriate to long-term capital gains. Modest as this tax may be, compared with the tax on ordinary income, it is less painful if accomplished in stages.

In the process of sale, real estate investors often join forces to seek leverage and deferred taxes through an installment sale. The seller agrees to take less than full sales price in the initial year of sale and receives the remainder of an agreed-upon sum over a predetermined installment period. If the period extends over ten years, for example, one can defer payment of his capital gains tax on the portion of the outstanding balance over that time frame. During the installment period, you can use the seller's capital at a rate normally lower than you could obtain through conventional institutional financing sources. The seller does, in effect, have the security of a first-mortgage lien against his own property, and any additional improvements to it would accrue to him if you, the purchaser, defaulted.

I recently purchased a subdivision on an installment sale. I paid the seller $25,000 down and agreed that principal and interest payments on the land would be made as each lot was sold, plus a percentage of the overall profits from the development. Since he was more interested in having a long-term contractual arrangement than he was in receiving all of his money up-front initially, and my intent was to structure an investment without any fixed timetable for payments, the transaction worked quite successfully for both parties.

How to Benefit from Tax-Free Exchanges and Annuities

Another method of deferring taxation is to set up an annuity among immediate family members or close associates, purchasing the property in the name of the annuitant and subsequently leasing the property back, channeling the rental income to the annuity holders in a lower tax bracket. Such an annuity arrangement need not be set up on a permanent basis, and can revert to you as the original grantor at a later date.

The most complicated and rewarding maneuver to delay the payment of capital gains tax is a tax-free exchange for a like property. This permits you to exchange or acquire tax-free an equity in another property that is usually larger than your original investment because of inflation and mortgage pyramiding, thus deferring any taxation until the eventual sale of the second or exchanged property. Through this means you can arrive at a new depreciable basis and be in a position to control a much larger asset with correspondingly greater deductions for interest and depreciation. Equities are seldom exactly alike in any tax-free exchange, as I am finding out in a recent exchange proposal that I received on an office complex involving a three-way trade. Under this arrangement, a third individual would exchange his $3,000,000 shopping center for my office complex, which I in turn would exchange for a $2,500,000 residential subdivision which I currently am in the process of developing, but have not paid for. In this case the equities are hundreds of thousands of dollars apart, and some portions of the three-way exchange will be taxable to the various parties. Whatever the complexities of this particular transaction, the only portion taxable to any of the parties on such an exchange is the decrease in mortgages or the imbalance of equities.

Determining the Optimum Yield

The optimum economic useful life of your project is determined by a blend of tax-sheltering components totally dependent upon your tax status, the commandable long-term rent increases, the projected escalation in operating expenses, and the reserves required for major capital improvements. These same factors are applicable whether the property was newly constructed or previously occupied at the time of purchase. Still another item contributes to the generalization concerning the seven- to ten-year maximum useful life, the probability that a short-range estimation of income, expenses, and potential appreciation on a real estate asset will be more accurate than a long-range estimate. A projection exceeding the ten years will probably not have much bearing on the income generated and the reversionary value unless you are speculating on the location of the development and the ability to re-lease at higher rental levels, rather than on the value of the structure itself.

More details on the intricacies of tax structure and the alternative loopholes real estate investment offers will be considered in the following chapters, as will the relationship between "financial leverage," a term we have loosely defined, and cash flow. Having painted the analytical picture early, we can explore together the alternative types of real estate investment possible to you the investor, the special talents necessary to manage them creatively, and many of the pitfalls peculiar to each.

Keeping a constant vigil over a project's real value—what it generates in cash flow and tax-balanced benefits—is the basic technique of the successful real estate investor. This is the yardstick to which you, the professional, will constantly return in determining the appropriate market value. Markets, in varying degrees, are fluid rather than static. What is available can be both exciting and overwhelming, as we will discuss in the next chapter. Only the investor who carefully sets his goals and closely monitors his own progress toward them can expect to weather the market's vagaries.

2

Determining
The Effective Yield
In the Marketplace

A country leveling off after a century of population boom must inevitably use more land, reassess beyond agrarian values, and revise land use to accommodate its shifting economic needs. While the basic needs for food and shelter are essentially unmodifiable, the means for providing them are subject to infinite economic variations. The rapid improvement of transportation and communication has provided industry with the fluidity to seek whatever advantages it can in labor markets. Where industry and society relocate, land values escalate.

This chapter will show you how imaginative investment in real estate eliminates speculation. Where you as an investor can anticipate changes in societal patterns, you can reap profits commensurate with the degrees of risk. You will be shown how predicting future values, timing their acquisition, and analyzing the potential risk and return will yield quick and exciting appreciation on most investment properties.

Systematically, we will outline for you how to analyze reproduction costs, judge comparable sales, and determine maximum and minimum income and expenses and break-even points that will guide you to the proven methods for arriving at the most profitable return on equity.

How Timing Affects the Investment Decision

We will mention the importance of economic cycles often in this book, and their relationship to success or lack thereof in real estate transactions. Basically, sound investment means acquiring during the downward cycles and marketing during the upswings. When markets are oversaturated or purchasing power is on the decline, even the best developments can fail.

I recently acquired a condominium project during the early phases of an upward economic cycle. Priced in the high $50,000's for purchasers with moderate incomes, the units had no particularly redeeming features except that many of them offered spectacular views. Due to the overall lack of demand for financing at that time, I was able to obtain a long-term commitment for all fifty units, which permitted me to sell out this $2,500,000 project in a relatively short time. Had I acquired this investment at a different and less desirable time in the economic cycle, or had I attempted to obtain financing in a highly competitive market, the sales picture could have been quite different, and the lack of distinguishing features connected with this project could have been detrimental.

This development, typical of many successful real estate investments, involved a one-time initial investigation to determine the appropriate timing of the acquisition.

How to Maintain a Successful Real Estate Portfolio

Accumulating a successful real estate investment portfolio consists of more than a series of properties involving one-time acquisition decisions. To maintain the value one creates and retains in a successful real estate portfolio requires a constant review of the changing elements in the marketplace. Adversely affecting long-term stabilized values are such factors as:

- large increases in operating expenses;
- depressing economic trends;
- rapidly accelerating property taxes;
- loss of the individual's purchasing power;
- sudden shifts or movements of population.

The benefits achieved through leverage must constantly be monitored in relation to the overall yield on your investment. A decline may indicate that your capital could be used to better advantage in some other form of real estate investment.

I was recently presented an attractive offer to purchase two major office complexes that I developed and own. Close analysis confirmed the competitiveness of the yield and the offering price. Closer evaluation also revealed other problems. My depreciated basis in the property was lower than the $2,000,000 mortgage, and my taxable obligation upon sale was so enormous that I would have suffered a major erosion of my capital if I had entered into a sale. This basic after-tax problem is what makes it so difficult to maintain a balanced portfolio by replacing older investments in areas of rapid appreciation.

Determining Your Investment Objectives

The first chapter concentrated on the theoretical aspects of real estate analysis. In this section we will relate investment decisions and objectives to the practical side of the marketplace from which you must operate. Basic to understanding this aspect is the variation found in the investment objectives of different individuals. Not every property is ideally suited to your investment goals. A younger person with the knowledge, energy, and desire to manage highly leveraged investments may be relatively unconcerned with the immediate cash flow because his near-term objectives might be to pyramid capital. On the other hand, older investors are normally more interested in cash flow, somewhat sheltered by depreciation, attained through properties that require less risk, time, and attention.

I attempt to diversify my real estate investment portfolio. Through condominium projects and land subdivisions I achieve the necessary cash flow. By acquiring or developing tax-sheltered properties I protect a good portion of my income from taxation, and in some years all of it. A combination of tax-sheltered vehicles and cash-generating ventures is an ideal way to build equity and retain those earnings tax-free.

What all real estate investors have in common is the desire to protect and increase their capital through the inflationary process. Over the years, real estate has shown such rapid appreciation that this benefit far outweighs the lack of liquidity and risk associated with real estate acquisition and development.

How Real Estate Compares to Other Investments

In the stock market, tens of millions of shares of stock are traded each day, often involving hundreds of thousands of shares in the same corporation. These shares are liquid, with established prices quoted on an exchange. Real estate of investment calibre lacks this fluidity. No simple formula exists by which the market price for an individual property can be established, as each holding is different.

Real estate involves a higher degree of risk than is entailed, for example, in investing in New York Stock Exchange high-grade corporate bonds. Because of this, real estate can command higher returns commensurate with the degrees of risk. I find in my real estate dealings that I can become involved in one or possibly two major real estate ventures a year and live quite comfortably on the proceeds. I often look at 40 to 50 separate proposals before I can structure an opportune situation. I don't believe that a person investing, say, in the stock market, can find the one company or opportunity that will provide the potential appreciation that you can find in the real estate field.

To arrive at the appropriate return on equity, real estate professionals use what is called "the band of investment theory." This method involves weighing the commitment of equity funds against the risk of their loss in relation to the amount of financing connected with the project. To the extent that leverage is an enabling factor in successful developments, it is the relationship between yield and this risk factor that we shall discuss in the following pages.

In order to achieve success, you as an investor normally have to commit a major portion of your equity funds. Down payments on temporarily unproductive properties can often be sizable and can absorb your capital that could be used for more lucrative and exciting opportunities. I recently had to syndicate a $3,000,000 residential condominium project, giving up one-third of the profits to outside investors in order to effectuate an accelerated closing. An anxious seller wished to expedite the closing at a time when many of my short-term investment funds were committed on other projects. To avoid passing up this choice opportunity, I had to reach outside for other investors' funds and expertise.

How to Adequately Compensate for Yield

To compensate for the drawbacks of real estate investment, you must, in my estimation, receive a cash return on your equity of four to five percentage points over and above what is available on liquid, relatively risk-free investments in the stock or bond markets. This return takes into consideration the advantages of depreciation but not the benefits derived from potential appreciation. I assign a risk value of 2% or 2½% to both the nonliquidity and financial exposure factors associated with real estate investments. If I cannot structure a cash return before debt service on any given property of at least 4% to 5% over the corresponding return I would receive on a quality New York Stock Exchange bond, I do not consider the asset to be a good investment.

If a property shows a great potential for appreciation, I sometimes make an exception to my 4% to 5% rule. Occasionally, you find a property that is undervalued or underrented to the extent that the potential resale value can be increased substantially in a short period of time. I recently found a small office complex that was leased at below market rentals, where the rents could be increased substantially over a short period of time. On this particular building, as on many others, I have settled for a lesser return up front, knowing that the long-term potential is there.

In calculating my overall return on investment, I have purposely excluded a management factor in that rate of return. I have done this since all properties should include an appropriate management fee in the operating statements, irrespective of whether or not the owners themselves are involved in the management. On most of my investment properties I seek out competent local management firms in order to conserve my time to acquire and develop additional properties. Special talent is often required during the initial rent-up periods. Once a respectable rental achievement has been accomplished, I then confidently turn over the management to a full-time professional organization.

Calculating the Appropriate Return on Equity

To return to the investment norm of cash return, our basis for making this calculation will be a quality corporate bond with medium maturity carrying a rate yielding 12%. To that base return on equity we add a nonliquidity and a financial exposure factor of 2% each, giving us a combined overall rate of return of 16%, 4% over the bond hypothetical rate.

Let us further assume that we can acquire a property with a 75% mortgage carrying a simple interest rate of 12%. For purposes of simplification we shall ignore mortgage amortization in our calculations. We would then calculate our yield as follows:

Source of Funds (1)	% of Property Value (2)	Interest or Rate of Return Required (3)	Combined % from Columns 2 and 3 (4)
First mortgage financing	75%	12%	9.0%
Equity contribution	25%	16%	4.0%
Combined totals	100%		13.0%

When we balance the debt service requirements and the desired return on equity, we find that we need an overall return of 13% on the project in order to achieve our 16% return on equity.

The foregoing analysis is geared toward a conservative evaluation without consideration for tax benefits or appreciation.

I recently used this band of investment theory in arriving at an appropriate return on an office complex that I own. At the time of analysis the corporate bond market was constantly fluctuating, and because the long-term potential for appreciation was considerable in this 45,000 square foot $2,500,000 complex, I had a difficult time determining an equitable yield. After weighing these two unusual factors, I arrived at 12.5% as the figure I considered a realistic market return on these buildings, even though the relatively risk-free bond rate was 11%.

How to Take Advantage of Rapid Appreciation Situations

Spectacular increases in values can be found in areas where supply and demand are not in balance. Where rapid growth is taking place and the supply of land or investment properties is limited, the creative and speculative real estate investor will discover interesting investment opportunities. Such was the case recently when I joined a group associated in acquiring a condominium site in a medium-sized city where approximately 4,000 new jobs had been created within a year's time. The value of the 9-acre tract was placed at $200,000 at the time of acquisition. Some two years later, the property was appraised at $620,000. In this particular instance there was no visible shortage of land, just an imbalance in supply and demand for improved ready-to-market residential lots.

During periods of rapid inflation, cash returns have little significance in making investment decisions. For example, an investor may acquire an apartment complex with as little as a 5% cash return on equity, knowing that a potential for conversion into condominiums is a distinct possibility within a short period of time, and that conversion might result in a tenfold return on his cash equity. In such a situation, you, as a creative speculator, can settle for a low initial return in contrast to a quality rated corporate bond, knowing that you have complete control over your investment and that your potential yield is limited only by your imagination.

By contrast, investing in the stocks or bonds of a publicly held company is passive. The investor is basically at the mercy of the corporate officers and directors whose function is to set policy and make day-to-day decisions. In my opinion, this is too high a price to pay for this liquidity factor.

Major fortunes in the investment world are made and established by individuals who control the leveraged assets that determine the destiny of their investment futures. Real estate investment provides the inherent stability, leverage, and appreciation through inflation that is not available to an individual who becomes involved with a form of investment controlled by management not of his own choosing.

How to Eliminate Risk by Determining Reproduction Costs

Thus far we have discussed the valuation of real estate, utilizing the income approach. While this method is the most widely used, considered the most accurate, and has the broadest application, two other ways must be considered in tandem. They have special application in determining the downside risk you encounter when acquiring investment real estate. You get a clearer picture of the value of a given property when you compare the income approach with the cost or replacement value and the comparable sales approach.

Knowing the cost or replacement value is important for two reasons:

- It determines the upper value you would pay for a given property regardless of the amount of income that investment generates.
- It also sets the upside potential for a property if you can acquire it at considerably less than its replacement value.

If an income-producing property can be acquired for less than its current replacement value, one of two things can conceivably happen:

- It can be sold at a premium to an owner-user who is not totally enamored of the income approach.
- It can be subdivided and sold to a multitude of different owners at a level approaching its replacement value.

Several years ago, I purchased, for approximately $20 a square foot, an older building that had been converted into an office complex. The building had been vacant for several years and I spent approximately $7 a square foot on this 6,000 square foot structure to renovate it and make it more habitable. The total cost of purchase and renovation amounted to $10 to $15 a square foot, considerably under the building's then replacement value. At a later date, I exchanged the building for another office complex at a considerable profit. The current owner recently resold the building for what I would estimate to be well in excess of the current replacement value.

How to Convert a Building to a Higher and Better Use

Similar appreciation is prevalent in many apartment complexes. Investors are acquiring these structures not for their income-producing abilities but for the prices they will command when they are converted into condominiums. Often, apartment buildings can be purchased at levels approaching 50% of their replacement value, leaving considerable upside potential for a developer with the expertise and financial staying power to convert them.

If an income-producing property is located in an extremely viable and expanding area, it can conceivably be worth more than its replacement value for one of two reasons:

- Rentals in the local marketplace are currently low, and a rapid increase can be predicted to eventually take place.
- If new properties under construction cannot justify a fair return on equity, development will cease and the market for existing properties will flourish with consequently higher rental rates.

Rentals can accelerate with surprising rapidity in expanding areas. Over the years, I have been associated with many developers who acquired apartment complexes for considerably less than replacement value with an eventual eye toward conversion. Yet they have delayed conversion on what they initially considered marginal investments, due to other developers converting apartments, which in the process removed a sizable number of rental units from the market. Many of these individuals are now receiving handsome returns on their initial equity and still have the lucrative option to convert at a later date.

I have had an extremely difficult time in the last several years locating apartment complexes that can be purchased showing a decent or respectable return on equity. I recently made an offer on a complex that showed an 8% overall cash return. However, the more I analyzed the situation, the more I realized that the project did not have conversion potential. Based upon this assessment, I was not willing to acquire that property at 8% strictly as a long-term investment.

Using Comparable Sales to Judge the Market

The second supporting approach to the valuation of real estate, through comparable sales, carries particular weight when you are purchasing or selling a single-family residence. Many investors, however, discount it in purchasing income-producing property. In my estimation, it has an important function relating specifically to the local market in which you operate, and it overlaps to some degree the income approach. The comparative sales method can provide an in-depth analysis of the local market by indicating the strengths and weaknesses that investment properties come under, thereby predicting the typical effective yield for investment real estate.

Strong markets exist, obviously, where excess funds are chasing a limited number of properties. In the Sun Belt, for example, large sums of foreign and eastern capital are being invested in almost any worthwhile venture. I have seen cash returns on apartment buildings in one major city drop from a 10% to 11% return as recently as three or four years ago to a 5% or 6% return currently. This sharp reduction isn't necessarily alarming, since the influx of new people is expected to continue, and property values and rentals will continue to escalate under these conditions.

How Yields Can Vary Drastically

Yields can fluctuate considerably from one area to another. In the major metropolitan areas of the Northeast, yields are considerably higher and less predictable in the long run than those found, for example, in the southwestern United States, where there is an almost predictable long-term potential for appreciation. For this reason, it is important to modify the band of investment theory with the comparable sales approach in specific markets. By the same token, it makes investment sense to bypass marginal growth areas and concentrate on rapidly expanding sections of the country.

Another factor to consider in applying comparable sales is the nature and amount of financing that passes with the sale of a project. Owner financing is often a necessity provided in areas where capital is short, often at rates considerably lower than those found in the conventional mortgage market. Lower rates on debt service have the overall effect of increasing the value of the property and your return on equity.

Several years ago I acquired an office building structured to include a submarket interest rate as an integral part of the transaction. My purchase price was $145,000, and the owner agreed to carry a $130,000 first mortgage. The rate of his existing mortgage was 6%, and he agreed to a wraparound mortgage at 9%, or 3 points over his existing smaller mortgage, and, for me, 2% under the then conventional market rate. Because of this consideration, I was able to pay him a slight premium for his property without affecting my yield substantially, in what turned out to be a mutually profitable arrangement.

How to Determine the Break-Even Point Accurately

An effective way to determine the leverage and corresponding effective yield of a property in the marketplace is to estimate the highest break-even point your investment can support. By this means, a prospective owner or investor is able to determine the occupancy level needed to support the fixed and variable costs that a project encounters. Examples of fixed costs are:

FIGURE 2-1

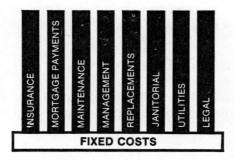

Additionally, a number of variable costs occur only when the property is substantially occupied by tenants. Some of these costs are:

- extensive janitorial services;
- full maintenance expenses;
- full capital reserves for replacements;
- utility costs;
- interior maintenance; and
- legal and accounting fees.

Charting the Break-Even Point

In Figure 2-2, I have charted the actual fixed and variable costs of operating a 45,000 square foot office complex housing nine tenants. During the period of my ownership, the key to the stability of the entire complex has been the major tenant, who occupies 26,000 square feet, or 58% of the building. The space occupied by the other tenants varies, with the next largest occupying 6,900 square feet, and the balance of the occupants leasing between 2,000 and 3,000 square feet each. Keep in mind that the two key tenants occupy almost 33,000 square feet, or approximately three-quarters of the total structure. It goes without saying that the leases by the two

FIGURE 2-2

Fixed and variable costs in operating a 45,000 square foot office complex housing nine tenants. The dotted lines indicate the break-even point.

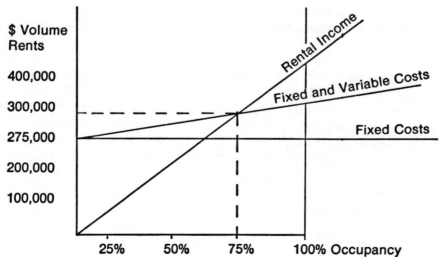

major tenants have to be solid and substantial or the office complex would not be a viable one. With the break-even point at $301,000 in annual rent at an occupancy level of approximately 76%, the smaller tenants constitute the obvious profit derived from this building.

With a $2 million first mortgage, this structure has an annual debt service requirement of $236,000. The graph illustrates that the ultimate answer to evaluating the value of a property in a given marketplace often does not come from using a hypothetical vacancy factor and figuring a corresponding return on equity.

Determining Maximum and Minimum Income and Expenses

Determining the break-even point means calculating backwards, since the actual return on equity reverts to the investor only after that break-even point is achieved. By analyzing the value of the rents, the duration of the leases, and the timing of the expiration of the leases, one should be able to accurately predict the vacancy factor and the break-even point after one additional calculation for the fixed and variable expenses. With this information, you can determine accurately:

- the yield on the property;
- the consistency of time the investment will provide the projected cash flow;
- the potential exposure if the building runs at an occupancy level below the break-even point.

Frequently, minor adjustments must be made in the gross income and operating expenses to reflect increasing costs at later dates. Sometimes it is important to chart or determine in advance maximum and minimum gross income and corresponding operating expenses, since wide variations can substantially affect the break-even point and the amount of leverage you will eventually use. Much depends upon how your leases are structured so that income can be raised expeditiously to offset increases in operating expenses.

To protect myself from having to absorb increased expenses, I attempt to keep my leases to a maximum of five years during inflationary periods. Although I have several leases with national tenants containing options extending beyond this period, these leases all incorporate direct pass-through increases in operating expenses. Additionally, I insert provisions under which, if the government cost-of-living index exceeds a predetermined figure and I am not protected, stop-gap clauses provide for either renegotiation or cancellation of the lease at my option. I currently have a lease with a major American corporation containing this cancellation provision which, if inflation continues in the double digit range, will have to be enforced.

If you are operating in a market where seasonal variations in occupancy occur, this factor must also be incorporated into your determination of the break-even point. These fluctuations do not normally occur in the office or industrial markets, although they are prevalent in the residential apartment sector and occasionally surface when one is involved in retail complexes where a majority of the rents are based upon a percentage of sales.

How to Predict Values Using Capitalization Rates

Inflation has had a significant impact on property values and the corresponding fortunes of most real estate investors during the last several decades. Positively, rental income and resale prices have increased considerably, reflecting the inflated replacement value of real estate. Negatively, inflation has raised operating costs, which can be quite detrimental if not fully absorbed by the tenants, such as:

- property taxes;
- management fees;
- insurance;
- janitorial;
- utilities; and
- maintenance.

Rising costs such as these have a major bearing on the overall appreciation you can eventually expect from a project.

All income-producing investments are analyzed on a stabilized cash-flow basis. Properties are most frequently valued at some particular multiple of earnings, commonly referred to as a capitalization rate, which is a direct reflection or multiple of the annual net income after operating expenses. This is quite similar to the price-earnings ratios used in the evaluation of common stocks.

This common multiplier or capitalization rate translates net income into market values. Because it is a direct reflection of the annual net income after operating expenses, it can also provide us with an approximate resale value in the future. As a simple example, suppose we purchase an apartment complex for $500,000 and receive a return of 10%, or $50,000 per year. The value of the property is then placed at 10 times the annual net income.

Over a ten-year holding period, we would then have to project the potential increases in income and offsetting rises in operating expenses. Accurate prediction of both categories would enable you to determine how much additional net income you would receive at the end of the holding period. If we could determine, for example, that our net income, after deducting increases in operating expenses, would increase by 5% a year (without, for the moment, calculating the effect of compounding this rate), we would have a 50% increase in net operating income. This would translate into operating income after expenses of $75,000 a year ten years after acquisition of the asset. Returning to the figure of 10 as an income multiplier, you could then establish a realistic resale value of $750,000 for the property at that point in time.

Having established that your property would appreciate by $250,000 over the ten-year holding period, you could augment your annual income by $25,000 for each year of holding reflecting the appreciation factor. If you purchased this property with a conventional down payment of 25% or $125,000, you can see that the additional $25,000 a year adds approximately 20% per year to the overall yield. When you compound this 20% per year you can see the astronomical effect inflation has on property values.

How to Effectively Combat Declining Yields on Properties

During inflationary periods, interest rates are pegged to the lender's increasing cost of money. As these rates rise, return on equity drops correspondingly, reflecting the increased burden of the debt service requirement.

I am currently in the process of refinancing one of my commercial buildings, a complicated process during an inflationary period. I am attempting to obtain a $1,200,000 loan based on a qualified appraisal of $1,700,000. To date, the financing proposals that I have received from several major life insurance companies either offer interest rates that can be adjusted every 3 to 5 years or contain long-term amortizations of 25 to 30 years with an option to call the loan at the end of ten years.

As long as inflation persists, I believe that the trend away from fixed-rate, long-term commitments will continue. In most cases, the overall free and clear capitalization rates will remain fairly constant, but the funds necessary to service the debt during periods of high interest rates and inflation will increase substantially.

Every major city in the United States has vacant or vandalized real estate testifying to the rampant effects of inflation and the corresponding decline in yields. The costs of holding and maintaining these properties can be astronomical, including such items as:

- mortgage payments;
- property taxes;
- maintenance;
- insurance; and
- utilities.

Many of these expense items have far outdistanced the ability of owners or occupants to maintain the necessary payments. Government-subsidized housing complexes in marginal areas have shockingly short lives. In St. Louis, for example, tens of millions of dollars were spent to construct a major project to provide housing for low-income occupants. That project had to be razed before it was even ten years old.

The silent testimonial of these vacant structures is a warning to real estate investors to closely analyze the ratio between potential income and operating expenses. Only a careful projection and a realistic analysis will prevent the deterioration of yields and the creation of more vacant, vandalized structures.

Pitfalls Found in Using Rules of Thumb

One discovers just how unique each piece of property can be when attempting to price comparable properties in the local marketplace. In spite of the fact that the real estate market is the largest investment vehicle in the United States, whose values far exceed those of stocks, bonds, or savings accounts, no individual has ever established a simplified proven formula for quick and accurate pricing. Of the many rules of thumb advanced in the industry, the majority are generally worthless since they disregard the pass-through ability of operating expenses, cost of living indices, individual tax brackets, and mortgage financing. A property with an annual gross of $100,000, for instance, might have a value that could vary between $500,000 and $1,000,000, depending on who absorbed the operating expenses that would reflect on the net income figure on the bottom line. Many individuals are totally inaccurate in applying the oft-quoted rule that fair market value equals 7 to 8 times the total gross annual income.

To illustrate a point, I own two adjoining office complexes which were completed within one year of each other. In the second building I obtained full cost-of-living escalation clauses in a majority of the leases. In the first I was less fortunate, settling mainly for direct pass-through expenses only. The cost differential in developing the two buildings was approximately $5 a square foot, and the buildings are currently in their second and third years of occupancy. The capitalized value of the income on the building leased with complete cost-of-living escalation clauses is almost $10 a square foot higher than that on the structure in which I am reimbursed only for increases in expenses.

Using this comparison, the income from a triple-net shopping center lease fully protected with overage rents would be one of the more attractive investment vehicles. An office complex with long-term leases and a multitude of services provided and paid for by the landlord would probably be one of the least desirable.

I have found in all the properties that I have developed, whether they were apartments, office or industrial buildings, mobile home parks or whatever, that if they were located in a geographic area that was expanding and had ample purchasing power to initially support my project, I could without exception pass on a majority of the operating expenditures to the tenants. Additionally I have found that any time these expenses run in excess of 35% to 40% of the gross income, profit margins will deteriorate substantially during inflationary periods.

Guidelines for Determining the Appropriate Rate of Return

The real estate industry provides little research or few analytical tools that can be accumulated on a national basis and applied to a local situation. In contrast, investors in recognized corporations in the stock and bond markets are guided in the direction of accurate pricing by charted trends and historic price-earnings ratios. As a consequence, most successful real estate investors rely on experience, judgment, and, in many cases, basic intuition.

Furthermore, the real estate industry lacks centralized and professional management to profitably maintain diversified investments under difficult conditions. For these reasons, you, as a successful investor, must develop a complete command of and feel for the local market by keeping in constant touch with:

- real estate brokers;
- property managers;
- mortgage bankers and lenders;
- mortgage brokers;
- consultants specializing in economic development;
- politicians and urban planners; and
- professional engineers, architects, and appraisers.

I have found that these groups can be quite informative, and can be some of the best sources of bringing in new viable investment opportunities. I have one associate who is not only an architect, but also a real estate broker. This individual is an outstanding source for new development projects as he has a feel for how to acquire and rejuvenate older buildings. On many of the projects he presents to me he will put in a great deal of up-front time and effort in order to convince me that the project will be viable.

The Importance of Understanding the Overall Picture

You, as a local entrepreneur, must be able to move in and out of various real estate investments based upon your overall knowledge of the local market, however large, unwieldy and misunderstood it may often be. Interesting opportunities will always exist for you when you comprehend the local picture totally and set your investment guidelines to fill gaps in the market that others always overlook. A short automobile drive of 10 or 15 minutes in any city will disclose the multitude of opportunities to acquire a simple city lot, a duplex, fourplex, or a larger apartment structure, not to mention the possibilities for developing subdivisions, office complexes, industrial buildings, shopping centers, and mobile home parks.

Like many other real estate entrepreneurs, I am less enamored of specialization and more challenged by diversification. The latter approach demands a knowledgeable command of the overall local market so that you can spot the lucrative gaps and capitalize on them before your competitors duplicate your efforts. The advantage of diversification is that it works anywhere you can find a strong local economy.

Just as familiarity with the local market is the key to recognizing opportunities in real estate development, it can also serve you well when you set out to find the financial backing necessary to implement your plans. A lending institution with strong community connections is preconditioned to projects that will improve the local economic environment. Even as financial backing for major projects moves further away from local sources, the mortgage institutions, guided by statistical generalizations, will profit from the talent that the local entrepreneurs can and do provide. When you establish an enviable track record in a locality, you can capitalize on your reputation for structuring imaginative investment opportunities to create a variety of financial bargains that we shall discuss in the next chapter.

3

Creative Financing Techniques

Financial leverage is essentially the control of money, another form of being in the banking business. If you can structure an investment to show a return substantially higher than the fixed cost of borrowing, you can theoretically leverage to infinity.

Step by step, this chapter will unveil the creative methods used by the professionals for utilizing leverage to its highest degree, substantially increasing your yield through the use of long-term permanent financing, accompanied by the unique tax benefits found only in properly structured real estate ventures.

This chapter will show you how to achieve maximum leverage by using long-term, fixed-rate sources of financing which permit you to repay mortgage obligations with dollars devaluated by the inflationary process. You will also come to understand how interim and permanent lenders make maximum commitments through the use of proven checklists and practical examples which demonstrate the unparalleled advantages of highly leveraged real estate investments during inflationary periods. The major vehicles used by real estate professionals to achieve leveraged financing—such as tax-free exchanges, wraparound mortgages, fixed and variable interest rates, advantageous owner financing, sale-leaseback arrangements and second mortgages, to mention a few—will be described in detail.

Understanding the Concept of Leverage

The concept of leverage is partially based upon the principle that the individual parts have more value than the whole. Acquiring an apartment building for $20 a square foot, and "condominiumizing" it at $35 to $40 a square foot to 5, 50, or 500 different purchasers, constitutes the same sort of fractionalization as developing a subdivision of 100 acres into half-acre tracts. Investing in one unit of a condominium or a half-acre of a subdivision constitutes only a portion of the overall degree of risk assumed by the developer of the entire project. Such an investment is indicative of the different sorts of interests and diversification of investment objectives. An intermediate degree of risk, associated with another objective, is assumed by the investor who bankrolls the venture during the critical development period. Large public corporations recognize the diversity of these potential investment interests by stratifying their offerings to include common and preferred stock, subordinated or convertible debentures, and mortgage and equipment bonds, to name only a few.

Several individuals who regularly invest with me in limited partnerships are interested primarily in projects with quick turnaround and no substantial ramifications for tax shelter, like the 50-unit condominium project, detailed in a later chapter, in which I returned the investors' equity in fifteen months. Others with whom I have associated have sources of long-term investment funds and want tax-sheltered benefits combined with appreciation of their capital through the inflationary process.

How to Calculate a Leveraged Investment

If we use an example of an investor who wishes a 13% annual return on $100,000 he has in available funds, he can acquire a property for cash, receive $13,000 a year net after operating expenses, and obtain some minimal tax benefits from the depreciation of the structure. In the process, he does not burden himself with mortgage obligations or monthly payments.

Alternatively, that same $100,000, if properly leveraged, could be applied as a down payment on a project having a value of, say, $750,000 showing an overall similar yield of 13%. Our investor then obtains a first-mortgage commitment on the $650,000 balance at a simple interest rate of 10%. He then achieves not only the 13% return on his initial equity, but he is also the prime beneficiary of the difference on the additional 3% return or spread on the leveraged portion of the $650,000. This amounts to $3,000 per $100,000 of financed debt annually, or approximately $19,500 per year on the entire $650,000. Of that 3%, approximately 1% will be used to reduce the principal if a normal amortization schedule is applied. Assuming that the $750,000 investment shows an overall yield of 13% before debt service, under these circumstances, our investor more than doubles his annual cash return ($13,000 versus $32,500), and in the process acquires 6½ times the depreciation deductions. In addition, the appreciation upon sale, which should also be adjusted upwards by a factor of 6½ times, is taxed at the favorable capital gains rate. Our investor's cash return in exchange for the risk of encumbering the project with mortgage payments, is $26,000 a year ($13,000 + $19,500 – $6,500 representing a deduction for the 1% amortization), and in effect he more than shelters the additional cash flow generated by the increased depreciation or cost recovery deductions on his leveraged asset.

How Depreciation Can Increase Your Yield Substantially

In the above example, the pre-tax ramifications of depreciation deductions would most likely increase our investor's return on equity from 13% in an unleveraged situation to an overall yield of 32% by acquiring a $750,000 asset. Our investor would receive a $50,000 annual depreciation deduction on the property, assuming that the underlying land was leased and that the entire $750,000 asset was depreciable on a 15-year basis, or at 6.67% per year, the new rate allowed under the Economic Recovery Tax Act of 1981. From this $50,000 we would have to deduct the $6,667 depreciation allowance for the nonleveraged $100,000 equity investment, leaving us a net difference of $43,333 to be taxed at the maximum rate of 50%. The net after-tax benefits of this additional deduction would have the effect of increasing our cash flow by $21,600. This increases our overall return on the investment to $51,000 before mortgage amortization. Through the use of leverage, our yield is multiplied almost four times, as illustrated in Table 3-1.

TABLE 3-1

The Effects of Leverage on Rate of Return

State of Investment	Equity Amount	Property Value	Return on Equity
Nonleveraged, cash return	$100,000	$100,000	$13,000/13%
Nonleveraged, after depreciation benefits	$100,000	$100,000	$16,333/16%
Leveraged, cash return before amortization	$100,000	$750,000	$32,500/32%
Leveraged, after amortization	$100,000	$750,000	$26,000/26%
Leveraged, after depreciation benefits, before amortization	$100,000	$750,000	$51,000/51%

How Inflation and Leverage Work to Your Benefit

If we can increase the rental income from a project at a rate that equals or exceeds the inflationary costs of operating that investment, we can substantially increase our cash return by using leverage. I recently developed a 45,000 square-foot office complex in which my cash equity was diminutive in relation to the amount of mortgage financing. I structured the leases in such a manner that the resultant cash flow justified a mortgage in the amount of $2 million, even though there was no substantial cash flow after· the mortgage payments. By using the straight-line method of depreciation, I obtained approximately $80,000 a year in depreciation deductions on this property. In situations such as this, the annual tax deductions often total more than the actual amount of cash invested in the project.

Returning to our previous example, our investor ends up, after leveraging his property, with an asset worth $750,000. How long would it take a person making $40,000 to $50,000 a year to acquire an asset of that magnitude? It is almost impossible to imagine accumulating any asset with such value during a lifetime through any vehicle other than investment real estate.

Capitalizing on Long-Term, Fixed Sources of Mortgage Money

The United States has a unique financial system which permits you, the real estate investor, to obtain a high degree of leverage over long periods of time that is not commonly found in other industrialized countries of the world. The fixed-rate, long-term sources of debt markets traditional in this country provide you, the leveraged investor, with a speculative and potentially lucrative vehicle to hedge against inflation. Fixed, long-term financing, combined with the proven concept that investment real estate commands one of the highest loan-to-value ratios for potential investors, permits the creative entrepreneur to control large amounts of property with small amounts of equity. Using other people's money through such familiar sources as owner financing, first and second conventional mortgages, and syndicated equity pools, permits you to control these sizable assets.

Three factors will dictate the degree of leverage you are able or should be willing to obtain:

- the stabilized cash flow that a project can generate will determine the amount of risk that you will encounter when utilizing highly leveraged mortgage financing;

- the degree of risk you are willing to take in light of the managerial abilities necessary to support the high level of mortgage financing;

- the safety factor that you are willing to accept, a margin often dependent on the economy and the number of potential vacancies a project can endure.

The effect of combining these factors is to weigh the economic risks against your financial resources and managerial abilities and the backup reserves you can obtain should the property require additional injections of capital during periods of uncertainty. These reserves can take the form of syndications with associates or of non-recourse potentially renegotiable notes.

I recently executed a non-recourse note backed by an agency of the federal government in which the amount of the note, $533,000, was equal to the total appraised value of the project. I subsequently sold the development and assigned the note to a highly leverage-oriented group, and in the process increased the price of the project substantially through this advantageous non-recourse note.

Beneficial Effects of Longer Mortgage Amortization and Lower Interest Rates

The two critical factors that determine the success of a leveraged investment are the interest rate and the mortgage amortization. As an example, let us take a building with a 9½% mortgage interest factor where the equity position or cash return is valued at 10%. From Table 3-2 we can see that by doubling the length of the mortgage from 15 to 30 years, you can generate an additional cash flow of $2,400 per year, thereby increasing the value of your equity position by $24,000. In other words, a building with a 30-year 9½% mortgage is worth 24% more to the investor than the same structure with a 15-year mortgage, based upon the annual cash it generates, excluding considerations for equity buildup.

TABLE 3-2

Effect of a Longer Amortization on Return on Equity

Amortization Period	Annual Mortgage Payment	Additional Cash Flow	Value of the Equity
15 years	$12,600	—	$100,000
20 years	11,280	$1,320	113,200
25 years	10,560	2,040	120,400
30 years	10,200	2,400	124,000

The effect of differing interest rates on your yield is similar. The same 10% cash return, when encumbered by a $100,000 mortgage, provides an interesting comparison between a 10% and a 13% mortgage on a 25-year basis. As we can see from Table 3-3, the difference between mortgage payments of 10% and 13% over 25 years is approximately $65,750, again increasing the value of the building by about 26%, if the cash flow is capitalized at 10%.

TABLE 3-3

Effect of Lower Interest Rate on Return on Equity

Percentage Interest	Annual Mortgage Payment	Additional Cash Flow	Value of the Building
10%	$10,900	$2,630	$126,300
11%	11,760	1,740	117,400
12%	12,640	860	108,600
13%	13,530	—	100,000

FIGURE 3-1

Percentage Increases or Decreases

In the Value of Residential Real Estate

And United States Dollars 100% Base Year 1967

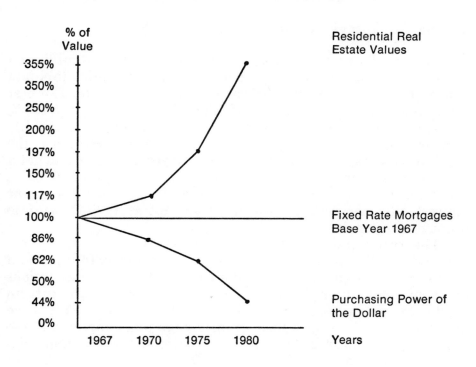

Taking Advantage of Fixed-Rate Financing

The leverage concept operates most efficiently when mortgage obligations are on a fixed-rate, long-term basis. This is evident from Figure 3-1, which indicates the effect of a long-term, fixed-rate mortgage compared to the actual purchasing price of the dollar, which greatly favored the values of real estate as an investment over the past 15 years. The increases in residential real estate values reflect the median price of a single family home as measured by the Government Consumer Price Index. The purchasing value of the dollar is also from that index, with 1967 as the base year for both figures. Both are presented to reflect percentage increases or decreases.

The applicable concept for long-term financing is changing for obvious reasons. Lending institutions are now requiring periodic interest adjustment factors, shorter amortizations, or equity participation either in the annualized cash flow or in the proceeds from sale in order to increase their overall yield as a hedge against inflation.

Taking Advantage of Variable Interest Rates

Recently I structured a mortgage well in excess of $1 million on one of my commercial buildings in which I was attempting to obtain a straight 25-year amortization at a fixed interest rate. The best commitment under the current inflationary conditions was a 12½%, 25-year amortization with a 10-year call, which gave the life insurance company the option to require that I refinance the building or renegotiate the terms after 10 years. In order to get a fixed interest rate on this 10-year balloon mortgage, I had to pay a premium of approximately 3/4 of 1%, as I was offered a 5-year interest-only mortgage for the same amount at 11-3/4% with no prepayment penalty.

The trend toward variable interest rates and short-term mortgages will probably continue well into the future. Inflation and the extremely high and fluctuating costs that lending institutions must pay for their funds are making fixed-rate, long-term mortgages virtually obsolete. It is obvious from Figure 3-1 that the individual who leverages through mortgage financing on a fixed-rate, long-term basis automatically achieves substantial appreciation as a byproduct of inflation. Debt service is repaid in depreciating dollars, having the net effect of reducing mortgage payments when current dollars are used to reduce those obligations. Lending institutions and their depositors are the losers, since the deflated dollars with which they are repaid will not constitute an ample return during inflationary periods.

I own an office complex which is encumbered by a long-term mortgage obligation of $1,200,000. One of the major tenants in that structure occupies close to three-quarters of the net rentable space. This tenant's base annual rental is $157,000, which is subject to annual C.P.I. increases for the full increase in the cost of living. Because these escalation clauses have averaged approximately 12% over the last several years, my bottom line income has increased by approximately $20,000 per year on this one lease alone. If I capitalized this $20,000 to show a 10% return, one can see that this portion of my building is increasing in value at the rate of $200,000 per year. What is more exciting is that I will be repaying the mortgage obligation of $1,200,000 with dollars that will be worth 50% six years from now, based on a continuing compounding of the 12% inflation factor. Many important trends are taking place with respect to these long-term, fixed-rate obligations which are delineated in detail in the final chapter of this book.

Understanding the Interim and Permanent Lenders

The transition from interim to permanent financing can be complicated if one does not understand the objectives of the various lending institutions. Basically, of the two types, interim and permanent, you must determine the proper source to accommodate your needs and structure the financing accordingly.

The prime objective of the long-term permanent lender is to fund sizable amounts of money at fixed interest rates, supporting these obligations with solid collateral. These lenders generally pay their depositors or policy holders a somewhat low rate of return on their retained funds, and profit on the long-term differential between the low depositor rates and the relatively moderate fees they offer on mortgages.

On the other hand, the interim or construction lender operates under a totally different set of guidelines. He pays his depositors considerably higher rates for short-term funds, often subject to withdrawal on demand. When his deposits fluctuate, the construction lender is often forced into the secondary market to cover these rapidly disappearing deposits. It is not uncommon for interim lenders to pay their depositors twice the rate of interest that long-term permanent lenders offer, and the rates on construction loans reflect these conditions. Normally, construction financing is structured to fluctuate from prime up to three or four points over the prime lending rate. This permits the construction lender to raise or lower his rates as his cost of money increases or decreases during the life of the loan.

The real profit to be derived from construction loans comes from the up-front points charged by the lending institutions. Because these interim loans are short-term by nature, most of them not exceeding 9 to 12 months, many are never fully funded, or at least are not completely drawn down until the final stages of development. This means that lenders, by seeking up-front commitment fees, can show income disproportionate to the funds they have actually disbursed.

The Importance of Obtaining a Permanent Commitment

I am currently developing a luxury condominium project with a total sales value of approximately $3 million. In shopping for my permanent financing, I approached a savings and loan which agreed to provide the permanent financing on the condition that they would also be able to fund the interim loan. Their strategy was to sell the long-term commitment in the secondary money market, receiving an up-front point plus a servicing fee. The really lucrative part of the transaction was to be derived from the interim construction loan, which was to encompass three phases. The up-front commitment fees and the short period of time their funds would be obligated during the three phases of the project were ample consideration for them to make both loans. From my standpoint, it was a comfortable relationship, since the transition from the construction to the permanent loans could be made without involving an additional lender.

For a multitude of reasons, interim lenders usually require that permanent financing be committed to prior to funding of the construction loans. The key reason is that their profits are generated by turning loans over every 9 to 12 months, as many projects cannot sustain these high interim rates for longer periods than this. If a permanent loan is not available upon completion, the project's cash flow will be inadequate to continue to absorb these high interim rates. Second, when interim loans mature before construction is completed or long term funds are obtained, additional points are difficult to extract on these loans to compensate the lender for continuing to support these projects until they are completed and funded. Construction lenders usually do not lack for new projects, and prefer to seek them out rather than renew existing commitments. With such an extension arrangement, the developer is also jeopardizing the value of the completed property, since the eventual value will be partially contingent upon the project's cost of financing.

Interim lenders are becoming quite conservative. At one time they would negotiate construction loans without firm takeout commitments for permanent financing. Knowing that a commitment might be fabricated or that the permanent lender had no intention of honoring it, interim lenders often provided financing mainly to profit from the up-front points. Those days have virtually disappeared. Currently, a developer must obtain a legitimate takeout that the cash flow from a project can realistically support before he can convince an interim lender to fund it.

I recently applied for interim financing on an apartment complex of over 200 units which I planned to convert to condominiums, subject to obtaining permanent funding for qualified buyers in the amount of $4 million. My interim lender required a large portion of that money to be pre-committed from mortgage authority funds, which are the interest-subsidized funds provided by local mortgage authorities selling tax-exempt bonds. Because of the difficulty of qualifying buyers at conventional rates, this provision of the interim commitment was quite important to the lending institution and to the project in general.

How to Find the Right Interim and Permanent Lenders

Both interim and permanent mortgagors have quirks about the projects or areas with which they feel most comfortable. Some deal only in geographic areas which they consider have long-term growth potentials, where their loans will remain solid and their collateral will be protected. Even though their geographical preferences may result from preconceived or erroneous ideas, their very existence can create difficulties for individuals trying to attract maximum loans. If the type of project or location is not on the lender's 100% list, the borrower may be denied the loan or penalized by the dollar amount.

This narrowness of vision is applicable to various types of projects, often because lending institutions were burned financially in the past or knew of other lenders who experienced foreclosures in certain types of ventures. High on the last-resort list of many mortgagors are mobile parks, speculative raw land deals, bowling alleys, car washes, and second-home resort or recreation complexes. Frequently, lenders refuse even to accept or to review loan applications for such projects. One finds that financial institutions specialize in areas where operations have been successful over periods of years and have established solid track records for repayment—in such areas as apartment complexes, office buildings, nursing homes, condominium projects and apartment conversions— and refuse to get out of their convenient and comfortable ruts.

I can recall several years ago when many mobile home parks were developed almost simultaneously in one state in the Southwest. At least half a dozen of these parks went into foreclosure due to a temporarily overbuilt situation, creating almost a domino effect, even though a majority were properly conceived. The impact of this upon the entire lending industry has been long and lasting, and many mortgagors still refuse to commit themselves to mobile home developments in that particular geographic area.

Obtaining the Permanent Financing Commitment

After screening the lenders with prejudicial preferences and zeroing in on those with an appropriate attitude and expertise for your project, you must take the complicated step of assembling the loan package to be submitted to either the permanent or interim lender. The background information required by either is similar, and should include the following:

- feasibility study and site plan;
- description of the site, including location maps and air photos;
- area demographics;
- existing rentals or comparable sales values;
- description of the improvements;
- amount of the requested loan;
- terms and conditions of that loan; and
- approximate schedule of funding.

A permanent lender who feels comfortable with this package after reviewing it on a preliminary basis will ask for the following additional detailed information:

- pro forma income and operating statements on new construction; or
- actual income and operating statements on existing property;
- cost of acquisition on an existing property; or
- detailed breakdown of construction costs on new development;
- qualified appraisals supporting sales values or rental income;
- access, facilities, parking, and conformity to zoning;
- availability of utilities, and building or occupancy permits;
- copies of existing leases, legal descriptions, and surveys; or
- prelease commitments on new construction combined with working drawings and specifications; and
- evidence of clear title insurance.

Checklist of Supporting Loan Documentation

Items in the foregoing lists provide the lender with a broad overview of the project and the development's ability to support the requested loan amount. In addition, lenders will require the following personal information about you, the development or acquisition team:

- complete corporate or personal financial statements;
- verification of income, operations and employment;
- personal and financial references and resumés;
- a breakdown of the sources and amounts of equity funds;
- complete identification of the vehicle or conduit that will hold title to the property;
- credit reports and certified income tax statements on the corporations or individuals involved; and
- verification of cash deposits and other assets included in the corporate or personal financial statements.

Special Requirements for Obtaining Interim Financing

If new construction is involved and a development loan is being requested in conjunction with the permanent financing, most interim lenders require detailed information regarding the type of construction, architectural contracts, schedules for completion, payment and performance bonds, marketing and sales expenses, phasing of the development, sources of equity funds, etc. Interim financing can also be complicated by conditions precedent to the funding of the permanent loan.

When permanent financing commitments contain rental achievement clauses, such as those found in shopping centers, office complexes, or apartment buildings, where a certain percentage of occupancy must be achieved prior to funding, an interim lender may not finance 100% of the permanent loan commitment. Since rental achievement clauses can produce additional exposure, interim financing may also involve a speculative bridge or gap loan to cover the additional funds which may have to be injected into the project as working capital, until the development achieves the level of occupancy predetermined by the permanent lender. It is also not uncommon for mortgagors to insert sales achievement clauses in projects such as condominiums or apartment conversions which require secondary gap financing to fully equalize the interim and permanent loan commitments.

Problems in obtaining gap financing always seem to proliferate in times of tight money. I recently obtained a $600,000 first mortgage from a conventional lender combined with an $840,000 second mortgage financed by the seller. Both encumbrances were necessary in order to complete development of this subdivision consisting of 104 residential lots. However, the municipal government required that I escrow $800,000, which was their estimated cost of completing the project. Since I had timed the construction and presales to insure that no more than $600,000 would be outstanding on the construction loan at any one time, I was able to satisfy the municipal regulations by submitting a $200,000 letter of credit to augment the $600,000 construction loan. My only equity in the project consisted of the down payment of $45,000 that was advanced to the landowner upon closing, and some initial up-front engineering and legal fees.

Proven Ratios for Obtaining Maximum Loan Commitments

Lenders commit themselves after extensive valuation of a project's stabilized net income after operating expenses, and their commitments vary with the risk of the venture and the stability of the borrower. On shopping centers with long-term leases for major tenants, they normally look for a cash flow of 1.15 to 1.25 times the

annual debt service requirement; on quality office complexes, 1.2 to
1.3 times; on apartments, 1.25 to 1.35 times; and on second-mortgage
financing, a minimum of 1.5 times the stabilized cash flow after first-
mortgage payments generated from the project. Several factors
reflecting the individual assessment of risk also have a direct
bearing on the capitalization rate. The standard formula used by
most sophisticated lenders is:

$$\frac{\text{Net Operating Income}}{\text{Debt Service Coverage Ratio}} = \text{Maximum Dollars Applied to Debt Service;}$$

then:

$$\frac{\text{Maximum Dollars Applied to Debt Service}}{\text{Loan Constant (Interest plus Principal Payments)}} = \text{Mortgage Amount.}$$

How to Obtain Higher Mortgages Through Inflated Appraisals

As a common denominator, let's take the example of an investor
interested in acquiring an apartment complex. The past record of
the complex is known to him, the vacancy factor is reasonably
predictable, and he can normally obtain 75% financing of the
acquisition price or appraisal through conventional lending sources.
How would this acquisition compare with the leverage he might
achieve if he decided to construct a new apartment complex?

One of the greatest advantages he achieves by contemplating a
new apartment complex is that he can obtain a considerably higher
loan to value. Since new apartment projects usually command
higher rents, his appraiser or that of the lending institution will
assign to the project the benefit of any possible doubt relating to these
higher rental figures. Income can be projected two or three years
into the future, reflecting a completed and occupied complex, at
which point that actual income will show the effect of continuing
inflation to the developer's benefit. If the lending institution operates
on this principle, and in most cases it will, the potential developer
attains a higher degree of leverage on a new project than he would on
an existing property. This is why rental achievement clauses are so
prevalent in permanent commitments.

In developing an office complex valued at $1,900,000, I successfully convinced the appraiser for the lending institution that the income would be approximately 20% over the then current market when the buildings were completed and ready for occupancy. One of my strongest arguments was that no new major office complex had been developed in the area for years, and therefore all existing rentals were artificially low. Shortly after commencing construction, I obtained two major American corporations as my key tenants. The appraiser and I both rightly guessed that these prestigious corporations would attract other tenants in smaller increments at levels that exceeded the existing market rentals. In fact, these key occupants attracted others so quickly that the complex was fully leased even before completion of the shell buildings.

To achieve these goals, an individual must be sophisticated not only in techniques of construction and development, but also in the marketing and sales aspects. The risks involved in new construction are obviously counterbalanced by the extra leverage achieved.

Creative Vehicles for Leveraged Financing

Among the more creative and rewarding tools for financing real estate transactions are tax-free exchanges, sale-leaseback arrangements, installment sales, and wraparound mortgages, to mention a few. We will offer examples of them all in the chapters that follow, together with unparalleled variations of these established techniques. In this chapter we will limit ourselves to the discussion of two: tax-free exchanges and wraparound mortgages.

A tax-free exchange is somewhat of a misnomer, since the procedure only defers the taxation until the second, or exchanged-into, property is eventually disposed of for cash. Well-conceived exchanges permit investors to pyramid real estate holdings by substituting properties after the depreciation benefits have been exhausted. When you enter into an exchange where an equal amount of debt is not assumed, which is normal for at least one of the exchanging parties, the difference between the debt that one party is relieved of and the other assumes, is considered taxable income to the first-mentioned individual. This is not as complicated as it might sound, since most exchanging parties normally do not have the same investment objectives.

Many investors whose prime motivation is to increase their depreciation deductions by acquiring larger and more leveraged properties, exchange with those who have owned properties for

FIGURE 3-2

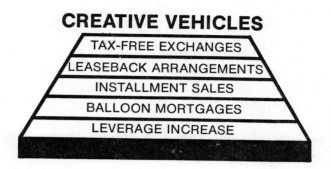

extended periods of time and are interested in cash or reducing their debt service and management obligations. Under these circumstances, a person interested in exchanging upwards can obtain not only the assumption of a larger existing mortgage, but often is provided with additional owner financing on the exchanged investment.

In order to effectuate a tax-free exchange, you have to trade like-for-like property. Tax laws differentiate between real estate used for trade or in business and that held for investment purposes. In other words, a person who is classified as a dealer in real estate cannot intermingle dealer property with long-term investment holdings and obtain the tax-free benefits of an exchange.

How to Successfully Structure a Tax-Free Exchange

The principle of balancing the equities in a tax-free exchange can be illustrated by a proposal I received last year. The owner of a shopping center offered to exchange a property for two commercial buildings that I owned. The basic economics of this exchange proposal were:

	Exchange Value	Existing Encumbrances	Equity
My buildings	$2,900,000	$2,000,000	$ 900,000
Shopping center	3,800,000	2,600,000	1,200,000

By my assuming the $2,600,000 note on the shopping center, the other party would have taxable consequences by reducing the debt obligation by $600,000. Since I would be assuming an encumbrance of $600,000 over my existing first mortgages, I would have no taxable liability in this exchange. In order to balance the equities, my contribution would consist of either adding $300,000 in cash or having the other party take a second mortgage against the shopping center.

The major problem with this exchange proposal was that the immediate cash flow from the center did not justify my full $300,000 equity contribution, so I asked the owner to carry a sizable short-term second mortgage. Under this proposal, she would have a taxable obligation on the $600,000 of debt forgiveness, with little cash coming out of the exchange due to the second-mortgage financing. Since the shopping center leases and income were fixed for, in some cases, as much as 20 years, and my buildings had considerable potential for increases in income and appreciation, I could not justify the investment of $300,000, even though it meant considerably more leverage.

Exchanges are used for a variety of purposes, some of which are unrelated to one's long-term investment needs. Sometimes exchanges are promoted under the misguided concept that a property which has been difficult to sell for various reasons can be swapped for another investment which is equally as difficult to move. A meaningless exchange such as this is normally promoted by an unsophisticated and self-seeking broker.

To determine whether you really can benefit from an exchange, you must completely analyze the cash flow, tax obligations, and the potential appreciation on your existing property and compare these factors with the potential leverage you could achieve by trading. The additional leverage and potential for appreciation gained through an exchange by acquiring a property of larger value are sometimes offset by a lesser amount of cash return on equity. The incentive for many an exchange is to pyramid your properties and increase the basis for depreciation, usually to the detriment of cash flow. Professional legal and accounting advisors are best equipped to deal with the complications of exchanging and the taxable consequences.

Increasing Leverage and Return Through Wraparound Mortgages

When first or second mortgages have existed for long periods of time, they usually carry lower than prevailing interest rates, and outstanding mortgage balances are commonly low in relation to their appreciated market value. As a potential buyer of property under these conditions, you can often persuade the owner to sell, structuring an arrangement lucrative to both parties. The seller agrees to wrap around the existing mortgage at a factor higher than the existing interest rate, but lower than you, as the buyer, would have to pay to conventional lenders. When these arrangements are beneficial to both parties, the seller often agrees to a larger loan than you could obtain elsewhere.

Several years ago, I purchased an old hotel with a history of marginal operations, which needed to be completely refurbished. The acquisition was financially unfeasible unless I could persuade the owner to continue to carry a low-interest second mortgage wrapped around his existing first mortgage for approximately 90% of the sales price. The terms of my agreement made it necessary for me to make the appropriate improvements in order to bring the property up to rentable condition, giving the seller the offsetting full claim on these improvements in the event that I defaulted. The combination of his highly leveraged situation, and my injection of fully tax-deductible renovation capital, was enough to turn the project around. Some two and a half years later I sold it as a profitable business operation.

Wraparound mortgages can generate benefits to the seller as well as those obvious to the buyer. If the seller is asked to carry a high percentage of the financing, he can normally dictate a higher sales price for his property. Since the existing permanent financing is normally at a lower-than-market rate, the seller can usually profit on the difference between his existing mortgage rate and the higher wraparound rate.

Using Wraparound Mortgages to Increase Cash Flow

Usually of short duration, these wraparound mortgages are quite frequently used when the rents generated from a project are not sufficient to justify a large conventional loan on a property at current market interest rates. Often, the purchaser can negotiate variable interest rates or reduced principal payments on these wraparounds, knowing that rents from the project can be increased to a level high enough to later justify the full wraparound mortgage payment. The seller often accepts this variable rate if, after a certain rental achievement is accomplished, the property is refinanced through conventional sources, at which time he is fully compensated.

Several years ago, I negotiated a wraparound mortgage on a vacant commercial structure in need of major improvements in order to achieve the current market rentals. I negotiated a six-month moratorium on all interest and principal payments, providing me with the time necessary to upgrade the building and achieve a rental income sufficient to justify the eventual wraparound mortgage payments. The owner agreed to this short-term moratorium because I was able to convince him that he had no other option on this vacant and non-income-producing investment.

During periods of tight money, when permanent loans are extremely difficult to obtain, or when market conditions will not permit maximum refinancing, wraparound mortgages are particularly effective. The deed to a property with a wraparound mortgage is not normally passed to the buyer until all mortgage obligations are repaid, meaning that the seller still has the collateral of the land and improvements in the event that the buyer defaults on his obligation.

In this chapter we have discussed the various financing techniques that are appropriate to you, often displaying different investment objectives. Our discussion has touched upon the tax shelter benefit as a major contribution to such transactions. The following chapter will concern itself with the after-tax consideration to you as the prime beneficiary of real estate investments.

4

Capitalizing On Tax-Sheltered Benefits

The substantial after-tax returns derived from real estate are generally not found in most other forms of investments. The special bonus of real estate lies in depreciation or cost recovery benefits and the corresponding tax-sheltering aspects it provides. Much, if not all, of the allowances for these deductions under current I.R.S. standards represent artificial or paper losses. In many instances, these depreciation or cost recovery deductions can be structured to exceed the reportable income from an investment property.

This chapter will outline for you the nature and types of these deductions by detailing the various methods used by the professionals for capitalizing on these unique tax advantages. Of special interest will be the new concepts enacted in the Reagan administration's Economic Recovery Tax Act of 1981. You will learn how to combine leverage and tax deductions effectively both as a first time and prior user of real estate. You will find out how to obtain quick writeoffs on residential and commercial rehabilitation, and how to capitalize on the 10% investment credit. A multitude of examples illustrates the successful techniques that will increase your deductions by shortening a building's useful life, by using the new accelerated cost recovery system, and by shifting depreciable

81

costs from land into buildings. Step by step you will be shown how to use the most advantageous methods of depreciation for any and all investments. You will also learn how to avoid the disastrous consequences of recapture when using accelerated depreciation, or the new cost recovery system as it is now known, and how the Economic Recovery Tax Act of 1981 makes tax-preference income extremely undesirable to you as an investor.

How to Profit From Combined Leverage and Depreciation

A property normally leveraged at 7 to 8 times over your equity investment provides a corresponding amount of depreciation and interest deductions, both of which are fully deductible. I recently completed a commercial building of some 25,000 square feet for which I obtained a 75% loan in the amount of $1,200,000. I exclusively handled the development and leasing aspects myself. The appraisal reflected 15% of the overall value as a developer's potential profit, which meant that I achieved 85% financing only by structuring and leasing the project with no outside help. With this high degree of financial leverage, I received a 200% return on my equity annually when I consider both the after-tax advantages and the potential appreciation of the property.

An important advantage of depreciation or the Accelerated Cost Recovery System (ACRS), as it is known under the Reagan 1981 Tax Act, is that these ordinary deductions from current income can be converted at a later date and taxed at a more favorable rate as long-term capital gains. Regardless of the taxpayer's income bracket, the federal capital gains taxes can now never exceed 20% of the total difference between the sales price and the depreciated book value when the straight-line method of depreciation or cost recovery is used. In addition, proven techniques such as refinancing or tax-free exchanging can be used to prolong the tax-deferred advantages during the later life of a property when these advantages become marginal and the investor's benefits decline.

In projects where substantially increasing cash flow after operating expenses can be achieved, you can acquire investments through the vehicle of leveraged mortgage financing, thereby substantially increasing your tax deductions and corresponding return. Leverage permits the acquisition of larger pieces of property than your personal equity alone could support, and the interest deductions consequent upon mortgage financing can substantially increase your after-tax yield.

I am currently refinancing a commercial building whose value, now estimated at $1,900,000, has increased considerably through the inflationary process. Many of the proposals I have received are tied to an interest rate that fluctuates with the lender's current cost of money. I do not begrudge lenders this attempt to hedge against inflation as, if it continues to accelerate, this property value and the corresponding rents will also increase substantially. Variable interest rates indicate a trend of the future, and sophisticated investors and developers of real property should be prepared to live with this concept perpetually.

Leveraged real estate also permits you to realize a tax-free cash flow from your investment and often provides additional tax shelter for other sources of personal or corporate income. The artificial losses derived from depreciation, or the Accelerated Cost Recovery System deductions, provide you with an additional return on equity that you could not obtain from most other conventional investment sources. In well-located projects, the paper losses bear no physical relationship to the actual depreciation, as a property that is well conceived, leveraged and is appropriately depreciated can often show a 50% per-year return on equity.

A Summation of President Reagan's Economic Recovery Tax Act of 1981

The Reagan administration's Economic Recovery Tax Act of 1981 represents a substantial, lucrative and radical departure from traditional tax accounting for real estate holdings. The Accelerated Cost Recovery System (ACRS) essentially replaces the useful life depreciation rules established by the IRS with a shorter, more uniform and audit-proof duration known as the asset recovery period. The concept and its implementation are tied to the increased inflationary cost of reproduction of assets and significantly accelerate the recovery of capital expenditures.

To qualify for recovery deductions under this act, the buildings must be depreciable tangible property used in a business or held for the production of income. Under the ACRS, capital expenditures are generally recaptured over a "recovery period" of 3, 5, 10 or 15 years. The recovery period depends on the classification of property into real or personal as outlined below.

- *3-Year Property Class* consists of tangible personal and certain other property (known as Section 1245 property) with a class life of 4 years or less.

- *5-Year Property Class* consists generally of all machinery and equipment and includes all personal property (Section 1245 property) not in other classes.

- *10-Year Property Class* includes certain public utility property and short-lived specialized real property (class life of less than 13 years).
- *15-Year Property Class* is essentially the cost recovery or depreciable program for real property holdings.

Under the last classification, the taxpayer can depreciate his real estate assets on a 15-year basis and has the option of increasing the recoverable life to either 35 or 45 years. These extended periods, however, are not generally advantageous, as will be discussed later in this chapter.

Depreciation Options Under the Economic Recovery Act of 1981

Under the 1981 legislation, the taxpayer has the option of electing one of the two following accelerated methods utilizing the uniform 15-year life applied to all property under the new Accelerated Cost Recovery System.

The New Straight-Line Method

Based upon the cost recovery system, a 15-year rate of recovery or depreciable life can be uniformly applied to all investment calibre real estate holdings. Under this approach, no ordinary income recapture provisions apply at the time of sale. This method permits an annual straight-line deduction in the amount of 6.667% of the depreciable portion of the asset, irrespective of whether it is new or used, and represents a great windfall benefit to real estate investors.

The New Accelerated Method

Through the use of the accelerated cost recovery tables, accelerated depreciation can still be utilized through the use of early acceleration deductions that eventually switch over to the straight-line method at the crossover point of diminishing returns. The most advantageous accelerated methods are still duplicable under certain conditions and can be calculated from the appropriate IRS tables.

The major change is the new 15-year life that one can depreciate real property. Under prior law, depreciation was recaptured only to the extent where the accelerated depreciation exceeded the straight-line deductions. The new 1981 law requires, on most property, recapture of all recovery deductions as ordinary income (including the equivalent straight-line portion) whenever any form of accelerated depreciation or cost recovery deductions are taken. Some exceptions to this rule apply to low-income housing and rehabilitation expenditures. This 100% recapture rule applies to all real property except property recovered under the straight-line method. Under the new legislation there is no recapture on real property if straight-line recovery is elected. However, the recapture provisions under the accelerated method can be catastrophic in almost all instances.

Under the Economic Recovery Tax Act of 1981, only two accelerated methods still apply. Neither offers any apparent advantages except for extremely specialized types of investments. Due to the severe recapture provisions under the 1981 Act, professional advice should be sought when considering any method other than straight-line 15-year cost recovery system.

Advantages of the New 15-Year Straight-Line Method

Under the straight-line method incorporated into the Economic Recovery Tax Act of 1981, a uniform annual depreciation deduction is taken each year over the 15-year life or recovery period of the asset. Applicable to both new and existing structures, it will be used for the vast majority of properties. As an example of its application, if you purchased an investment valued at $500,000, of which $100,000 is attributed to the value of the land and $400,000 is allocated to the cost of the building, the land itself is not depreciable; however, the building is depreciable at 6.67%, reflecting the 15-year anticipated life or cost recovery period. You can therefore deduct 6.67% of the $400,000, or $26,000 per year, using the new straight-line method of cost recovery. This amount is allowable regardless of the age of the building, the amount of your equity investment, or whether you had personal liability on any of the mortgages securing this investment.

This new legislation provides many of the lucrative tax benefits of the old accelerated depreciation method without the disastrous consequences of the ordinary income recapture provisions upon sale. Because the Economic Recovery Tax Act of 1981 changed the recapture provisions and accelerated the straight-line deductions to 15 years, I am currently using the straight-line method of depreciation on all my newer acquisitions. This conservative and extremely attractive approach to calculating depreciation best provides the investor with the means of protecting himself from the potentially burdensome taxes upon the sale of his asset. As we will discuss in the section of this chapter on recapture provisions, any accelerated depreciation or cost recovery taken under the new law in excess of that allowable under the straight-line method means that the entire amount of the deductions taken over the years will be taxed as ordinary income rather than as capital gains upon the sale of the asset.

How the Most Advantageous Method Worked Prior to the 1981 Act

A quick review of the old accelerated methods will give us some insight as to their application under the new legislation. If 80% of a new building was intended for residential use, depreciation on it could be calculated by using the 200% declining balance approach. This treatment permitted the maximum amount of deductions allowable under the old IRS Regulations.

Using our previous example of a $500,000 property with $400.000 worth of depreciable value, you could have taken twice the deductions obtained under the old straight-line method, assuming a 25-year depreciable life, for a first-year writeoff of $32,000. Thereafter, the depreciation base would be reduced annually, reflecting the amount of depreciation deduction taken the previous year. After the first year's $32,000 deduction, your depreciable base would have been $368,000 ($400,000 – $32,000), and your second year's deduction would have been $29,440 (8% of $368,000). Since the depreciable base and corresponding deduction decreased with age, the deductible amounts were obviously more substantial in the earlier years.

The up-front deductions achieved through the 200% declining balance approach were extremely important to individuals in high income tax brackets. An associate and frequent partner of mine develops government-subsidized rental housing units exclusively. His properties carry a high degree of leverage, financed through non-recourse mortgages, and qualified prior to the new legislation for this most accelerated method of depreciation. His investors used this 200% approach as the ultimate way to achieve maximum depreciation on carefully structured investments which were lucrative because they also provided for capable long-term financing and management. Many of these projects were leveraged through industrial revenue bonds carrying below-market interest rates. The federal interest exemption from taxation and the non-recourse provisions attached to these bonds made this an extremely attractive investment vehicle. Some of these accelerated tax advantages are still available under the new 1981 Act.

The Other Methods of Accelerated Depreciation Prior to the 1981 Act

Three other methods of accelerated depreciation existed prior to the 1981 Tax Act. The 150% declining balance method functioned like the 200% approach, except that the rate of depreciation was 1½ times that obtained under the straight-line approach. This was appropriate for use on new commercial and industrial property, just as the 200% method was reserved exclusively for new residential developments.

Existing residential housing with a useful remaining life of 20 years could be depreciated by the accelerated 125% declining balance method. Allowable deductions here were 1¼ times that found under the straight-line approach.

The last method, the sum of the year's digits, also applied only to new residential construction. Under this technique, one would create a series of declining fractions in which the numerators were the years' digits in declining order. The denominator was the sum of the number of years of the property's depreciable economic life. As an example, using an asset with an estimated life of 25 years under the old law, the denominator of the fraction would be 325 (the sum of the numbers 1 through 25), and the numerator would be 25 in the first year, 24 in the second year and so on. In the first year, the fraction 25/325 would be 7.7%. Again, with our depreciable $400,000 asset, the first year's deduction would be $30,800, in the second year it would be reduced to 24/325 or 7.4%, and so on. As with all methods of accelerated depreciation, the benefits decrease substantially as the years advance. The sum of the year's digits, again, had application only to new residential construction. These four accelerated methods either have all been eliminated or consolidated under the 1981 Act and can be determined and accurately calculated from the accelerated cost recovery tables issued under IRS regulations.

Determining the Impact of Depreciation Under the New 1981 Act

The Accelerated Cost Recovery System (ACRS) completely changed the economic lives assigned to investment real estate property. Under the new legislation, all property has a uniform 15-year depreciable life. The advantages found in the new straight-line 15-year method are illustrated in the following table. The accelerated cost recovery deductions under the new act apply only to specialized situations where independent tax advice should be sought from competent advisors and are therefore not presented in the following table. For the purposes of illustration we shall use our previous example of a $500,000 asset with $400,000 worth of depreciable value.

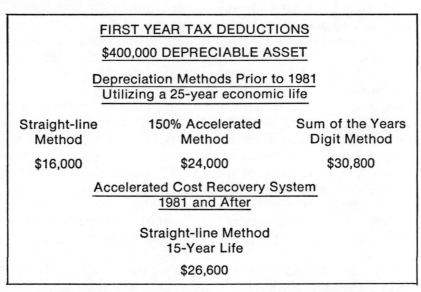

FIRST YEAR TAX DEDUCTIONS

$400,000 DEPRECIABLE ASSET

Depreciation Methods Prior to 1981
Utilizing a 25-year economic life

Straight-line Method	150% Accelerated Method	Sum of the Years Digit Method
$16,000	$24,000	$30,800

Accelerated Cost Recovery System
1981 and After

Straight-line Method
15-Year Life

$26,600

From the above presentation it becomes evident that the new 1981 legislation offers as much tax shelter using the straight-line approach as the old accelerated methods did without the recapture provisions at the time of sale.

FIGURE   4-1

DEPRECIATION DEDUCTION CHANGES

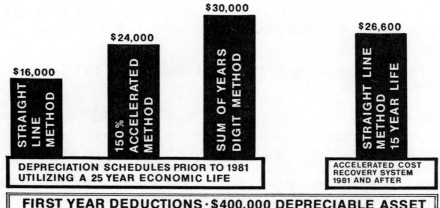

FIRST YEAR DEDUCTIONS · $400,000 DEPRECIABLE ASSET

How Depreciable Building Lives Were Changed Under the 1981 Act

Historically, for tax purposes, the useful life of a building was not determined by how long the brick and mortar held up or remained in place. Rather, the useful life of a property was calculated by the length of time it served a mandatory economic function and, obviously, single-purpose buildings had shorter economic lives than did structures that could be readapted to changing market conditions.

The pre-1981 guidelines that the Internal Revenue Service used were not cast in stone, as the depreciable life of any structure varied with the age and type of building, the economic conditions of the immediate area, the trends of the neighborhood, the purchasing power in the area, the shifting mobility, and the employment base as well as a multitude of other fluctuating needs and demands for investment real estate. All historically affected the useful life of a building which conceivably varied from 20 to 60 years. Due to the escalating nature of calculating future replacement values caused in large part by rampant inflation, President Reagan's Economic Recovery Tax Act of 1981 established a uniform depreciable or asset recovery life for all investment real estate at 15 years, irrespective of whether the property is new or used, by totally ignoring its current or eventual economic use or value. This not only simplifies the entire depreciable process, but provides substantial tax benefits as delineated in the previous section.

Major Effects on Component Depreciation Under the 1981 Law

Another major change that affects real estate investors is the elimination of the component method of depreciation. This, historically, has been the most effective way to maximize depreciation benefits prior to the enactment of the 1981 Act. Even though this approach no longer has complete application, a full review of how the component method was historically applied has considerable merit in understanding its residual benefits for building renovations for older structures under the new 1981 Act. Its use still has application for corporations or partnerships holding assets currently depreciated on the component method, should these holding entities be acquired expressly for the purpose of retaining these beneficial tax advantages.

To illustrate the ramifications of component depreciation, we will use an example of an office building having a useful accounting life of 30 years, which cost me $1,250,000 to construct several years ago. Under the old straight-line composite method, I could take an annual depreciation deduction of 3.33% or $41,600. By using the old component method, which is not accelerated and had no ordinary income recapture provisions, the annual depreciation deduction would have been $69,594, as itemized in Table 4-1.

TABLE 4-1

Useful Lives of the Components and Their Depreciation Deductions on A $1,250,000 Office Building

Value of the shell: $776,000.   Value of the Improvements: $474,000.

Component	% of Cost	Depreciable Life/Years	Annual $ Depreciation Deduction
Building shell	62%	30	$25,840
Electric	5%	15	4,168
Plumbing	2½%	15	2,084
Roof	5%	15	4,168
Mechanical	10%	10	12,500
Ceiling duct work	5%	10	6,250
Landscaping and paving	2½%	15	2,084
Tenant Improvements	8%	8	12,500
			$69,594

Under the new Accelerated Cost Recovery System, utilizing a 15-year straight-line depreciable life or rate of recovery, I would be permitted to deduct $83,300 ($1,250,000 × 6.667%), a sum considerably more than that allowed under the antiquated method.

Under the Economic Recovery Tax Act of 1981, newly installed building improvements or renovations can still be depreciated on a component basis by establishing an appropriate economic useful life. This is applicable provided these renovations do not exceed 25% of the depreciated book value of the structure over a 2-year period. If they exceed this 25% figure, their depreciation or cost recovery period reverts to 15 years, the standard time frame for all real estate structures under the new act.

FIGURE 4-2

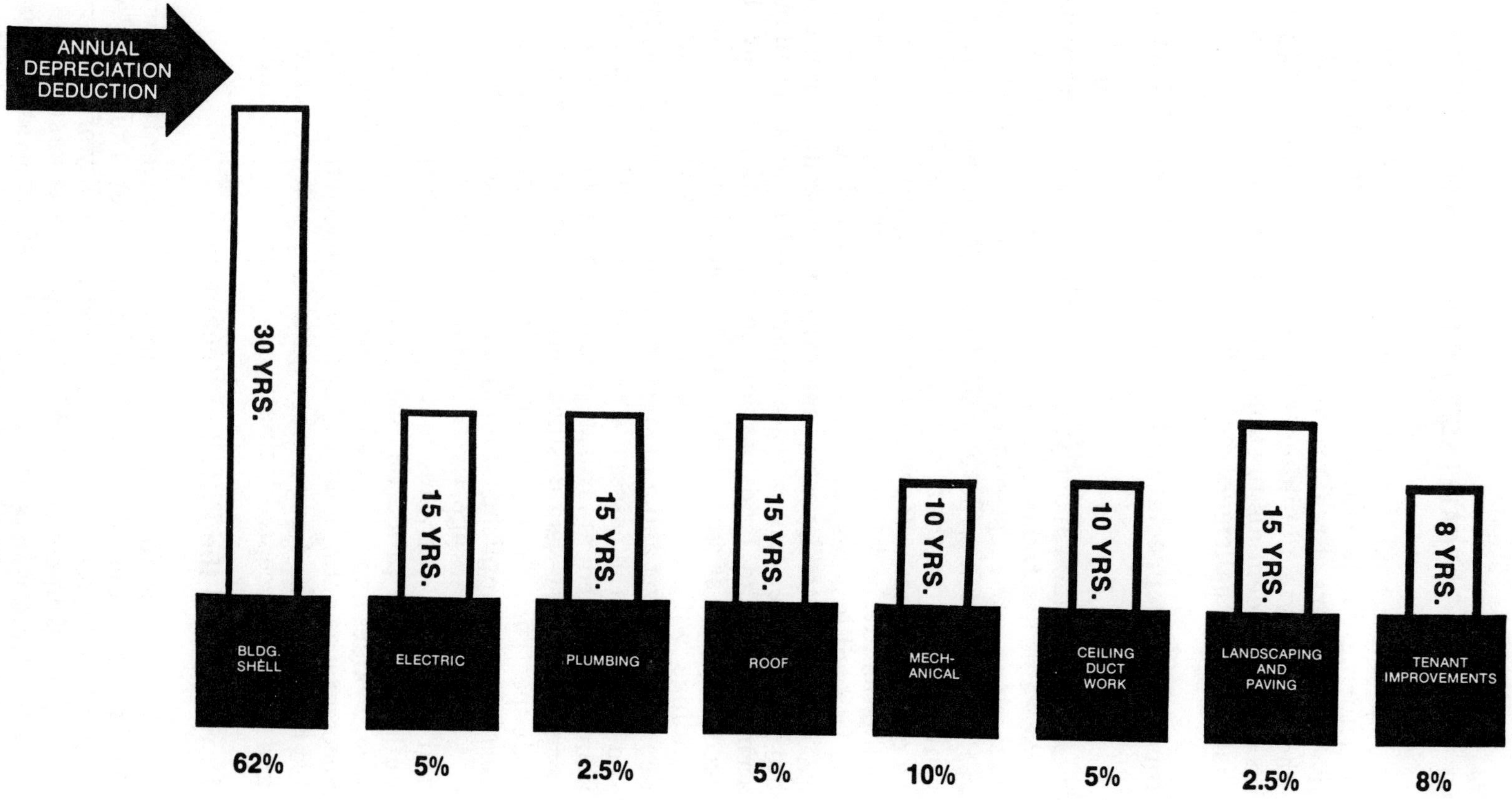

ANNUAL DEPRECIATION DEDUCTION

Component	Years	Percent
BLDG. SHELL	30 YRS.	62%
ELECTRIC	15 YRS.	5%
PLUMBING	15 YRS.	2.5%
ROOF	15 YRS.	5%
MECHANICAL	10 YRS.	10%
CEILING DUCT WORK	10 YRS.	5%
LANDSCAPING AND PAVING	15 YRS.	2.5%
TENANT IMPROVEMENTS	8 YRS.	8%

Several consulting firms in the United States specialize in structuring component breakdowns and corresponding economic lives for owners of real property. Their staffs consist of individuals who can analyze a building, isolate its components, and possess the necessary credentials to support or justify your claim in the event that the IRS challenges your deductions.

Increasing Depreciation by Allocating More of the Costs to the Building

Since the land underlying a building is not a depreciable or cost recoverable asset, the acquiring investor should place as little value on the land as is respectably possible, allocating as much as possible of the acquisition or development costs to the structure. Normally, you can determine the relationship between land and building values by consulting an independent, qualified appraiser for an impartial evaluation. If the appraiser is well respected within the community, the IRS will use his ratio and will very rarely question it.

Sophisticated investors can vary this procedure. For example, a buyer and seller can contract separately for the land and buildings, structuring the land portion on an artificially low basis to accomplish these same goals; or, by comparing the ratio of land to buildings with the tax assessor's office you can calculate the depreciable asset and its deductions before you acquire a property. If you find that the assessor's ratio is beneficial, you can forego the above-mentioned appraisal. The tax assessor's valuation always carries the most weight, since that office is involved in appraising a wide spectrum of comparable properties in a given market area, and normally accomplishes it on an impartial basis.

Several years ago, the IRS audited a group of properties I owned and questioned the value that I placed on the land in relation to the buildings. The properties were located in an older neighborhood where values had increased over a short period of time and where the accessor was delinquent and had not updated those newer values on his tax rolls. His figures were quite favorable from my standpoint, and the IRS accepted his authority in settling the audit.

How to Avoid the Pitfall of Recapture

All accelerated depreciation, more recently known as the Accelerated Cost Recovery System under the 1981 Act, will eventually expose the investor to the possibility of ordinary income recapture. The concept behind recapture is that it prevents the investor from converting the benefits of accelerated depreciation deductions into long-term capital gains. Under the new law, you must declare as ordinary income at the time of sale any and all tax deductions that you have taken over the holding period of the asset if you have used an accelerated method. This varies drastically from the old rules where the recapture provisions only applied to the accelerated portion of the depreciation taken over and above the straight-line deductions.

For example, under the old rules, during the first 100 months of the holding period of an asset, you as owner were subject to 100% recapture on the accelerated portion only. During the next 100 months the recapture provisions were phased out at 1% per month so that they were completely eliminated at the end of the 200th month. The gradual reduction of this recapture exposure no longer applies under the Economic Recovery Tax Act of 1981.

Under the new rules, an investor who takes accelerated depreciation or cost recovery is subject to 100% recapture for all tax deductions no longer limited to the accelerated ones, taken over the holding period of the asset. These recapture provisions, applied at the time of sale, can conceivably accelerate you into an extremely high tax bracket. If the property being sold was acquired primarily for tax purposes rather than for appreciation, a major and potentially disastrous tax obligation could also arise at the end of the holding period without the corresponding funds to satisfy it. This situation is not uncommon on highly leveraged tax-oriented properties where the total tax ramifications are not always completely understood. These new accelerated cost recovery tables are extremely complicated and difficult to interpret, and competent tax advice should be sought prior to their use and application.

Determining the Most Advantageous Method of Depreciation

The method of depreciation or cost recovery that one chooses should be directly correlated with the projected economic life and the net income a property will generate after carefully calculating the potential for reducing that income through increased operating expenses. The economic value of a project at the end of the anticipated holding period must always also be evaluated in light of the potential tax liability. A project with a relatively long economic life and a predictable and positive cash flow is the only likely candidate for using the accelerated cost recovery approach since these types of assets will normally show sizable appreciation when offered for resale. Investments with a less predictable economic life and corresponding cash flow will ultimately command a lower sales price. If accelerated depreciation or cost recovery is used in these instances, you will find yourself in trouble at the end of the holding period, with too little profit from the sale to cover the tax obligations incurred through the stiff and almost prohibitive recapture provisions of the 1981 Tax Act.

The new accelerated cost recovery approach has the overall effect of eliminating all the advantages found in accelerated depreciation by reducing the maximum long-term capital gains rate now set at 20%. Many ill-advised investors use the accelerated cost recovery approach on single-purpose buildings, especially buildings like motels and drive-in restaurants, to initially offset the large amount of cash these operations generate in the early years. In attempting to shelter the cash flow early in the life of the project, they face the ultimate probability that the resale value of their single-purpose buildings will not be adequate tax-wise when their business operations start to decline.

From time to time I have been associated with low-income government subsidized housing syndications. Most of these projects tend to maximize their tax deductions during the initial years. Unless these investments are located in quality neighborhoods, and most of them are not, I have advised my clients not to take the maximum accelerated tax deductions. The long-term ability to increase income after expenses usually does not exist in these marginal areas, and the potential appreciation to cover the short-term recapture consequences will normally not be there at the time of sale, especially if the general partner participates in the proceeds of sale. However, the tax-deferred exchange provisions discussed in Chapter 3 can conceivably negate the economic sting of the recapture provisions of the 1981 Act if properly understood and applied.

Increasing Deductions Through the 10% Investment Tax Credit

The 10% investment tax credit, which was made permanent by the Tax Reform Act of 1978, is extremely important for individuals in the higher tax brackets. This one-time up-front deduction, which can be carried backward 3 years and forward 15 years, is applied to and directly offsets your personal tax obligation. According to the general guidelines, deductions can be taken on tangible personal investment property. Two types of assets qualify; property with a three-year life qualifies for a 6% investment credit and property with a five-year life qualifies for the full 10% credit. There is a limitation of a maximum one-time annual deduction of $125,000 for used property with no limitation on newly acquiried assets. In the real estate field, several items qualify for this credit including:

- office machinery and equipment,
- office furniture,

- movable partitions,
- floor and window coverings,
- retail fixtures, and
- industrial machinery.

Buildings and their structural components are excluded from the 10% tax credit. The 1981 Act also includes an "at risk" provision meaning that the total deductions are limited to the amount of the investment capital you have at risk. In summary, the 1981 Act provides the following benefits:

Property Class	ITC Rate
3-Year Life	6%
5-Year Life	10%

The ordinary income recapture rules have also changed under the 1981 Act. The investment credit is "earned" with the passage of time under the old law; one-third of the 10% credit earned after the third, fifth and seventh years. The advantageous changes under the new legislation can be summarized as follows:

Years Property Held	Cumulative Old Law	ITC Earned New Law
1	0%	2%
2	0%	4%
3	3⅓%	6%
4	3⅓%	8%
5	6⅔%	10%
6	6⅔%	10%
7	10%	10%

The 1981 law tends to decrease the importance of holding an asset until the credit is earned because it is earned ratably over a shorter period.

Some time ago I purchased an office complex, structuring the building as an executive suite. Each of the 22 offices was served by a common reception area and enjoyed the use of a centralized conference room. Each office was fully furnished, the contents of which I leased on a five-year basis from the manufacturer's distributor. The lease was structured giving me the option to purchase the furniture at the end of the lease for 10% of the initial purchase price. By structuring the lease in this fashion, I was successful in obtaining the 10% investment credit even though I did not own the furniture until the end of the leasehold period.

How to Advantageously Adjust the Economic Life of a Project

Earlier in this chapter, we discussed the new 15-year economic life established under the Economic Recovery Act of 1981. We mentioned that the remaining life of a specific project could still be changed on existing properties acquired prior to and not subject to the new legislation, with relative ease if the appropriate supporting material were properly presented to the IRS. Where an investment is marginally located or subject to adverse changing economic circumstances which could diminish its viability, taking accelerated depreciation or cost recovery is obviously not prudent.

Several years ago, an associate and I were acquiring properties near an urban university in a neighborhood that was beginning to show initial signs of deterioration. Because our properties were purchased reasonably and rented to college students, the cash flow was quite substantial. Our accountants took the position that, in spite of the positive earnings, a strong argument could be made for shortening the economic lives of the properties in this area which was showing overall signs of deterioration. Because of the condition of the neighborhood in general, we were successful in our appeal to shorten the economic lives of our investments, increasing our tax deductions without being subject to the recapture provisions. In this instance, my associate and I deliberately chose not to take accelerated depreciation, even though we might have completely sheltered our cash flow. This possibility still exists on properties acquired prior to the 1981 legislation.

We have returned with some regularity in this chapter to the 1978 and 1981 Tax Reform Acts and the severity of their recapture provisions. A major change in the Reform Act of 1978 dramatically affects you as a real estate investor. Under this legislation, a minimum tax of 15% was enacted affecting the profits on certain tax preference items. The real estate areas directly affected by this minimum tax of 15% was enacted affecting the income on certain tax depreciation on real property and accelerated depreciation on personal property under lease.

The ramifications of the appropriate sections of these two acts are too complex to permit a full discussion here. The subject should be thoroughly reviewed with your accountants, tax and or legal advisors.

Capitalizing on Quick Writeoffs for Residential and Commercial Rehabilitation

The Economic Recovery Tax Act of 1981 authorized new deductions for rehabilitation of older buildings. A new three-tier investment credit for rehabilitation of buildings has been adopted in the new law of 1981 to replace the old 10% regular investment credit. The old investment and the energy credits will no longer be allowed in addition to rehabilitation credit on the same expenditures. The new investment credit percentages with respect to qualified rehabilitation expenditures are as follows:

30-year-old building	15%
40-year-old building	20%
Certified historic structure	25%

The 15% and 20% credits are only applicable to nonresidential buildings. However, the 25% credit for certified historic structures applies to both residential and nonresidential buildings. In addition, taxpayers will be allowed the credit only if they elect to recover the cost of the rehabilitation expenditures using the straight-line method of depreciation or cost recovery. The expenditures must be capital in nature and have a recovery period of 15 years in order to qualify.

Additionally, the recoverable or depreciated basis of rehabilitated buildings (except certified historic buildings) must be reduced by the amount of the credit that is taken. The 60-month amortization of certain rehabilitation expenditures has been repealed under the 1981 law. However, there are some interesting transitional rules that an accountant can interpret for those who are currently utilizing the tax advantages of this interesting program.

An associate of mine who specializes in reconverting moderate-to low-income housing projects has, over the years, analyzed the construction compilations of these programs and mastered many of the complicated tax rules and regulations. Investors continually line up to commit equity funds for his projects. He often purchases the shell buildings and land for less than 25% of the total cost of their replacement value and achieves sizable up-front deductions on the improvements. Even before this new legislation was enacted, his business was extremely profitable. Now it is a virtual gold mine.

How Rehabilitation Projects Can Return 100% on Equity Annually

The 15%-20%-25% provisions of the Economic Recovery Tax Act of 1981 discussed in the last section were designed to provide an incentive for the private sector to rehabilitate buildings in older metropolitan areas of the United States. Buildings qualify for the program as long as the improvements have a useful life in excess of five years.

Many of the rehabilitation tax deductions, when combined with the relatively low acquisition prices of these older properties, coupled with the redevelopment authority tax-free bonds issued by many municipalities as an inducement for rejuvenating our major metropolitan centers, can often provide a relatively risk-free after-tax return of over 100% per annum.

After purchasing an old abandoned school building at a public auction, an associate of mine rejuvenated the structure and leased it to several prestigious national tenants. A majority of the renovation improvements qualified for the accelerated writeoff provided for in the new legislation, and my associate was successful in attracting several outside investors to the project because of the associated tax advantages. Although the acquisition price of the building cannot be included in the accelerated deduction schedule, similar projects have proved to be very lucrative for many real estate investors since the Economic Recovery Act of 1981, and will result in the restoration of many dilapidated structures in the older metropolitan areas of this country.

Before you acquire an older building with the intent to rejuvenate it, using this advantageous legislation, you should engage a structural engineer to analyze the exterior of the building for its soundness. A restriction of this legislation as it applies to historic buildings is that only a certain percentage of the exterior walls can be replaced. If major improvements are needed on the exterior shell of a building, the investor risks losing many of the accelerated tax advantages.

Buildings with historic preservation value designated by the United States Government, or by recognized historical societies, show the most lucrative tax benefits if you can work around the restrictions on exterior improvements which are sometimes financially prohibitive. Much greater latitude in rehabilitation is possible in buildings without historic designations and these often, over the long run, prove to be better investments.

The rejuvenation of older buildings and the redevelopment of projects within the inner cities will become increasingly lucrative during the decade of the 1980s. Incentives for urban renewal will most likely be provided by the United States Government, often in the form of additional tax credits or tax-sheltering devices. Local municipalities have and will continue to look favorably on urban redevelopment which will broaden their tax bases without adding appreciably to the costs of municipal services through the "in-fill" process. Because of the tax advantages inherent in these inner city projects, you will find them increasingly important in attracting the financial backing that we shall discuss in the next chapter.

5

Limited Partnerships: A Simple Vehicle For Raising Equity Capital

Limited partnerships can be profitable for investors and syndicators alike. This vehicle will permit you, as a syndicator of the partnership, to control sizable assets by investing only time and effort and by capitalizing on your ability to locate real property and take it under option.

This chapter will show you, systematically, how to structure syndications and locate the investors by offering dynamic and exciting returns to yourself and your investors. We will outline the important tax benefits and full disclosure provisions associated with successful syndications, and differentiate between private and public methods for raising equity capital. These concepts are illustrated by dozens of successful examples and techniques. These and a multitude of other strategies constitute the inside secrets of using other people's money successfully to everybody's mutual advantage.

How to Locate the Investors

Individuals who purchase interests in real estate limited partnerships are normally in high income tax brackets. Their prime interest is in finding tax shelters, paper losses built up over a period of years to offset their income from other sources. You as a syndicator interested in attracting such investors can intentionally shift or disproportionately allocate these deductions in relation to the investor's income in order to show sizable after-tax benefits for many years. When the deductions decrease or evaporate altogether, you can exchange the equity in the tax-sheltered property into a new vehicle, thus avoiding for your investors the eventual day of reckoning with the Internal Revenue Service. Most partnerships can be structured so that deductions can be accelerated, especially if the cash method of accounting is used where front-end expenses are paid and deducted during the early years.

In all my experiences I have found that (if I syndicate sound properties), the more front-end tax deductions I can offer the investors, the easier it is to sell them.

Obviously, individuals in the highest tax brackets will be the biggest beneficiaries from the tax-sheltering of such deals, and will have the least to risk if one's projects do not fully materialize, or if investors partially lose their equity. For instance, an investor-taxpayer in the 50% bracket who commits $1,000 to a limited partnership venture can save up to $500 in taxes, for a 50% return annually, if he receives $1,000 annually in artificial tax deductions taken against his other ordinary income. If the project totally fails, this same investor in the 50% bracket will lose only $500 of his $1,000 investment after tax considerations. The basic reason for stressing and structuring the important tax-sheltered ramifications of limited partnerships is that high-income individuals are prone to acquire high-risk situations because of the overall tax ramifications.

I was recently associated with a tax-shelter syndication involving a 576-unit apartment complex bought out of bankruptcy from an eastern real estate investment trust. The limited partners received a staggering amount of tax losses in relation to their initial equity investment. These artificial deductions were over five times the initial investment. The project itself was located in a marginal area and most of the investors would have been satisfied just to recoup their initial contribution after a four-year holding period in light of these unusual tax benefits. Later in this chapter, I will give the details of this transaction, in which the limited partners received a $2 million windfall when the project was sold to an apartment converter.

What Constitutes a Good Return to the Investors

The syndicator of a limited partnership normally has to offer between $3 and $4 of tax deductions for every dollar of invested capital put into a project. These figures can be adjusted depending upon the nature and quality of the venture. Obviously, a sound development that will show appreciation combined with a positive cash flow and substantial tax benefits can be marketed with ease.

Several years ago, I syndicated an investment opportunity with a group of limited partners whose equity contributions were based exclusively on the direct tax deductions they received. Basically, with predetermined maximum and minimum equity contributions, the investors were to contribute $1.00 in equity funds for every $4.00 in direct tax deductions they received. The investors achieved their maximum tax benefits and made a full contribution of equity in the fifteenth month of this project.

Many tax-shelter deals involve new construction, especially if accelerated depreciation is an important part of the investment package, since accelerated depreciation or cost recovery can be taken only by first-time users of a structure. The element of speculation obviously lies in completing the project on schedule, and being able to provide ample funds for completion and start-up expenses.

I was associated with a project in which a group of 25 investors had purchased for $8 million a 576-unit apartment that had gone through foreclosure in 1976. The partnership acquired the project and sold it four years later to a converter for $12 million, for an approximate gain of $4 million over the initial purchase price. Each of the 25 limited partners contributed $18,000 for a total equity contribution of $450,000. Each investor eventually received $99,000 worth of cumulative tax deductions over the four-year period, all being in the 50% plus tax bracket. The limited partners received 50% of the proceeds of the sale after conversion and after repayment of the first and second mortgages. This approximated $2,300,000 or $87,000 per limited partnership unit. The cumulative benefits totaled $136,500 per partnership unit when calculating the after-tax ramifications for a 750% overall return on equity, or 190% per year— not a marginal return by any investor's standards.

The general partner in this project did quite well considering he had no equity investment and received a 5% management fee on the annual income of $1,500,000, or $75,000 per year plus an additional 25% of the profits upon sale, or $1,000,000. His combined earnings were $1,300,000, or $325,000 per year. The remaining 25% of the profit upon sale, or $1,000,000, went to the real estate investment trust, as they held the first and second mortgages in the amount of $7,550,000 or 94% of the acquisition price as their only means of merchandising a highly leveraged non-recourse situation. Obviously, all parties involved showed substantial profits on this venture.

The Important Tax Benefits of Limited Partnerships

Limited partnerships offer an extremely important benefit to investors in that they can convert deductions from ordinary income into long-term capital gains. This translates basically into deferred tax-free income during the holding period of the asset. Excess depreciation from a syndication can be offset against one's ordinary income, a direct benefit without a corresponding taxable obligation, until the asset is sold. Since real estate by its very nature is a capital asset, any recognized gain is taxed at the favorable capital gains rates.

A limited partnership is governed by the regulations of the state in which the partnership is formed. The express intent of its existence is to permit passive investors to contribute funds to a general partner who subsequently invests in real estate ventures and provides the limited partners with the same flow-through singly-taxed benefits they would have if they had the status of a general partner. The added attraction of this vehicle is that limited partners' exposure is limited exclusively to the funds they have invested in the partnership. In effect, if a limited partnership meets the simple guidelines set up by the Internal Revenue Service, the partners can achieve the same limit of exposure a corporation has, without the double taxation to its shareholders.

Limited partnerships are not in themselves tax-paying entities. The general and each limited partner are taxed each at his own individual rate. For this reason, these vehicles have wide-ranging and interesting tax ramifications for the participating investors, especially when tax deductions can be passed through directly to the partners in amounts often far exceeding their initial investment, depending of course upon the "at risk" factor of the transaction. In real estate limited partnerships the "at risk" aspect relates not only to the contribution of the limited partners, but also reflects the amount of non-recourse financing that the partnership assumes as it develops or holds a given investment. The 1976 Tax Reform Act eliminated many of the excessive and accelerated writeoffs, especially those that related to non-recourse financing.

Before this legislation was enacted, I syndicated an interesting project that was financed by a non-recourse note in the amount of $530,000, which was guaranteed by a branch of the U.S. Government. The interest on the note and the high degree of non-recourse leverage permitted the investors to obtain large deductions in relation to their equity contributions, some four to five times the size of their original investments. Similar non-recourse notes were the key to many successful syndications prior to the Tax Reform Act.

Understanding the Important Capabilities Necessary for Syndication

When forming a limited partnership, you as a general partner must carefully explain to your limited partners that they basically have no voice in the operations or the management of their investment. The limited partnership agreement must specifically outline the functions in which they can participate, as any active management participation can destroy the single taxation benefits found in these vehicles. To operate successfully, and to continue to syndicate real estate projects, you as general partner must not only have the capability to package the initial offering, but must have the ability and the management talents to operate a major real estate venture. Some of the more obvious characteristics you need to possess in order to maintain a viable syndication are:

- locating the appropriate property;
- providing the necessary equity and mortgage financing;
- justifying a realistic compensation for you as general partner;
- providing competent tax advice and realistic profit projections;
- determining adequate working capital and reserves for contingencies;
- supplying annual reports and making cash distributions;
- providing a vehicle to enable limited partners to transfer or sell their interests;
- knowing when to liquidate the partnership, refinance the investment, or exchange into another tax-sheltered property.

I recently reviewed a proposed major syndication on an apartment complex in the Southwest where a 500+ unit $10,000,000 apartment complex was financed through government-subsidized funding. The project was in what I considered a marginal area; however, the track record of the management combined with the tremendous tax shelter advantages, in my estimation, made this a respectable investment. Without these two necessary ingredients I do not feel that this project would have been viable on a long-term basis.

How to Meet the I.R.S. Qualifications for Pass-Through Tax Deductions

To qualify as a limited partnership having the benefits of direct pass-through of losses, and not being subject to double taxation as are corporations, the limited partnership must not possess more than two of the four I.R.S.- designated corporate characteristics:

- continuity of life;
- centralization of management;
- limited liability;
- free transferability of interest.

The first and last characteristics are always specifically excluded in all limited partnership agreements. The second and third items must be incorporated. When forming a limited partnership it is important to understand that this vehicle is a creature of statute. Failure by the general partner to file a Certificate of Limited Partnership can cause revocation of the limited partnership's status, resulting in the entity's being classified as a general partnership in which the limited partners would have the same unlimited liability that the general partner has.

Because of the passive role the limited partners must play in the management of a project, combined with the concept that they are investing based upon expected profits, a limited partnership is considered by the Securities and Exchange Commission to be an investment contract or security. If the general partner fails to comply with federal or state securities laws or is not exempt from registration, his limited partners have the option to rescind the contract and sue the general partner for a return of their invested funds. The S.E.C. regards limited partners in much the same way as it views stockholders in a corporation, protecting their interests by emphasizing their lack of actively participating in the management. They require full information and disclosure to the investors involved regarding all the negative ramifications and the illiquid nature of these investments.

I came close to developing a problem on a syndication of a 181-unit mobile home park in which one of the limited partner/investors also served as the partnership tax attorney. There was a sizable amount of interplay and dialogue by this individual acting as the partnership counsel and also holding a limited partnership interest. If this professional relationship had been challenged, it is quite conceivable that this individual could have lost his status as a limited partner.

I make a special effort in all my syndications to oversimplify the potential risk factors, urging my investors to seek out competent legal and investment advice. In addition, I provide supporting materials to their financial consultants, should it be required in their making a decision.

How to Maximize Tax Deductions for Your Investors

A limited partner can claim a tax deduction for his prorated share of the partnership losses only to the extent of his basis in that partnership interest. For instance, if an individual contributes $10,000 to a limited partnership and over a period of years accumulates tax losses of $11,000, he can deduct only $10,000, which represents his original investment, on his personal tax return unless you as the general partner are in a position to increase his tax-deductible basis. You need to make a distinction between a tax-deductible basis, a partner's capital contribution account, and finally the partnership's basis in the asset. A limited partner's tax-deductible basis can be increased by encumbering the property in such a fashion that the mortgage debt is a direct obligation of the partnership. If the partnership is personally liable for the debt, the limited partners can increase their tax deductions by their proportionate share of the recourse financing, taking these additional writeoffs in excess of the capital contributions to the limited partnership. This is what is known as the "at risk" provision. Increased responsibility for partnership liabilities is considered for tax purposes as an additional contribution of funds to the partnership which increases the partners' tax-deductible bases. By the creative use of recourse financing, a limited partner can deduct losses in excess of his actual cash contribution.

For example, a limited partner who invested $25,000 for a 5% interest in a project with a non-recourse mortgage, could not deduct losses in excess of that $25,000 contribution. If this same equity investment were structured on a property in which a recourse mortgage of $5 million was obtained, our limited partner would receive an artificially boosted tax-deductible basis of $275,000, representing his 5% interest in the mortgage obligation, potentially claiming deductions up to that figure. You as the syndicator must, of course, fully realize the interrelationship between recourse and non-recourse financing. When you are involved in an "in-and-out" cash flow type of venture and the tax benefits are minimal, the choice of non-recourse financing is not important. When immediate cash flow is not at issue and tax deductions are, mortgage interrelationships should be discussed in considerable detail with your financial advisors.

How to Advantageously Structure the General Partner's Taxable Obligations

In determining profit and loss allocations and structuring the appropriate fees to you as the general partner, it is important to seek competent counsel, as in some cases the services provided by the general partner can be considered taxable without your receiving the funds to meet these obligations. An interesting way to shift distributions is to prioritize allocation of profits or losses to the limited partners until their initial investment has either been recouped or a fair return on their investment has been received. One such arrangement is for the general partner to be compensated for his direct services during the lifetime of the project, or to receive an initial up-front fee for the syndication, taking a disproportionate equity in the partnership until the project is sold. At that point, the profits of the partnership revert equally to the limited and the general partners. This coordinates the cash received with the taxable obligation to fund it.

I recently structured a limited partnership with an initial 2% interest for myself, the remaining 98% of the cash flow and depreciation going to the limited partners. When the full capital contribution of the limited partners was returned with a reasonable interest rate, the partnership equity reverted to a 50/50 arrangement in which I controlled 50% of the assets and was entitled to 50% of the cash flow. Such an arrangement can be an effective selling tool in that the limited partners get the majority of the benefits from the venture until they have been repaid and receive a fair return on their equity. Nonetheless, the general partner is additionally compensated during the development or holding period for his services. If you as the general partner take a sizable up-front equity position, a taxable situation might surface.

How to Shift Short-Term Income into Long-Term Capital Gains

A general partner's percentage of the partnership interests can be considered compensation for your services, and you run the risk of being taxed at the rate of ordinary income without any corresponding distribution of funds. It is important, even before approaching potential limited partners, to draw up the partnership documents structuring the general partner's compensation to appropriately meet Internal Revenue Service requirements. This can be accomplished by designating your participation in the partnership as an exchange for your eventual contribution, giving you the contractual option at a later date to obtain a larger interest in the investment. When you exercise your option for a larger interest in the capital asset, you are then taxed when the total gain is payable and declared. If you as the general partner can demonstrate that the partnership interest you received was in exchange for a transfer of real property, your profits will not be taxed as ordinary income but as a long-term capital gain when the asset is disposed of. Only a competent tax attorney or accountant can assure your protection in such a situation where large sums of limited partnership funds are involved and you as the general partner risk a sizable tax obligation, if the venture is not structured properly.

In every major syndication that demonstrated considerable tax implications, I have been audited by the Internal Revenue Service in recent years. So far, I have not suffered any major setbacks on these audits because of the precautions I have taken in consulting competent attorneys and accountants in drafting the appropriate documentation for each limited partnership transaction. A major possibility of error lies in assuming that documentation for one limited partnership can serve as a blueprint for a similar transaction. Superficial similarities often mask important differences which surface under I.R.S. scrutiny.

The Important Accounting and I.R.S. Aspects of Limited Partnerships

The taxable years of most limited partnerships are based on a calendar year since the initial benefits go to the limited partners who calculate their tax liabilities and file their returns on a calendar year basis, one exception being that the Internal Revenue Service will permit a limited partnership to have the same fiscal year as that of its general partner. A sophisticated general partner can predetermine when it is most beneficial to pass through the profits or losses by establishing a newly formed corporation as the general partner, utilizing an advantageous fiscal year end.

Recently I structured a limited partnerhip in which I specifically formed a Subchapter S corporation to be the general partner, thereby giving the partnership a different fiscal year end than the calendar year. I did this specifically because it was a newly constructed for-sale condominium project in which I could predict with a degree of certainty when the sales would close and the income would be generated. By setting the fiscal year of the corporation to terminate prior to the income being generated from the project, I deferred the taxable income to the following calendar year for the general and limited partners.

Historically, most limited partnerships have used the cash method of accounting, declaring all income when it was received and all expenses when they were incurred. By utilizing this method, partnerships could expend up-front cash outlays for prepaid interest and syndication fees, passing these accelerated and artificial deductions on directly to the limited partners. The Tax Reform Act of 1976 changed this by eliminating most of these accelerated writeoffs. Since then, many limited partnerships are using the accrual method of accounting which gives a more accurate picture of the partnership affairs. This method reports income and deductions in the year in which they are incurred, regardless of whether or not cash transfers are involved.

The Importance of Obtaining Advance I.R.S. Rulings

Occasionally it is imperative to seek out advance I.R.S. rulings on the tax status of a proposed partnership to assure that it will not be subject to double taxation as a corporation. This is especially prevalent in large real estate syndications where tax shelter is a major consideration in the formation of the partnership. The I.R.S. has issued a statement of conditions under which it will agree to provide advance rulings on the classification of limited partnerships. The four major conditions for issuance are:

- The general partner must have at least a 1% interest in the income, gain, loss, or deductions of the partnership.

- The total deductions claimed by the partners in the first two years of the partnership's life must not exceed the amount of equity capital invested by the limited partners.
- The use of non-recourse loans owed by the partnership to outside interests cannot be converted into an equity interest in the limited partnership at a later date.
- The limited partnership must make available to the I.R.S. all appropriate documents supporting the above three points.

From time to time I have applied for and received these advance rulings on limited partnerships. I find that if one's legal counsel is competent, an application can be processed and a ruling obtained within 90 days. This is often a good hedge if large amounts of syndicated funds are involved, as these larger projects automatically get close scrutiny from the I.R.S. once they are formed and operational.

How to Syndicate Projects Without Offering Tax Advantages

A general partner can raise equity funds for project acquisition and development through a limited partnership vehicle. These projects normally do not provide tax shelter, and must be structured to provide a sizable immediate return on the limited partner's capital contribution. Development is risky by nature, and many limited partnerships can provide a cushion against a catastrophic loss in case a project does not fully materialize.

On several occasions I have used limited partnerships to fund development-oriented projects. The process commences with the analysis of the completed value of the project, the anticipated profits that can be generated, and the wholesale or residual value of the venture should a disaster occur and the development have to be aborted. Having accurately determined these three figures, I personally borrow an amount equal to the wholesale value of the project from a lending institution and use a limited partnership syndication as a cushion for completing the balance of the project. Under such circumstances the limited partners can normally expect a minimum of 30% to 40% per-year return on their equity investment.

I am currently involved in such a syndication where I am financing a project being constructed on leased land. The project is an 18-unit luxury condominium. Because of the tight nature of the money market, combined with the fact that the leased land is unsubordinated, I syndicated this project through several limited partners to whom I guaranteed a 30% return on equity before any profits would go to me as the general partner. The partnership is structured in expectation that the limited partners will receive between 40% and 50% return on their equity after the first half of the project is completed. Utilizing this approach, I can go to the interim lender and borrow only approximately 60% of the total value of the completed venture. With this structure, the lender feels comfortable with the unsubordinated lease, I am at ease with the amount of my personal exposure, and the limited partners will receive a return of approximately three times what they could obtain in the current money market.

Mechanics of a Successful Non-Tax-Sheltered Syndication

Several years ago I completed a syndication on a 50-unit semi-completed condominium project. I acquired this out of foreclosure from an East Coast real estate investment trust for $860,000, representing a purchase at thirty cents on the dollar. I acquired the property in 1978 and syndicated $250,000 in up-front money through ten investors with $25,000 each. I had the use of the investors' funds for approximately 15 months in order to complete the initial phase of this project, which was acquired and developed under these basic parameters:

Income:

Sellout value—Phase One, 50 units	$2,375,000
Value of Phase Two, Land—9 acres	300,000
Total income generated	$2,675,000

Development Expenses:

Cost of Acquisition	$ 860,000
Cost of Completion/(Construction)	1,040,000
Marketing and Closing Costs	155,000
	$2,055,000

Profit to the Limited Partnership

Cash on Phase One	$ 320,000
Land Value on Phase Two	300,000
	$ 620,000

The limited partners received 9½% interest on their outstanding invested funds plus the first $62,500 in profits generated from the project, representing a projected 25% return on their equity prior to my company as the general partner receiving any cash distribution. In addition to the full return of their equity contribution, the ten limited partners received a total cash distribution as follows:

Percentage of profits guaranteed	$ 62,500
Interest at 9.5%	31,000
Additional 10% interest in profits after deducting $62,500	25,750
10% interest in Phase Two, land	30,000
	$149,250

This represented a 60% return over the fifteen-month sellout period, 4% a month or 48% annualized return on equity.

The large amount of equity funds in relation to the acquisition price afforded me the luxury of acquiring this project for thirty cents on the dollar. This venture is typical of many others in which distressed lenders take the first legitimate, cash-oriented deal presented to them.

How to Be Exempt from State and Federal Registration

The complications and costs associated with registering with the Securities and Exchange Commission are beyond the scope of description in this chapter. Yet limited partnerships, depending on the number of limited partners and dollar amounts involved, can be required to register. The S.E.C., through its Rule 146, defines a private offering that is exempt from federal registration. Of the points to which you have to conform in order to be exempt, the first two below are tailored to exempt the small limited partnership application. The balance apply to all exempt issues, irrespective of their size.

- There can be no general solicitation, which includes newspaper, magazine, radio or television advertising, promotional meetings, etc.
- There can be no more than 35 limited partners who must invest less than $150,000 each. There can be an unlimited number of purchasers who invest in excess of $150,000 each.

- The potential limited partners must have access to all pertinent information on the project.
- The potential investor must have sufficient income and assets to be able to afford the investment risk.
- The shares cannot be offered to an underwriter or other persons whose basic intent is to resell the partnership units.

In order to exempt a limited partnership offering from the various states' securities commissions, one must scrutinize the particular state statutes that affect these new offerings. Generally speaking, the state exemptions are fairly easy to obtain; however, competent legal counsel should be retained prior to drawing the limited partnership agreement and structuring the syndication offering prospectus.

General Parameters of Public Syndication

Although public syndications are too complicated to permit full-scale consideration here, we will, however, examine them briefly. Public syndication is required for such entities as real estate investment trusts, publicly held real estate corporations, and many other associations devoted to raising public funds for mortgage or equity participation or for investment pools designated to acquire future properties. Most of these public vehicles are structured by individuals having expertise in real estate brokerage, development, mortgage financing, or property management. They involve acquiring properties near wholesale values and reselling them at higher, often retail levels, collecting in the process sizable fees for acquisition, construction, management, and financing. They are promoted and distributed through professionals with securities licenses who specialize in a multitude of tax-sheltered or leveraged investments including oil and gas syndicates, leased equipment trusts, and commodity futures. Up-front fees on these syndications can fluctuate from 10% to 20% of the value of the equity raised, which means that the syndicated investor automatically reduces or dilutes his equity by the amount of these up-front syndication fees.

From time to time I have had the opportunity to review many of the prospectuses of these public syndications being promoted by various members of the New York Stock Exchange brokerage houses. When the commissions that the brokerage firms receive are taken into account, this specialized area of syndications can be quite lucrative, especially when one is dealing with properties that utilize sizable amounts of leverage. By the same token, such activities are highly regulated and require more experienced individuals than do private syndications. These syndicators who are experienced in management, construction, and the potential tax ramifications make these investments less risky in the long run and less likely to develop financial problems than private syndications.

All my syndications to date have been privately placed. I do this primarily to retain more control over the syndication with less bureaucratic red tape than one encounters in a full-blown public offering. I find that private syndications have immense value for the local or regional developer who from time to time needs up-front equity funding.

In my estimation, many of these major public syndications merely trade dollars. The properties they purchase are usually conservative in nature with long-term, fixed-obligation leases. They offer little long-term potential for the investor during inflationary periods, except for a predictable cash distribution that is relatively assured and fully tax-sheltered. Since many of the major public syndications are relatively new, no record of their long-term potential or resale value exists at this point.

How to Syndicate Without Utilizing One's Own Funds

Limited partnership arrangements can be structured so that the general partner is a corporation, as was the case with a previously cited example in which a Subchapter S corporation was set up to establish the desired fiscal year for one of my partnerships. In such instances, the general corporate partner maintains the minimum net worth, usually a percentage of the total amount contributed by the limited partners, this normally being the only contribution except for one's time and managerial abilities. Whatever the nature of the general partner, individual or corporate, the general partner maintains full control of all the financial and management aspects creating an interesting vehicle for acquiring large properties with little personal equity.

Some of the major public syndications are attracted to this leveraged aspect of limited partnerships. As the general partner, they retain substantial up-front fees for brokerage, syndication, management and insurance, distributing part to the limited partners and retaining a predetermined and preferential portion of the cash flow themselves. When the assets are sold and the partnership is dissolved, they entitle themselves to a certain percentage of the profits over and above the initial cost of the asset to the partnership. If the asset is sound enough to appreciate considerably over a period of years, they also acquire an immediate and increasingly valuable equity which is not taxable until the asset is sold. Many general partners also receive leasing or sales commissions, profits on construction, and contributions towards corporate overhead that can be extremely beneficial to these syndicators.

As an indication of the confidence I have in my projects, I normally structure a preferential return to the limited partners in my syndications. This return can be in the form of a priority on the cash flow or tax benefits, up to the point where the partners have received a fair return on their invested equity. Limited partners are attracted and impressed by a general partner who is willing to wait until completion of a project to be compensated for his time and effort. I recently did this on a condominium project in which the limited partners received a return of approximately 20% on their equity prior to my taking any profits.

Understanding the Full Disclosure Provisions of Limited Partnerships

Whether a limited partnership is registered with the Securities and Exchange Commission or exempt from registration, it is extremely important to provide your investors with sufficient information in order that they fully understand the risks and rewards of that investment. If insufficient information is provided and the contract is rescinded, investors have legal grounds to seek and recover pecuniary damages.

Many limited partnership offerings stress only negative concepts in an attempt to forestall possible disapproval by the S.E.C. I believe that the prospectus for a limited partnership should stress the positive as well as the negative aspects of the offering as an impetus to the prospective investor who needs a balanced view of the entire risk-reward features of that offering. My presentations cover such important items as a general description of the financial risks involved, stressing the speculative nature of the real estate investment and the lack of liquidity. I also cover any areas of potential conflict of interest between the general and the limited partners, such as:

- management fees;
- fees for corporate overhead;

- brokerage or syndication fees;
- real estate brokerage commissions;
- contracts involving corporations in which I have an equity interest.

From time to time I have either controlled or had equity interests in companies that specialize in real estate brokerage, real estate syndications, maintenance or janitorial services, and property management. I feel that it is necessary to outline and specifically name the corporations involved and their potential conflict, as most investors do not find this offensive if they are fully informed initially, and the companies provide a worthwhile service.

On the positive side, the capabilities and respectable track record of the general partner should be strongly emphasized. If the general partner is developing the properties for the limited partnership, his profit on the development or construction should not be minimized, as the proven capabilities of the general partner should be brought forth. The investor, always without exception, should be invited to consult competent advisors if he is not knowledgeable on investment matters.

Supporting Documents That Help Sell Limited Partnerships

If the tax ramifications of a project are important to the viability of selling a limited partnership, the prospectus or brochure should appropriately include the name of the accountant who prepared the pro forma projections, or, in the alternative, the presentation should include a pro forma projection on the Certified Public Accountant's letterhead. Associating the projections with a reputable C.P.A. independent of the general partner will add a great deal of credibility to the overall presentation. This is extremely important when the property is under development, since depreciation schedules are most favorable for new construction. When projections of income or resale values are the essence of the profits to be derived from the partnership venture, the substantiating testimonial of an independent third party is essential. On an existing project a statement from an M.A.I. appraiser carries more weight than a corresponding statement from an accountant.

I recently circulated a prospectus for developing a 21-unit condominium project to a group of associates indicating a projected pre-appraisal sales figure. Shortly afterwards, I received the M.A.I. appraisal on the units; it was approximately 15% higher than I had anticipated. I subsequently sent a copy of the appraisal to the individuals who had received the initial prospectus. The effect was impressive. My initial underestimation of the potential income from the project considerably expedited the selling of the balance of the partnership units.

In many limited partnership ventures, accurate projections can be as important as the actual operating figures. In fact, obtaining commitments from limited partners would be extremely difficult, if not impossible, without projections. Statements of projected taxable income and cash flow, and corresponding tax consequences, gain enormously in credibility if they are fully supported by a qualified C.P.A.

Although most limited partnerships are born of necessity to serve as temporary vehicles, the association of persons involved may survive the project that united them originally. Over a period of years, after some of the tax advantages have diminished, many successful general partners find other projects, reutilizing the proceeds of the first successful venture to invest in the second. Not only is a pleasant and profitable association preserved, but a highly leveraged vehicle for additional development, which we will discuss in the next chapter, can result from these valuable financial allies.

6

Understanding The Development Process

A successful developer reacts to fulfill a need in a given marketplace. In a previously undeveloped country, speed of reaction time and accuracy in perception were the only essential prerequisites. Historically, the developer entity has been inexperienced and undercapitalized, building simple products for an uncomplex market. The environmental impact of development came to issue within the last decade, changing the uncomplicated relationship between supply and demand. Lenders, planning and zoning departments, sales and marketing people are demanding more and more sophistication of the developer.

This chapter will outline for you the need for scientifically selecting a site, pricing land, locating the most lucrative markets and obtaining the maximum price for your product in both the upward and downward segments of the market. Procedurally, you will learn how the pros design and lay out projects and how they effectively deal with zoning and planning departments where rezoning for profit is a way of life.

This chapter will guide you through the complete steps involved in the development process to include successful methods for bidding construction contracts, choosing the appropriate architects and engineers, and structuring the interim financing, to mention a few.

How to Use Feasibility Studies Profitably

Historically, developers conducted market research studies in order to impress their financial institutions. Backed with an impressive accumulation of local statistics, these artificial documents established the credibility necessary for building a successful track record. Less than objective, the market research often reflected the slant of the developer who contracted and paid for it. This attitude toward market research still persists to a large degree.

I recently reviewed a feasibility study contracted for a hotel which was to be incorporated into a major franchise chain. Prepared for and financed by the developer's firm, the study only too clearly betrayed its origin. Even with my limited knowledge of the market and this particular project, I knew that many of the local competing hotels were not operating at high enough levels of occupancy to justify the high costs of adding this new structure.

Because of the financial problems and attendant bankruptcies among many of the larger development corporations in the mid-seventies, greater emphasis is being placed upon reliable and accurate market feasibility studies today. Not only are lenders becoming more critical of such studies, they are more demanding of objectivity, as are the developers themselves who are closely analyzing these market feasibility studies with increasing care. Specific to the design of an individual project under consideration, a market feasibility study will help you profit by determining market absorption, the type or size of the units to be developed, the proper types of financing and marketing techniques to be employed and the phasing, budgeting and scheduling aspect of any proposed development. Furthermore, if the study is specific to the area, and concludes that the economic base shows a sound, sufficient market with enough depth to support the project, you are well on your way to a successful venture.

Major Benefits Derived from Feasibility Studies

Among the statistics to be generated from a well-conceived feasibility study are:

- the local version of the gross national product, the total of all goods and services produced;
- the number of housing or building permits and starts in the area;

- the current housing and commercial development volume;
- a summation of the new construction project entities coming into the area that directly affect the venture;
- any legislation adversely affecting new development, such as no-growth statutes; and
- the local housing occupancy trend and its effect on the overall market.

Other factors are pertinent and deserve consideration. They will include:

- the number of local mortgage foreclosures;
- the unused inventory currently on the market;
- a profile of the average buyer or user of the property;
- the funds available locally for purchasing housing or leasing commercial space; and
- the typical household formation in the area.

FIGURE 6-1

Proven Techniques for Selecting a Site

Once a given area is determined favorable for the development of a particular concept, the promising sites should be analyzed for such things as:

- topography;
- suitable size and configuration;
- soil conditions;
- existing zoning; and
- availability of utilities.

In addition to acquiring at an attractive price and being able to have under option during the planning stages, a given site must be in close proximity to all the supportive facilities necessary to make the development a successful one. Some of the demographics pertinent to location of a site are:

- the quality of the neighborhood as it relates to the proposed development;
- the location in relation to public and private transportation; and
- proximity to cultural centers, schools, recreation facilities, country clubs, restaurants, and neighborhood shopping centers.

Optioning the Land Advantageously

Once you have found one or more appropriate sites, you must then determine the price you can allocate to that land. While the lowest price for land is obtained by a cash offer with no contingencies, this is not normally the method of acquiring a major development site. Customarily, the developer options the land subject to obtaining the proper platting or zoning, raising the appropriate mortgage financing, and completing the final marketing analysis, construction estimates, and engineering work. You determine what will be a reasonable price for the land by structuring the entire development backwards, beginning with the eventual value of the developed property and offsetting the costs of development, and incorporating a reasonable profit.

In the past, I have found that optioning a site is the most logical and realistic way to compensate the owner for his land. For the additional consideration the landowner receives above the price that cash could command, he is usually willing to give you the time to complete all the necessary steps in the development process before closing. Since the actual value of the land will be contingent upon the type of improvements to be installed, I very rarely purchase a property with no contingencies in the contract.

Recently I made an offer on a property subject to obtaining the appropriate rezoning. The project, a potential subdivision of 218 units, required medium density rezoning to be feasible. If I had offered to acquire the tract without the rezoning contingency, the price could have been considerably lower. However, there was a sufficient profit margin in the project to pay a premium for the land. This way I could acquire it with the assurance that, if the right density were not obtained, I could cut my losses to include my up-front costs only.

How to Value the Cost of the Raw Land

The logic of working backwards applies to residential subdivisions as well as to other types of properties. The following elements should be analyzed:

- the size of the units or tracts;
- the construction costs;
- the engineering or architectural fees;
- the costs of holding and marketing; and
- the anticipated profit.

When these figures are projected conservatively, the value of the land should become quite obvious and this is the appropriate price to offer to the seller of the land.

In analyzing a rental property, either an apartment or a commercial building, we start with the capitalized value of income. We then deduct the cost of the construction, development and marketing to arrive at a per-unit or per-square-foot cost for the land.

The analytical process is similar for any development, and the raw acreage cost must be adjusted for whatever unusual site problems may exist, such as utility extensions or special grading or drainage requirements. Regardless of these adjustments, it is important to offer the seller a realistic price up-front and not try to chisel him by overnegotiating. Openness and fairness in dealing with a seller are especially important when the site is particularly desirable and the profit can be predicted with reasonable accuracy. If you are satisfied with the profit margin, it is unrealistic not to offer the landowner an equitable price.

I just concluded an offer to acquire a 91-acre tract at a figure that was twice the appraised value of his land on a 36-unit condominium project. I did this for two reasons: (1) the seller permitted me the necessary time to structure the financing, and (2) he eliminated a major share of the up-front money by taking the majority of the purchase price, not upon the initial closing, but when the units themselves were closed and the funds received. I was also fortunate enough to work out an arrangement with the seller whereby I could use some adjoining land for recreation facilities, and the combination of these three factors made my deal quite attractive, and in the end obtained an unusually high compensation for the seller.

Important Considerations for Site Design and Layout

Once you have obtained control over the site, two additional factors must be considered:

- to design the project for the specific location; and
- to determine the type of product to be placed on the site.

Designing for the site may mean departing from the traditional grid pattern and opting for planned unit developments, density transfers, or other creative methods of site layout utilizing the more obvious building sites and leaving the less desirable ones as open or undeveloped areas. The type of unit to be placed on the site will be determined by the preliminary market feasibility studies. Knowledge of the levels of demand in the area and purchasing power of the potential buyers is essential in determining the size and composition of the units that are generally appropriate to the local market.

I know a major developer who, through the years, has been successful in developing nondescript subdivisions consisting of houses with minimum square footage and virtually no landscaping. He caters to the low end of the market, utilizing FHA and VA financing. Because of the current rising costs of land and construction, combined with higher interest expenses that must eventually be passed on to buyers, this organization is encountering major financial problems. Their excess inventory of lots and houses has little appeal to today's market of sophisticated buyers who desire more than the stripped-down products they have for sale. This developer has been totally priced out of the market because he took a short-range economic view and did not revise his product to meet the changing needs or demands.

When to Rezone for Profit

Most residential land is priced on a per-unit basis. The higher the density, or the more dwelling units the land can contain, the higher the value. Some preliminary engineering work on a site is usually enough to determine whether the existing zoning is sufficient or whether an upgrade in zoning would permit better use of the site and a more desirable and lucrative project. The basic ingredients of this determination are a contour map, a quick analysis of the utility picture, and an assessment of the buildable sites and the various slopes found on the tract.

Obviously, rezonings have tremendous effects on land values. This is even truer with rezoning for commercial use, since commercial values can be extremely high in relation to values for residential land.

Two years ago I did an analysis on a property that I eventually developed as a low-density subdivision. Although the 45-acre tract was zoned for one unit per acre, scattered rezoning had taken place in the immediate area, indicating the possibility of zoning for half-acre lots. The one-acre lots had a value of approximately $40,000; the half-acre lots were valued at $25,000 to $30,000. However, the municipal building codes required that half-acre lots have paved roads, sidewalks, curbs and gutters, whereas one-acre lots did not have to incorporate these improvements. When I balanced the development costs and sales figures, I quickly saw that rezoning this tract would not be materially beneficial.

Effectively Dealing with Planning and Zoning Commissions

After you have determined the density believed to be appropriate to your tract, it is important to discuss your preliminary concept with local public building and zoning officials. Bringing these people into the development in the early stages helps make them feel part of the overall process. Rough outlines of your preliminary site plan and master plan are all that are needed to initiate an early dialogue that will permit them to make suggestions. Their sense of early involvement and contribution to the overall plan can simplify the rezoning process if opposition from the general public should surface at a later stage.

Many well-conceived projects which would be good additions to communities have failed at public hearings because the developers and their associates did not lay the proper groundwork with the planning and zoning staffs. The most convincing argument that can be made at a zoning meeting is a recommendation by the professional municipal staff that your project will be a welcome addition to the community, one that can easily be incorporated into the master plan of the city. Since most protestors argue toward special interests, a professional, unbiased testimonial carries enormous weight. A developer who does his homework with the city staff and/or appropriate committees will stand a good chance of overruling the protests of neighborhood groups.

Last year I received an expedited approval on a 32-lot subdivision in which the neighborhood associations attempted to block my approval by associating my project with a rezoning request for a 450-unit planned unit development adjoining my parcel. The thrust of their argument was that both projects, if approved, would create too large a demand on the existing utility systems. As I had established a working rapport with the city staff, they easily convinced the planning commission, over the neighborhood opposition, that they had studied my project in great depth, and that no adverse effects would result from its approval and implementation.

Choosing the Appropriate Consulting Architects and Engineers

Once a project has received preliminary municipal approvals, qualified consulting architects, engineers, and surveyors must be retained without delay. Since time is critical to most real estate developments, an accurate schedule must be established within which consulting professionals will be able to perform their aspects of the work, within which construction can also be completed. You should interview several prospective engineers and architects in order to compare their methods, prices, and time schedules. Normally, a competent engineering firm can also provide the survey work required to initiate the project, and most qualified consultants can come up with fairly accurate cost estimates and projections of time needed to complete a project.

Specialized engineering consultants should be retained through the architect, who will have the responsibility for coordinating and paying for their services. Most major projects require the services of a mechanical engineer to design the heating and air conditioning systems. Problems of floor loads in high-rise residential and commercial buildings can become extremely complicated, requiring input from structural engineers. This is especially true with massive buildings using the free-span method of support. Because of changing codes instituted by many municipalities, it is also imperative to coordinate your project with an electrical engineer.

Before retaining an architect, ask for a written proposal as well as a rough sketch or rendering of what he would recommend doing with the site and the project. Many architects have preconceived ideas about design and development which emerge early through a preliminary sketch. If these ideas do not complement your own, you might wish to reconsider the relationship. I recently picked an architect from a group of three submitting architects, in which an extremely rough piece of land was involved, for a low-density, highly clustered condominium project. The average density was 1 unit for 2½ acres. However, the units were clustered in groups of 6, each site occupying no more than 15,000 square feet, or 1/3 of an acre. One can see that on this difficult site where the units occupied considerably less than 5% of the overall acreage, a special type of talent in the architect was required. Be certain, in choosing an architect, that he is in focus with current consumer demands and can design a building for construction within a moderate and salable budget, and, most important, that he has the ability to work with contractors and lending institutions from start to finish. In addition, the architect must obtain all the necessary building permits and be responsible to the municipality for all final inspections, as well as have the ability to assure the interim and permanent lenders that the project is complete and meets all plans and specifications. Considering the complexity of the architect's involvement in the project, it is important that you have a cancellation provision in your contract with him, including an arbitration clause permitting you to continue construction of the project during the arbitration phase.

Understanding the Steps in the Development Process

The architect's involvement with agencies and officials outside the project is only one facet of the service he performs. The sequence of his major activities is as follows:

- schematic plans, to include site and/or floor plans;
- preliminary plans for presentation to municipalities;
- preliminary construction bid-obtaining plans;
- complete architectural drawings containing structural, mechanical, and electrical plans;
- construction supervision and change orders throughout the construction process;
- final approvals of county, city, and lenders; and
- approval of all construction draws during the period of building.

FIGURE 6-2

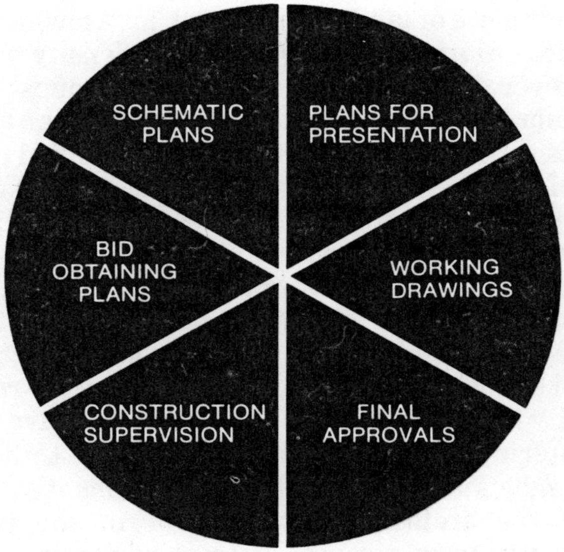

SCHEMATIC PLANS

PLANS FOR PRESENTATION

BID OBTAINING PLANS

WORKING DRAWINGS

CONSTRUCTION SUPERVISION

FINAL APPROVALS

DEVELOPMENT PROCESS

Proven Methods for Bidding the Construction Work

Once the appropriate architectural and engineering firms are retained and the project is put out for construction bids, several approaches can be used in obtaining a general contractor. Usually, a full set of contract drawings and specifications are presented to the contractor, who is asked to quote a firm price (guaranteed so that it can be bonded) and a firm schedule for completion in a predetermined period of time. The contract price normally covers the cost of all the work, the contractor's profit, overhead, and his general requirements. Sometimes this contract can be negotiated with an upper ceiling, with any cost savings being equitably prorated between the contractor and the owner.

Another method involves reimbursement for the cost of the work plus a predetermined fee for the contractor's profit and overhead. A maximum ceiling is normally attached to the expenditures of the general contractor and his subcontractors. This method can be extremely difficult to monitor, especially if the contractor has several different projects under construction simultaneously. Under these circumstances, accounting methods are extremely complicated and funds for the various projects can easily be commingled. This concept is most effective when approached on a joint-venture basis where the contractor receives both his overhead and a percentage of the profits on the project.

Last year I completed a $2,500,000 condominium project on a joint-venture basis with three general contractors. We purchased the project, which was about 60% complete, out of bankruptcy. Since the previous subcontractors had several liens filed against the project, it was reasonable to assume that they would not return to the job. This joint-venture arrangement with the contractors permitted me to complete the job at the lowest cost. As partners, they provided the margin of safety needed to complete the units without the high exposure that might have resulted from inheriting a multitude of construction problems created by dissatisfied subcontractors.

A third method of contracting for construction involves bidding by units rather than by an aggregate price. The basis for bidding is a quantity takeoff prepared by the engineer or architect in which all the materials and labor that will go into the development of a subdivision are enumerated. For example, such items as the lineal footage of the sewer, water, electric, and gas lines, and the total amount of paving, concrete, and dirt to be moved are all calculated separately. The contractor then submits his bid at a fixed price per unit, with the assurance that, if his unit prices are accurate, he will have no cost overruns. This method enables him to be more competitive since many of the unknowns are eliminated.

I have found that this third method works well for the developer since it facilitates comparison of unit prices and enables him to equalize the higher portions of his bid more easily than he could with an overall lump sum estimate utilizing one of the other two methods. I used this method on a subdivision with just over one hundred lots with a construction budget of approximately $750,000. When the subdivision was completed and I tabulated the quantity takeoffs, my cost figures were within 5% of the preliminary estimate prepared by the engineer. Unless you are convinced that your contractor and engineer are competent and trustworthy you should not use this method.

Structuring the Development Contract Advantageously

Certain basic provisions should be incorporated into any contractual arrangement with a general contractor. The American Institute of Architects has included many of them in the standard forms it makes available. The following basic concepts should be drafted into your contracts:

1. All contractors should be paid for the work completed, less a 10% retainage, and waivers of lien rights should be obtained before that payment.
2. Before the contract is terminated, all lenders and governmental authorities should have inspected and approved the work.
3. All materials are to be of specified quality and all workmanship guaranteed to be free from defects.
4. A definitive time schedule should be set up for completion of each aspect of the project.
5. The owner and the architect should have specific rights of approval and dismissal over all contractors on the job.
6. The owner should be coinsured for liability and vandalism during construction.
7. The owner should have the contractual authority to withhold payment in the event that the work is not completed satisfactorily.

8. The owner should have the right to take over and complete the project upon the contractor's default deducting the completion costs from his contract.

The owner and the architect should have broad powers of decision-making during construction of the project, including the right to substitute additional contractors. There also should be a provision for liquidated damages for untimely delays and a bond for lack of payment and performance by the contractor. A penalty clause should be specifically inserted if construction work is not completed in a timely fashion, normally calculated on a per-day basis, since interest expenses accrue regardless of construction delays, and a project cannot normally increase its rentals or sales price to offset these additional interest expenses.

Several years ago I developed a 181-unit mobile home park in which the gas lines were improperly installed. The financial status of the general contractor was marginal, and I called upon the bonding company to make restitution and re-install the defective gas lines. When I brought litigation to force the issue, I found that the bonding company was insolvent and could not make restitution. Since then I have taken great pains to analyze the financial capabilities of the bonding company as well as those of the contractor.

Advantageously Structuring the Financing Package

Financing the development begins with the preparation of an elaborate loan package for the potential lender. Included in this presentation should be:

- a detailed outline of the developer's organization;
- financial statements of the developer;
- the types of projects the developer specializes in;
- a projected sales and marketing plan;
- site and landscaping plans;
- pro forma statements of income and expenses;
- market and feasibility studies;
- construction schedules;
- a detailed set of architectural plans; and
- letters from municipal authorities stating project compliance with local ordinances.

The dialogue accompanying this loan package and the documents supplementing it should outline the existing improvements and the total cost of the proposed improvements, together with sources of the funds, and the amount of the mortgage loan being requested. The amortization schedule, the interest rate, and the dates for repayment installments should also be specified. The terms of prepayment and the collateral used to support the loan are important and necessary inclusions in the package.

When requesting the loan, you must specify whether you personally plan to sign the note, whether the signature will be corporate, or if the signature will be exculpatory and guaranteed by the real estate only. Both borrower and lender must agree on the funds to be advanced and the repayment schedule before certain portions of the property are released.

On investment properties, many lenders require that rental achievements be met before permanent funding is allowed, as rental projections are strictly pro forma. When these clauses are effective, funds from the interim lender will normally be insufficient to complete the project, and the developer will have to borrow additional monies from other lending institutions to complete the development.

An associate of mine had difficulty meeting a rental achievement clause during a period when the mortgage market changed considerably. His interim loan on an apartment complex had an expiration date cancelling the lending institution's obligation for permanent financing if the rental achievement was not timely met. His rental achievement deadline came and he closed on the permanent financing with no time to spare. If he had been delinquent, efforts to obtain another permanent commitment would have been impossible, given the high interest rates that surfaced during the periods of construction.

Advantages of In-House Versus Outside Sales Organizations

Weighing the advantages and disadvantages of in-house versus outside sales organizations will be inconclusive for any but the most active of developers specializing in a given type of development. Recruiting an in-house staff and gearing up a large sales and marketing force for a project is difficult at best. The obvious advantage is that all members of the sales staff know the product, the developer, the architect, the construction, and the planning that went into the project. They are also in a position to devote full time to the venture and to anticipate the kind of rapport most appealing to potential buyers or renters.

On the negative side, a developer can often get into a major project without realizing the incompetence of his in-house staff until it is too late and the image of the project has suffered. Furthermore, in-house staff members must be compensated during the development period, often before sales are even feasible, whereas outside real estate sales people work on a commission basis only.

If a project is well-conceived and in a viable area, it is quite possible to set realistic quotas and goals for an outside staff and monitor their activities during the sale or rental process. I use a combination of in-house and outside independent brokerage firms for marketing my various developments. Sometimes problems arise with in-house sales organizations in that individuals lose interest in a given project and hard feelings arise when the project is given to a competing firm in order to restimulate sales activity.

The most successful condominium sales program I have done to date was with an outside independent brokerage firm employing some 18 to 20 individuals. I listed with them a $2.3 million condominium project that was completely sold out in one weekend with a sizable waiting list over and above the initial purchasers. This waiting list was quite welcome, as many of the original purchasers did not qualify for loans. However, between the initial sales and the backup sales prospects, the entire development was successfully marketed in an extremely short period of time.

How to Survive Downward Market Cycles

The length of the economic market cycles is shrinking drastically. A decade ago, one could operate in a strong local market without being concerned about or affected by the national outlook. All this has changed through a combination of inflation, financing and energy shortages. Currently, you as a developer must understand more than your local market for survival. You must also chart national cycles and be aware of their high and low points.

Surviving in the development business means operating on a counter-cyclical basis. Planning, acquisition, and financing of projects must take place during the low or recessionary end of the cycle so that you are able to come out of recessions with sufficient inventory to market during the rising part of the cycle. The timing of any development is probably the most critical aspect and is governed by the concept of buying low and selling high, so familiar to investors in the stock market.

During the last recession, I acquired several residential condominium projects and land subdivisions. Since relatively few people bid for projects at such times, I obtained bargain prices or was given ample time to structure my package and financing. I managed to tie up one specific condominium project for nine months with only a $16,000 letter of credit, and that investment shows a net profit in excess of $500,000.

By acquiring projects when nobody is interested and reselling them when total optimism prevails, you can virtually create a short-term monopoly and enjoy the advantages of rising values during the upward end of the cycle. With careful and correct planning, you can acquire enough inventory during the recessionary period to take you through the upward lucrative part of the cycle. When the cycle peaks, you should theoretically have sold off your complete inventory, attaining the liquidity to enable you to acquire more bargain properties when the market bottoms.

Most large corporations look for immediate earnings, since their key to continued success is accounting to stockholders on an earnings-per-share basis. Diametrically, most small or medium-sized privately held companies or individuals look for developments that provide substantial residual value and generate earnings and tax shelter over longer periods of time. Unfortunately, smaller organizations cannot take major risks that lead to large profits as the shortened nature of current economic cycles carries with it too much of a financial burden. These factors limit the profitability of small companies in that they cannot tie up large tracts of land or undertake large drawn-out projects where economics of scale are available in labor, materials, and land costs. The skill of many small and medium-sized developers in overcoming these handicaps testifies to their tremendous expertise and well-seasoned judgment.

Selecting the Most Lucrative Market

Two basic approaches to real estate development are employed, respectively, by small and large developers alike. The first is to select a strong market that will be viable for years, study it carefully, find an opening in that market through the patient process of elimination, and then capitalize on that market void. The second approach, that preferred by many of the successful national and regional developers, is to refine a basic concept and look for specific projects in many markets where that concept can be duplicated and applied. Once the concept is refined, developers normally find that lending institutions will follow them to different markets with relative ease, perpetuating their money machine in many places.

I use the first approach in my organization. It demands, as the price paid for existence, the time, efforts, and imagination needed to jump from office complexes to land subdivisions to residential condominiums as given voids in the market open up. It permits me to keep my basic operation small and efficient so that I maintain the financial liquidity to acquire bargain investments during cyclical downturns. By employing outside consultants for the financial, legal, engineering, and construction aspects of my various ventures, I am able to keep my permanent staff small and my overhead low, which I find preferable to concentrating staff efforts on keeping marginal projects going during unprofitable times. This approach will permit you to make mistakes without endangering your overall chances of success if your timing is good and your market analyses are accurately predictable.

In many respects, the approach you and I take, and the corresponding risks, are totally dependent upon the overall size of the market and our own imagination. One approach which has proved successful time and time again requires more courage than thought process. Basically, it involves repeating what the competition is doing, by eliminating the obvious errors and mistakes. This can be done, for example, by structuring a different unit mix which is more competitive within the marketplace, or offering different floor plans, unit or lot sizes, or basic amenities. Sometimes this takes the form of duplicating the concept with a lower price accompanied by a quicker absorption rate, or determining that a similar building can be constructed on an ideally located site. The approach works better for a small to medium-sized developer who can normally move into and out of local markets quickly than it does for slow-moving bureaucratically controlled large development corporations.

I am currently employing this approach by constructing a condominium project located within 100 yards of a highly successful completed condominium project. I used basically the same floor plans, retained the same architect, and duplicated the competing units with some minor upgrading in patios, skylights, room sizes, and bathroom and kitchen amenities. The major difference was that

I constructed my project on leased land. My units are currently being appraised at higher values than those found on the adjoining property, and my costs are considerably less than what one could purchase the competing condominium units for.

The same concept can be applied to either a larger or a smaller market, zeroing in on a different type of clientele. For instance, a large apartment complex with all the luxury trappings can be duplicated on a smaller scale, creating the image of greater exclusivity; or, a larger project can be patterned after a small, successful venture, with enough additional amenities to make it considerably more desirable.

Establishing a Maximum Price for Your Project

Many well-conceived projects lack curb appeal; their developers emphasize brick and mortar to the detriment of the overall aesthetics. A project located strategically on the right street and designed to capitalize on the environment will attract purchasers or tenants more readily than a structure at odds with its environment, even though it may not be as well-constructed or conceived.

Establishing a price for a new product is always difficult, as new developments must be priced before construction is completed to allow for the variables that may arise from the long lead time involved. Furthermore, residential units offered in a new development may be so dissimilar to those previously offered for sale or rent that comparative figures might not be available or reliable.

I am formulating a policy of limiting the number of presales on any given development. This was an antiquated practice, prevalent in the industry. Developers historically presold as much of the project as they could, eliminating what they thought was the majority of the risk. I have found, especially in land subdivisions and in my recent condominium developments, that the further I progress, the more value these individual units have. I have seen that many of the units I have sold early in the development stage are commanding prices 15% to 20% above those initial sales prices as I approach the end of the development.

Irrespective of whether the units are for rent or for sale, the price analysis begins on a square-foot basis. You begin with the basic product and analyze the comparable square-foot rentals or sales in the area, adjusting either upward or downward. When enough comparisons are made, a median or trend line can be established for comparable projects, and that median can be adjusted for a project's unique characteristics, including such things as its location, the attractiveness of surrounding areas, special amenities, and its convenience with regard to public transportation, schools and shopping.

I encountered a unique pricing situation in a recent condominium project. Approximately a year elapsed between completion of the first phase and the construction of 75 units contemplated for phase two. Resales did not materialize as rapidly in phase one as anticipated because of the desirability of the units and the long-term intention of the buyers to retain them. Comparable units in the area were selling for between 12% and 15% over my resales, even though my site was more attractive. The increased cost of construction and the area's comparable sales on new competing projects had not caught up with the older units in the first phase of my project, and I therefore had to go to an outside appraiser to establish a higher value on the units in the second phase.

Pricing the Upper and Lower Ends of the Market

In a highly competitive market, one has less flexibility in pricing upward than in a less competitive situation where prices consistently exceed the median trend line. Establishing prices successfully involves comparing a variety of projects. If comparable developments do not exist in the immediate area, you must use other areas or cities and adjust your sales or rental prices according to an income equalization factor. The difficulty in adjusting and establishing the price for a product not fully completed is overcome by many sophisticated developers, who can convince lenders that higher prices a year or two in the future can be achieved when the development is completed.

At the low end of the market, sales prices are not necessarily as important as they are in the higher or medium to high segments. Purchasers at the low end of the market have fewer alternatives, and here the developer can almost dictate his price, assuming that the prospective buyers can qualify financially. Similarly, sales prices at the uppermost end of the market are less significant than they are toward the middle. Here a potential purchaser, if he really is enamored of the product and has the wherewithal to afford it, is not particularly concerned with the analytics of square-foot pricing.

I have consistently found that in my developments I have much more flexibility in pricing at the upper range of the market, where I have been structuring my projects either on leased land or on land where terms and conditions are quite favorable, even though I often pay a premium for the land to get these terms and conditions. I am finding that on a recent land-lease condominium project where I have the flexibility of low lease payments, I am raising my prices considerably during the development and sellout period—a luxury that I would not have been afforded had I been at the lower spectrum of the market.

The small to medium-sized developer must look at the general market and then isolate the appropriate submarkets in order to be successful. Submarkets are not identified by large quantities of statistical information, as is prevalent in the general market. A developer who is knowledgeable about an area can search out marketing opportunities with enough depth to support a project for an extended period of time, maneuver into the special situations he uncovers, and capitalize quite rapidly. In isolating and developing such submarkets, you can obtain a decided advantage over the larger corporate developers.

In the next chapter we will discuss apartments, the vehicle of real estate that is most accessible to the average developer. In learning the secrets of merchandising apartments by spotting the appropriate niche in the market, you will gain the basic experience needed to advance to other forms of development as well. The need for apartments exists among people of all income levels, in all geographical areas. The logical first step for anyone wishing to understand the development process with limited financial funds, is through an apartment investment.

7

Dollars and Sense Of Apartment Investments

Many consider apartments one of the major growth areas in real estate, primarily because of the vast demand created for them by the rising cost of single-family housing combined with the advantageous use of similar design, marketing and construction techniques that can be applied in metropolitan areas throughout the country. Apartments were relatively uneconomical to develop during the latter part of the 1970's. However, the conversion boom has created a shortage of rental units that will soon be reflected in escalating rents and property values, again making apartments a lucrative vehicle for real estate investing. This chapter will point out the major markets that are being created by the changing population profiles found in most major suburbs and metropolitan areas, as separations and divorces increase and more women enter the professions. You will discover how to capitalize on the new markets for smaller, more efficient apartment units that are replacing the large, leisure-oriented homes of the past. Systematically, we show you how to predict costs, spot fabricated operating statements, determine unit size and composition, accurately predict maintenance costs and vacancy factors. This chapter will also enable you to accumulate sizable amounts of information on conceiving, designing, and

137

leveraging apartment complexes catering to young professionals and "empty nesters," the most affluent and expanding segment of the apartment market.

How to Accurately Predict the Market

More than 50% of the households in the 1970's consisted of between two and three occupants. Since many of today's average wage earners cannot afford to occupy a single-family detached home because of increased construction costs, soaring land values, and higher interest payments, they find the general life style of their small household best served by a rented unit. I was recently involved in a 200+ unit apartment project which was acquired specifically to capitalize on the young professional market. Even though the apartments were converted into condominiums catering to that same market, we initially had a unique low-end rental product. We could almost dictate the amount of rents that we could obtain for the units, as it was a desirable complex with no immediate competition.

These stratified groups combine to create a tremendous market in suburban areas for garden apartments, moderately comfortable to luxurious. Such complexes are often welcomed by communities since they increase the municipal tax base, and normally do not put an excessive burden on existing municipal services and educational facilities, at least in relation to the tax revenues they create.

Finding the Appropriate Location

An apartment complex located in a prime area retains its value if it is accessible to the employment centers of its tenants. Discounting public transportation, since less than 20% of the working people in the United States utilize it, means that distance must be measured in terms of driving time to the prime place of employment. Secondarily, the location must provide after-work accessibility to shopping, night clubs, restaurants, and other leisure-oriented functions.

Prime markets for apartment complexes exist where people are being transferred into areas where they will occupy apartments for several years before determining whether their employment situations are stable enough to warrant the purchase of houses. Ideal locations are near areas of:

- Research centers
- Light manufacturing complexes

- Universities
- Hospitals
- Government complexes
- Major office buildings
- Service-oriented businesses

These particular locations offer accessibility to places of employment and provide a living atmosphere for people to get acquainted and socialize with others of like interests or employment.

When the location chosen for an apartment complex is a metropolitan area, the maturity of the area must be considered. Look for areas in which additional growth patterns will exist for years, and where a steady influx of people can be relied upon. I also look for the potential buys in older stabilized parts of major metropolitan communities that can be revitalized. Many years ago, I purchased several medium-sized apartment buildings in a major metropolitan area near a newly formed and rapidly expanding urban university. I found, by slightly rejuvenating these projects, that I attracted students who lived together and paid rents considerably over and above the normal market rate. These students were not concerned with the marginal appearance of the neighborhood, as the convenience factor was more important. I purchased many of these apartment buildings for approximately 40% of their replacement value. I encountered a somewhat higher turnover and additional management problems; however, when the area stabilized and the university matured, I sold these apartment projects at a considerable profit.

Determining Feasibility and Unit Size

In analyzing the feasibility of a project, it is important not to have any preconceived ideas as to the size and composition of the units you plan to develop or acquire. It becomes important not to be enamored of the physical structure to the point of not looking objectively at the market. Success in the apartment field means finding the appropriate niche in the market to maximize rent and occupancy in order to have a worthwhile long-term investment.

I have a colleague who in the past 10 or so years has exclusively developed small efficiency, almost motel-room-like apartment units. He has done this successfully in several major cities. Many real estate developers feel he is taking on excessive management duties that are not common to the apartment industry by developing these small high-turnover units. However, my colleague has almost every major lender willing to commit himself on his new projects, and he has made millions developing these transit-type units, many of which rent by the month or the week.

From your standpoint, apartment projects are normally the easiest types of ventures to syndicate or finance. It is normally a simple process to attract equity-money investors into large syndications for apartment projects since limited partners put up small amounts of money as an overall percentage of the value of the project, receiving large tax-deductible allocations in relation to the amount of equity funds invested.

In order to determine the market initially, you must analyze the current income within the general vicinity, allocating 20% to 25% of a family's gross income for rent. In other words, a family having an annual income of $15,000 a year will normally spend between $250 and $300 per month on residential shelter. If an apartment is located in a developing area where less than 25% of the average individual's income is being applied to rent, rents normally can be increased over a period of time. If costs of operating the project later increase, difficulties can arise without this cushion for increasing the rents on a proportionate basis to offset the increased operating costs.

How to Profit from Accurate Cost Analysis

From the perspective of new construction, the cost analysis of a multi-family housing project is considerably different from that of a single-family dwelling. When one purchases a home, the price generally reflects the value of the current cost of construction, the land and financing costs, the sales commission, and promotional charges, which are generally added to the cost of the project by the developer. The value of the house usually reflects these total costs plus an additional figure representing a profit to you, the builder or developer. I use this approach on most of my for-sale condominium projects, where I take the total cost, add a reasonable profit, and then attempt to convince the appraiser that this is the current market value. Surprisingly enough, this is quite easy to accomplish.

To summarize, the builder of a single-family dwelling is concerned with:

- current cost of construction;
- land and financing costs;
- sales commission and marketing expenses;

- developer's overhead expenses; and
- developer's profit.

How Apartment Analysis Differs from Single-Family Housing

Diametrically, in determining the feasibility of constructing rental housing, analysis starts, not with cost, but with the economic rent that the proposed structure will generate or support, given the composition of the units and the market demand and services to be provided. You, as the apartment developer, must determine:

- occupancy level,
- projected operating revenues,

and balance or offset them against:

- operating expenses,
- mortgage financing, and
- tax-related benefits.

The overall market demand must be analyzed and translated into square-foot rental in order to determine the size and composition of the unit mix. Generally, smaller units will command a higher monthly rental per square foot and will be correspondingly somewhat more expensive to develop, since the heating, plumbing, electricity, appliances, and bathroom fixtures must be equally prorated over these smaller units. Some of the most profitable buildings that I have owned or managed have been one-bedroom and studio apartments. In these units, it is not uncommon to obtain 10% to 15% additional rent over and above the typical two-bedroom standard size unit that the major lending institutions insist on for permanent financing. Often, you can rent these apartments furnished, putting together groups of investors to acquire the furniture and lease it back to you. On occasion, I lease directly from financial institutions, retaining the tax benefits of the furniture, and increasing my rents substantially in the process. Rent, vacancies, expenses, and profits must be calculated on a per-square-foot basis at different cost levels for efficiency, one-, two-, or three-bedroom units. You then can set your unit mix according to the potential market and the profitability of each particular type of apartment.

Spotting Underrented Markets and Extreme Vacancy Factors

In order to evaluate a rental unit correctly in the existing marketplace, you have to explore and comprehend the location, neighborhood characteristics, and competition from existing projects. The rents in the project to be acquired or constructed must compare favorably with or be less than the current market for the immediate area in order to determine the long-term stability of the project in a potentially competitive marketplace. Current income alone on a given project should not be the sole criterion for acquisition. The unit renting at an undervalued price in a desirable community has more long-term potential than a high-rental property in a less desirable section. A property of mediocre design which is not even fully occupied, in a fashionable part of a suburban community, will generally be worth more over a period of time and command a higher resale premium than an attractive, well-designed apartment project in a middle-income or less fashionable part of the city. My colleagues and I have found this to be true, especially when properties have been acquired and converted into condominium units. The newest and potentially the largest segment of apartment dwellers, the young professionals and the "empty nesters," will be attracted to apartment complexes in fashionable areas.

Tenant turnover is probably the most important aspect to consider in analyzing the potential income in an apartment complex. From the rent receipt book, a qualified bookkeeper can calculate the average stay of the occupant within the complex. High tenant turnover may indicate:

- structural or design defects,
- unusual management problems,
- a highly competitive or overbuilt market,
- poor quality of tenants.

Tenant turnover is both expensive and one of the key indicators of long-term stability. Most studies indicate that the average tenancy in an apartment complex is approximately two years.

One must also be cognizant of the actual vacancy factor within the existing market, especially in older units that are in reasonably good condition. If the market deteriorates, or generally becomes overbuilt, and if you have not analyzed the older units in the area, you will find yourself competing with apartments having a lesser cost and, subsequently, a lesser break-even point.

How Accounting Methods Can Distort Income

Owners of existing buildings have a tendency to present financial statements which do not reflect rent concessions, especially when the cash, not accrual, method of accounting is used. Under the cash method, all income and expenses are accounted for when paid; under the accrual method, they are reported when incurred. For example, leases do not normally reflect the concession of one month's free rent to an individual signing a long-term lease, a practice not uncommon in areas of competitive rents. Sometimes, operating statements may be distorted by prepaid rentals, for which owners offer discounts, thereby artificially ballooning the gross income from one operating period to another. I recently had an option on a building from a major real estate investment trust, in which, according to the rent roll, there always appeared to be close to full occupancy. However, on further examination prior to closing, I found that many of the units had deposits and no tenants, or the units were being rented several times each month. In this case, the rent roll was quite misleading in regard to the actual number of rent-paying occupants. Individual lease agreements must be examined for predetermined contractual arrangements for future rent increases and undesirable clauses that might hinder a new owner from maintaining a positive cash flow during a period of rising operating costs.

How to Spot Phony Operating Statements

Many owners, agents, or brokers, when presenting operating statements on apartments, exaggerate income and understate expenses, especially through the cash method of accounting, in which receipts and disbursements are accounted for upon their receipt. This is a typical way for owners to defer expenses and balloon operating income figures. Most certified public accountants will not attest to the accuracy of the cash method of accounting, and one has no way to verify such figures unless a complete and detailed inspection of the books is made. Recently, I acquired an option on a 216-unit apartment building which I had initially planned to convert to condominiums. Gross misrepresentations were made as to the occupancy, as the rent levels were realistic for the overall metropolitan area but not stable in this particular project. A closer look at the existing leases in the complex indicated that the tenants were breaking their obligations prior to their fulfillment of the term, and the last month's rent and damage deposit was misleadingly represented as rental income. In this particular case, I declined to exercise my option. The project was not suitable for conversion, since it was showing an occupancy rate of 10% less than that found in the community. The accrual method of accounting, however, does permit a certified public accountant to attest to the accuracy of the income and expenses of the project. Statements should be backed up with annual income and operating expenses submitted to the Internal Revenue Service for the past three to five years.

When acquiring a property, one must be completely convinced that the rentals or pro forma projections are not substantially at the market peak. If they are fully priced for the current tenancy, you, as the potential owner, cannot calculate a rent increase or build one into your projection. If rents are increased to catch up with the value of the project, the resulting vacancies will create a negative cash flow, as the apartment market is quite sensitive to rental adjustments.

Rules of thumb involving gross income multipliers for appraising apartments can be quite misleading, as most values tend to fall in the six to eight times annual gross income range, depending upon who pays the utilities. You should only use them for preliminary analysis, and completely ignore them after that. Low rentals may also indicate that the project is located in a less than desirable or deteriorating neighborhood, or in an area where apartments are so competitive that the owner no longer feels he can command a premium for the project.

Analyzing Tenant Profiles and Property Taxes

From the application forms executed by all tenants before occupancy, you can verify such important things as:

- Current income of the tenants
- Number of children
- Number of parents supervising children
- Stability and length of employment
- Average length of occupancy
- Current status of rental payments

A profile of existing occupants will reveal the type of tenants the project can be expected to draw from in the future. Generally speaking, a project should not have more than one person in a small efficiency unit. You can assume an overcompetitive situation if there are more than two people physically occupying any given bedroom in a complex. Gross rentals must be adjusted in anticipation of vacancy factors, if these conditions exist, as the economic rent for the holding period of the project will fluctuate accordingly if these conditions prevail.

The local property tax is one of the most important areas to concentrate on in the operating statement. Even under ideal market conditions, an apartment building would not be feasible in many communities in the United States because of local property taxes. Unless there is an unusually tight rental picture, where future rents can be increased considerably, real estate taxes exceeding 15% of the total gross rental income will work as a direct liability against the project and you as the owner. While this 15% tax figure may not sound alarmingly high, it will probably eliminate new construction in 40% to 50% of the larger cities in the United States.

Several years ago, I was acquiring apartment complexes for a group of individuals in a major metropolitan area, where the tax rate was the second highest in the nation. Real estate taxes were averaging between 22% and 29% of the gross income. Some of the properties started to become marginal. The group then shifted to a different geographical area where real estate taxes were in the 10% to 15% of gross income range. The resulting 10%, naturally, all went to the bottom line.

Herein lies the reason for the rapid growth of the suburban apartment complex. If an apartment complex to be acquired is in a community where this tax ratio exceeds 15%, the current rent schedule must be considerably under the prevailing market rate in order to accommodate any rent increase and still remain under 15% of the gross rental figure. The taxation picture on new apartments can be distorted further if the assessment is based on partial cost of completion rather than full completion or if political favoritism enters the tax picture.

A venture is normally feasible if it shows 10% of the gross income expended on real estate and personal property taxes. If a reasonable vacancy factor is included, a 5% to 7% profit margin on gross income in a highly mortgaged situation might be all a venture will ever show you initially as cash flow.

Pricing Land as a Percentage of Rents

A second important factor to analyze is the cost of the land. In existing units, the land-to-building ratio forms the basis for the depreciation allowances. In units to be constructed, the land cost should be in the area of 10% to 15% of the completed value of the units, which includes all costs of interest, construction, and architectural fees.

Many value judgments can affect analysis of land cost at the time of property acquisition. Value is based on the fully improved site, which includes unusual site preparation, utilities, drainage and permanent roads. As a general guideline, you can estimate the price you can pay for a fully improved underlying piece of ground normally as ten times the monthly gross rental. I have analyzed and acquired a multitude of apartment sites and, generally, this ratio is considered fairly accurate. I have made exceptions where tight zoning and extreme market demand will eventually raise the rentals of the units considerably.

The Importance of Cost and Availability of Utilities

Another important factor found in the operating statement is its reflection of the cost and availability of utilities, which have played and will continue to play an important function in the future valuation of an apartment investment. Since the Arab oil embargo, the fall of Iran, and the recent Congressional deregulation of natural gas and oil, the historic calculation of $15 to $20 per month for utilities for the average-sized apartment is no longer realistic. Since tenants resist direct rate adjustments for utilities less than general rent increases, most owners and developers of apartment buildings are installing separate utility meters. The result is usually less turnover and more conservative consumption by tenants.

Traditionally, the annual rent increases of 3% to 5% have covered the increased cost of operation. An apartment renter finds it difficult to absorb or comprehend a large one-time rent increase to cover utilities, especially if he has been occupying apartments a good portion of his adult life.

I have also found that single-metered utilities can create problems when you attempt to convert apartments to condominiums. I recently encountered such a difficulty with the FNMA organization, as the permanent loans on the individual condominium units were to be sold in the secondary market. The hurdle was eventually overcome. However, lenders in the secondary market are not normally sympathetic to local problems you will encounter with these single-metered utilities. A respected mechanical engineer will know the policies of the local utility companies and their long-term rate situation.

Analyzing Building Codes, Construction Costs and Unit Composition

Just as tax rates and charges for utilities vary with locality, so do construction costs, either for new buildings or for remodeling older units. Availability of general contractors and architects is extremely important to the developer, as is the labor picture in terms of unionization.

In certain localities, municipal code restrictions and environmental restraints are excessive. In addition to these constraints, a truly no-growth community is distinguished by planning commissions, building departments, and elected officials dedicated to making it difficult for you to operate profitably. I recently found myself developing in two metropolitan areas that were approximately 60 miles apart. The cost differential, surprisingly enough, between these two areas was approximately 15%, even though neither area was highly unionized. Many arbitrary restraints and restrictions caused this price differential.

Restrictions regarding building height and excessive code requirements frequently rule out construction of luxury apartments, which tend to be high-rise in nature. Developers use a minimum figure of $5 per square foot of land cost as a justification for constructing a high-rise building, since construction costs are considerably more than those of garden apartments. Anything less than such a land cost would not justify the installation of elevators, the construction of underground parking, and higher construction costs per square foot. Most high-rise complexes disguise smaller square footage with large glass windows to give rooms a feeling of openness, as these units generally have fewer rooms. The norm is a blend of efficiency, one-, and two-bedroom units.

Garden apartments are normally found in the suburbs, where lending institutions are quite sensitive about land coverage and in many cases will dictate the details of well-landscaped open areas to you the developer. Generally, about a third of the units have one bedroom, another third have two, about a fourth have three, and the remainder are either four-bedroom units or efficiencies. About 60% to 70% are occupied by young married couples, of whom about half have families. The elderly and young singles occupy the remaining percentage. In most such units the ratio of building to land coverage is about 25%, even if this means constructing a second or third story and providing an elevator.

As we mentioned earlier, only 20% of the nation's populace uses public transportation. Private vehicles driven by the tenants of most structures necessitate a parking allowance of between one and a half and two cars per dwelling unit, varying with local ordinances, the size of the unit, and the number of bedrooms or bathrooms within the complex. A normal car and its turning radius takes up about 300 to 325 square feet of asphalted surface, so that the paved area for parking might very well equal or exceed the gross livable area of the units themselves, if they are small. In downtown localities of large cities, the parking requirement is considerably less than it is in suburban areas. However, the conversion of a rental project into a condominium will increase the need for parking, and lack of these facilities can be a real detriment to potential sales, irrespective of the location of the complex.

Spotting and Funding Maintenance Costs

A potential buyer of an apartment complex must analyze the maintenance expenses of a project, as sometimes deferred maintenance is not immediately obvious. Generally, it is not necessary to inspect every unit before purchase when the appropriate formulas in an analysis are applied. If the owner budgets and spends ample funds on maintenance—an average of 9% of the gross income should be required—the units, generally speaking, should be in satisfactory condition, and this will also be reflected in the tenant turnover. The buyer should budget an additional 1½% of the gross income as a reserve for replacement for:

- Heating and air conditioning units
- Elevators
- Hot water heaters
- Ranges, refrigerators, dishwashers

Deferred maintenance is probably the toughest area for an outsider to analyze. Several years ago, I purchased a 12-unit apartment complex which was then approximately six years old. This was built by a builder/developer, and all appliances, disposals, hot water heaters, etc., were of the minimum quality required by the architect and the lending institution. Most of these appliances needed replacement during the sixth or seventh year, as many builders and syndicators construct apartment projects knowing that they will sell their projects immediately after the depreciation benefits run out. Prior to purchasing the complex, I had the appliances checked and reduced my offering price correspondingly to cover their eventual replacement.

In analyzing deferred maintenance, you have no authoritative source to approach, such as a utility company for rates, or the local assessor's office for the tax assessments. The key is to retain a qualified individual, such as an appraiser or a property management firm, to estimate the cost of maintaining a project, either on a per-unit or on a square-foot basis, calculated on the area's historic trends and the type of your particular structure. A low maintenance figure on the operating statement of an existing property will probably mean that you, as the prospective buyer, should reduce your offering price by the amount of the deferred maintenance.

A person selling an apartment complex is not necessarily interested in maximizing the project's expenditures if he anticipates that the project is going to be disposed of. This has the multiple effect of distorting the true picture with additional artificial cash flow and deferred maintenance having to be funded at a later date.

Relationships Between Operating Expenses and Gross Income

In order to analyze and fully understand the potential return on the apartment structure, you must know the relationship and percentages of operating expenses typically used within the industry. These expenses on a percentage of gross income basis can vary from area to area, and more so with the age and type of construction. However, in analyzing the potential income, you must be completely realistic about the economic rent that the project can generate. Table 7-1 is an itemization of the typical expenses of an apartment building as they relate to 100% of the gross operating income. Expenses will vary anywhere from 35% to 45%, depending upon four key factors:

- Maintenance
- Taxes
- Utilities
- Reserves for replacement

If utilities are metered separately and the cost passed on directly to the tenants, both the gross income and operating expenses are reduced accordingly, and the bottom line figures remain approximately the same.

TABLE 7-1

Typical Expenses of an Apartment Building

GROSS OPERATING INCOME	100%
Vacancy factor, bad debts, and collection losses	– 5
Gross income after vacancy factor	95%
Operating Expenses	
Real estate and personal property taxes	10%
Utilities (heat, air conditioning, electricity and water)	11
Management	5
Advertising and sales promotion	1
Maintenance	9
Insurance	2
Legal, accounting, and professional fees	0.5
Reserve for replacement	1.5
TOTAL OPERATING EXPENSES	40%

On the average, operating expenses will be in the 40% range, and in many instances they should be less. If these expenses exceed 40% of the gross, either the project is not feasible or the current market rents are not at the highest economic level.

Important Ratios of Debt Service to Income

Debt service payments based upon first-mortgage financing at 75% of appraisal take into consideration the above ratio of operating expenses to gross income. A properly structured debt service payment should approximate 45% of the gross income after a normal vacancy factor. In other words, the vacancy factor of 5%, the debt service of 45%, and the operating expenses of 40% combine to leave a normal profit margin of 10% on the investor's equity. This is not an alarming figure in a highly leveraged situation, where thin equities and large depreciation are paramount. If the property is showing a 10% vacancy factor instead of the projected 5%, the situation becomes somewhat uncomfortable. If such operating expenses as taxes and utilities combine to rise an additional 5% and you cannot successfully pass these costs on in the form of increased rent, suddenly, after you have gone through all the effort and expense to acquire or develop a

FIGURE 7-1

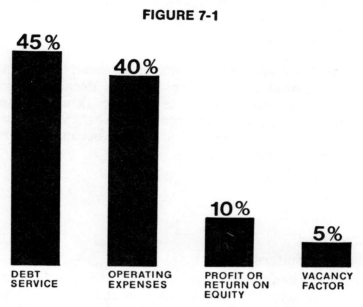

RATIO OF OPERATING EXPENSES TO GROSS INCOME

project, your equity position substantially evaporates and the value of the project only equals that of the first mortgage. In every apartment complex I have either acquired, been associated with, or acted as a consultant on, I have attempted to get at least a 70% loan-to-value ratio on the permanent financing. Sometimes this is done by refinancing, and often it is accomplished by having the seller carry the balance over the existing first mortgage. In order to obtain the right amount of depreciation and corresponding return on equity, this 70% figure should be met.

Many projects have been foreclosed where the owners have sacrificed their equity positions because of increases in the costs of utilities and real estate taxes in markets where they could not pass these additional operating expenses on to the tenants. I know of at least two dozen apartment projects in the Southwest that, in the mid-1970's, went through foreclosure shortly after the Arab oil embargo, as the increased utility costs could not be wholly absorbed in an overbuilt rental market. Many of these projects had occupancy rates in excess of 95%, and most were developed by sophisticated people involving investments of millions of dollars per project.

Key Expenses Affected by Inflation

Your analysis of operating expenses before acquisition or development is imperative. Over the last decade, it has been customary to raise apartment rents between 3% and 5% annually, based upon normal inflationary trends. In recent years, apartment expenses have been rising faster than income because of increases in the following major categories:

- utilities,
- janitorial,
- maintenance,
- taxes, and
- mortgage interest.

If you as an owner can stabilize or eliminate utility costs by metering each unit separately, establish yourself in an area of moderate real estate tax increases, and correspondingly reduce operating expenses to approximately 30% of gross income (excluding utilities), you can be relatively assured of a workable apartment project and a respectable cash flow.

Other areas of possible reduction in expenses exist as well. The management fee of 5% balances against the vacancy factor of 5%. Obtaining top management by paying a full 5% management fee in larger complexes should considerably reduce the vacancy factor. The 1% advertising expense is probably realistic, certainly not during the initial leasing-up period on a new building, but over the lifetime of the project. If your venture is well-conceived, located in a good area, and has a low turnover factor, this 1% figure should be realistic.

Importance of Reserves for Replacement

The reserve for replacement is an extremely important item to analyze, not only for bookkeeping purposes, but also as a realistic expense at a future date. Most developers of new apartment complexes tend not to escrow these funds, at least not during the initial period of the building in tenancy. In a majority of owner-provided operating statements, this figure is either not reflected at all, or is present on an artificially low basis. However, once the project is established and leased, provisions for this reserve factor are important, especially where furnished units are prevalent. Even in unfurnished apartments, such items as carpeting, ranges, refrigerators, window coverings, elevators, air conditioning units, hot water heaters, and other mechanical equipment will not last the full duration of the twenty-five to thirty-year mortgage. In the furnished apartment units that I have owned, I have found that the carpeting and the major items of furniture need to be replaced approximately every fifth year. The ranges, refrigerators, dishwashers and compactors consistently need replacement sometime between the seventh and ninth year. In some of the projects I have owned, the 1½% reserve for replacement is quite low, and on occasions, especially with furnished units, I have budgeted 5% or more, especially in older buildings where I can predict that the increases in cash flow will not generate sufficient funds to meet these expensive and recurring replacement costs.

As a building ages, it becomes increasingly difficult to extract large amounts of money from current cash flow to cover these major improvements. Establishing an escrow fund to meet these potentially large obligations is extremely critical in older apartment buildings.

Obtaining Maximum Mortgage Financing

Apartment financing is based on a cash-flow analysis by means of a realistic existing or pro forma operating statement submitted to lending institutions. On new developments, the lender will generally require a summary of the project's cost, which includes a breakdown of:

- construction costs;
- architectural fees;
- cost of interest and financing;
- land cost;
- cost of furniture and appliances;
- title insurance; and
- operating deficit and leasing commissions.

Normally, the above costs will all be included and itemized in the appraisal. Additionally, lenders usually require air photos of the site, location maps, plans, specifications, resumes of the owners and general contractors, appropriate personal and corporate financial statements, copies of the offer to purchase, target dates for acquisition, completion, and leasing of the project, and a summation of the sources of the equity funds. Whenever I submit a financing package on a project, whether it be new or on an existing building, I detail the amount of equity funds and the sources from which I plan to obtain them. Historically, I have provided all start-up equity money myself, and then follow this with a presentation of the equity funds required for development or acquisition of the project. I provide a complete breakdown as to whether my personal funds are involved or whether I am syndicating equity investors. Conventional sources of financing normally require a larger equity position than do some of the government financing agencies, such as the Federal Housing Administration (HUD) or the Farmers' Home Administration. However, federal agencies have a tendency to control rents, and, therefore, profits.

The pro forma, or in many cases, actual operating statement will be submitted to the lending institution, showing the operating expenses ranging in the 40% to 45% area, including utilities and reflecting the traditional 5% vacancy factor. This information then becomes the basic tool for the lending institutions in analyzing the value of the project and the subsequent loan that the project and you as the owner can economically support.

How Lenders Figure Maximum Mortgages

Many permanent lenders insert rental achievement clauses which dictate that a given rental per unit be achieved and a predetermined level of occupancy be set before the long-term mortgage is funded. This complicates the interim financing, as most interim or construction lenders will commit a lesser percentage of appraised value if a rental achievement is required in the permanent mortgage. The interim lender will also want assurances that sufficient funds are available to fund any potential operating deficit during the initial rent-up stage. A lender then analyzes the package and applies a constant loan factor to the stabilized cash flow generated from the venture. If the financial institution is committing funds at 11% for a twenty-five-year period, they will arrive at what they call a "constant repayment factor." This factor is arrived at by determining the amount of interest as well as the annual funds necessary for principal reduction over the duration of the mortgage.

If the simple interest is 11%, the constant factor for principal amortization on the typical mortgage would be about 3/4 of 1% more. The lender takes the available cash flow after deducting the operating expenses and vacancy factor and applies the 11.75% constant factor to the remaining cash flow, thus arriving at a mortgage amount, with some cushion known as a debt service coverage ratio to the lender, that the cash flow from the project will support. Basically, this is a simple and universal formula that you and your lending institution use to arrive at a realistic mortgage amount within a matter of minutes. Most sophisticated lenders commit apartment funds on a multiple of 1.2 to 1.3 times the recognized debt service coverage. For every $1.20 to $1.30 available for debt service, lenders will apply $1.00 toward the first mortgage to provide an ample cushion in the event of default. Said differently, they will commit the reciprocal of 120 to 130 times the debt service coverage, or 70% to 80% of their appraised value. This cushion is built in to cover unforeseen vacancies or abnormal increases in operating expenses. I have found recently that financial institutions, when providing extremely leveraged first-mortgage funding, are now asking for an equity interest in the project. Often it relates to a percentage of the overage cash flow after the mortgage is funded, which has the effect of increasing their overall yield. Sometimes it relates to an actual equity position in which they not only participate in the cash flow, but also have a residual interest in the investment when it is disposed of.

Apartment acquisition and development offers you, the small to medium-sized real estate investor or developer, the easiest access into the complicated development field. This vehicle provides the most potential for accumulating projects and the means for establishing a sophisticated pattern to be used over many years for other successful ventures. As you gain experience with apartments and establish a track record for management and financial responsibility, you may find that by making full use of the experience you have gained with apartments, you may decide to follow a lucrative trend of the times and venture into the field of developing residential condominiums, which we will consider next.

8

Lucrative Opportunities in Residential Condominiums

Condominium projects are a relatively new vehicle for real estate development in the United States, surfacing during the early 1960's and coming into maturity during the 1970's and the early part of the 1980's. In many respects they will replace the detached, single-family tract houses that have been developed so successfully since World War II.

The shortage of land available for detached single-family subdivisions, combined with the fact that many municipalities lack funds to extend services and utilities to far-reaching places, has led to in-fill policies in many communities. Such policies are designed to encourage utilizing improved land to its fullest extent before expansion to outlying areas, and in-fill sites are usually high-density tracts ideally suited to condominium projects.

This chapter will show you how to locate the lucrative markets and zero in on the potential buyers, how to find the 100% location and design your project to obtain maximum sales prices. You will benefit from the proven methods used by the professionals for marketing condominium projects and the successful techniques used to accurately determine costs and take advantage of the economics of scale found in large developments.

You will also see how apartments designed for conversion to condominiums are extremely lucrative, such as in the 300-unit apartment complex I am currently attempting to structure, which, if successful, will be converted to condominiums when the initial tax benefits are exhausted. The development will be structured so that I can sell off small numbers of units during the initial years to cover any operating deficits. When the balance of the units are eventually converted and sold, I will, hopefully, see the major profits from this project.

Variations of the Condominium Theme

For investment purposes, residential condominiums can be categorized into three major types:

- cooperative apartments;
- "pure" condominium projects;
- townhouse condominiums.

The first can be dealt with briefly. The other two can best be explained by comparison.

Cooperative apartments have been phased out during the last decade or so, at least in terms of new development. This form of ownership is similar to purchasing a share of stock in a corporation which entitles one to a percentage of the overall complex rather than to any physical claim to a unit or to the air space within a unit. This method of structuring communal ownership has, in the majority of instances, proved to be no longer viable. For all practical purposes, lending institutions generally disapprove of this as a valid form of ownership.

The major difference between pure condominiums and townhouses is that, under the latter arrangement, the purchaser of a unit owns the land underneath the building, the air space within the structure, and in many cases half of the adjoining common walls. Townhouse ownership is preferred by most lending institutions and is the prevalent method of development where low-rise construction prevails. Where high-rise units are developed so that one unit physically occupies the air space over another, the pure condominium concept prevails since it is not feasible for each buyer to own the underlying land or common facilities such as elevators, stairways, heating and cooling systems, ductwork, and common hallways.

This chapter is concerned primarily with the townhouse concept of condominium construction and ownership. Lenders, in most instances, resist the pure condominium approach, especially during periods of tight money, unless the units are extremely desirable, as they become quite selective when interim and permanent funds evaporate. Under the pure condominium approach, an individual purchaser acquires only the air space within his dwelling unit and a proportionate interest in the common areas based upon his overall percentage of ownership. This form of ownership is obviously complex from the legal and engineering standpoints, and the fees for developing pure condominiums are consequently higher than those for townhouses.

Several years ago, I encountered some additional expenses on a project that I was involved with, in which nine buildings contained condominium units, all consisting of two stories. The additional engineering and surveying work was considerable, as the inside air space had to be totally delineated and the common areas within each one of these buildings also had to be well defined. Such things as common party walls, stairways to the second floors, the heating and air conditioning rooftop units and ductwork were all intermingled and expensive to survey. Had this building contained one-story townhouse units, the engineer could have quite easily depicted the common walls and drawn the appropriate documents with relative ease.

Zeroing in on the Potential Buyers

The movement away from apartment complexes and detached single-family suburban houses is creating a viable, expanding, and lucrative market for condominium developers. The buyers constituting the prime market are normally the same as those for luxury apartments—the "empty-nesters" who have moved from large detached houses and the young professionals who have traditionally occupied apartment complexes—all anxious to obtain the qualities of home ownership.

Successful condominium projects carry financing as high as 90% to 95%, which is often higher than an investor can obtain on conventional detached housing. With proper financing, you can achieve presales commitments early, eliminating much of the speculation in a given development. Even the small- to medium-sized investor who can visualize opportunities finds this lucrative market accessible and quite easy to define.

A condominium unit can normally be constructed and developed for 20% to 25% less per square foot than a single-family detached house. Competitive benefits of condominium development relate specifically to:

- land costs;
- repetitious construction;
- utilization of common walls;
- site work and utility extension;
- clustering of units; and
- common roads and driveways.

The rising cost of land and construction of detached housing primarily accounts for the rapid increase in condominium development. Adding to this, the major and, I believe, permanent upward adjustment in interest rates means that the developer who formerly built single-family detached houses must channel his efforts into smaller, less costly, higher density condominium units. In many respects I have shifted my operations away from single-family detached houses and subdivisions into condominium projects, as I am finding that some of the land costs in these subdivisions are running 20% or more of the price of the finished house that is being offered for sale. When these conditions prevail, I normally rechannel my efforts, selling the land only, offering terms and conditions on the remaining lots in these subdivisions, preferring to concentrate on the higher density, lower land cost condominium projects.

How to Locate the Characteristic and Lucrative Markets

The segment of the condominium market appealing to buyers with moderate to upper incomes has extreme depth. If you are specializing in a well-conceived, well-located project designed for these buyers, you can readily achieve a 15% to 20% return on sales and can eliminate many of the risks through presale commitments. A large percentage of the buyers in this income range are young professionals born after World War II. As first-time buyers, they have lived with inflation for most of their adult lives and fully recognize the value of real estate as a hedge against inflation. They are also cognizant of the fact that, if they wait until they can afford what they ultimately want at the income level they will hopefully achieve, inflation will eventually price them out of the market.

Even though the market for moderate-income buyers is the most expansive, it can also be the most volatile. For instance, I recently completed the first 50 units of a condominium project which will total 125 units on completion. In arranging my financing package for the second phase, or 75 units, I find that the 3-point rise in long-term interest rates since I financed the first phase will eliminate a large share of the market I intended to attract. The potential buyers are totally dependent upon qualifying for monthly payments, and the second phase of this $6,000,000 project must be timed carefully and brought to the market when interest rates make this profitable. In my estimation, the project will again become viable when long-term rates drop by 1½ to 2 points, at which time it should sell out in a relatively short period of time, due to the pent-up demand for units in this price range.

Against the depth of the moderate-income market, you must balance the shallower but more lucrative segment to be found among buyers of substantial means. Here your sales efforts must be designed to convince these older, more sophisticated buyers of the advantages connected with luxury condominium living over the continued occupancy of their expensive single-family residences. The sophisticated developer who cultivates this niche can constantly show a 20% to 25% profit on sales; however, you must cater to buyers who purchase out of convenience rather than necessity and have the means to pick and choose from projects which are tailored to their individual needs. If you can succeed in anticipating the needs and whims of this clientele, you can dictate almost whatever price you want for your product.

While the in-fill sites zoned for high density are potentially the most suitable for a condominium project, purchasers of luxury units often want the convenience of townhouses combined with the appearance of rural retreats. Satisfying this requirement often demands much ingenuity in your selection of site in a relatively low-density development. I am currently constructing 18 luxury condominium units in a project located on 2.9 acres of land. By adding some relatively minor cosmetics to the construction of the units and budgeting $25,000 per acre for landscaping on this prime site, I find that I am obtaining sales prices in excess of 25% over what other condominium projects in less desirable areas are commanding.

How to Accurately Determine the Costs of Development

The most substantial costs in a condominium project, those for land and construction, normally equal about three-quarters of the overall expenditures in any given venture. As a rough rule of thumb, the normal breakdown of these development costs is as follows:

Land cost	10%
Offsite Improvements	2%
Construction of the units	65%
Construction of recreation facilities	3%
Architectural and engineering fees	4%
Interim financing	6%
Sales and overhead	5%
Landscaping	2%
Contingency	3%

FIGURE 8-1

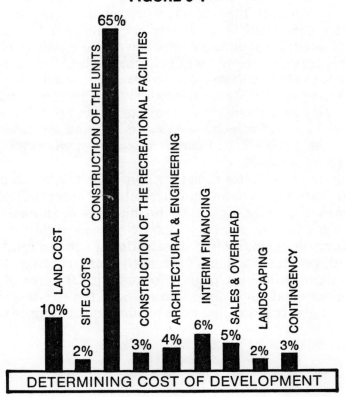

These figures can vary considerably with the type of market and the size of the project. In a luxury condominium development, the location is obviously of prime importance and the land cost can often exceed the 10% listed above. By the same token, construction costs of units may be secondary, well under 65%. Extensive land costs can also be complemented by increases in architectural fees and landscaping expenditures to create a particularly pleasant environment. I am currently developing a luxury condominium project on leased land where the capitalized value of my leasehold interest exceeds this 10% figure. Since individuals are essentially buying the location in these luxury condominium projects, exceptions to this land cost rule can be made quite frequently, especially in the upper income ranges. I anticipate that when this project is completed, I will be more than compensated for the highly capitalized cost of land in relation to the finished product.

How to Select the Location and Site

Convenience to shopping, places of employment, recreational and cultural facilities are extremely important aspects of selecting the site for a condominium. Equally important are the acceptance of condominiums in that particular area and the nature of the existing competition. Undercurrents of residents' resistance can develop, especially in prestigious neighborhoods where continuous development of condominiums persists and you must monitor local conditions carefully when you contemplate a new luxury project. No-growth attitudes followed by restrictive zoning can solidify communities rather rapidly. Any offer to purchase a tract of land intended for condominium development under these conditions should be subject to obtaining all the appropriate approvals before the transaction is concluded.

A luxury $3,000,000 condominium project which I am currently developing was the cause of a recent controversy. Although commencement of the project did not involve rezoning, it did require approvals of an architectural styles committee of the city zoning department. Although they had no means of blocking the issuance of a building permit, many of the neighborhood associations protested my project. The momentum they achieved carried over to another project in the same general vicinity being planned by another developer. Month after month of hearings involving literally hundreds of protesters have so far blocked the necessary rezoning for the other project, and it is now questionable whether it will ever receive zoning approval. This example is not untypical of what can

happen in well-to-do communities when a certain stage of
development is reached. Suddenly the powers that be emerge to
eliminate or effectively stop all further condominium development.

Designing a Condominium to Achieve Maximum Sales Prices

The design of a residential condominium project should create a
sense of privacy within a unit while offering common or recreational
facilities for an open life style that one could not obtain in a
comparably priced private residence. Such things as roads, patios
and entryways into units should create the impression of total
privacy and the feeling that the project was designed exclusively for
the individual occupant. The layout of the private roads is extremely
important since they do much to project the feeling that the complex
exists exclusively for the use of its owners and not for the general
public.

Condominiums do not generate the pride of ownership
comparable to that found in single-family dwellings. Cultivating
that sense of pride should be a major factor in the activities of the
homeowners' association and, even more fundamentally, in the basic
design and construction of the dwelling unit. There should be no
restrictions that will limit what an owner can do to individualize his
unit, and, especially, no regimentation of exterior features such as
patios or courtyards. When purchasing for investment purposes,
many buyers realize how much pride of ownership they are
sacrificing specifically for resale value, and they are particular
about flaws in design which may permanently limit their privacy.
They will search widely, choose carefully, and become renters rather
than sacrifice their life styles to the permanent commitment of
purchase. The absence of facilities to insure privacy and pride of
ownership is one of the reasons that so many apartment complexes
will never be converted to successful condominiums.

I am currently involved with a group of individuals who own a
large 300-plus-unit apartment site, which we are eventually
contemplating as a condominium project. Given the current market,
the economics of the development would not justify a conventional
apartment building; however, the group is designing the buildings
as apartments with an eye towards potential conversion into a
condominium project. We will syndicate the required up-front
equity funds, as a considerably larger amount of equity money is
needed, as the current economics do not justify the cost of the
structure. However, our group feels that the tax benefits in the first

five to seven years will be substantial, and that the conversion possibilities at the end of that period will provide more than the necessary overall desired return on the project.

Capitalizing on the Economics of Scale

One of the more salable aspects of condominiums is that they offer amenities to purchasers at a fraction of what each facility would cost if purchased individually. We have already discussed how the economics of scale apply to land, construction, and other improvements such as landscaping, utility extensions and roadways. Similarly affected are:

- maintenance,
- management,
- security, and
- recreational facilities.

Aesthetics and economics can be compatible in condominium developments. Some sites are well worth the hundreds of thousands of dollars the land commands because so large a percentage of units can be oriented to command a variety of attractive views. Only the economics of scale permit the acquisition of such sites, which in turn lead to premium prices.

I recently had a 9-acre condominium tract I own appraised. The remaining land was the last phase of an $8,000,000 development. The site is sloped and elevated to provide spectacular views of a nearby city. The appraiser valued the tract at $620,000 for the 75 units, or 25% over the going per-unit rate in that metropolitan area. In effect, he put a premium of $150,000 on this site based upon orientation of the project toward the urban horizon.

The ratio of density to the supporting facilities must be considered prior to the conception of a development. Moderately priced condominium projects must be fairly large in scale since recreational facilities, management salaries, security provisions, and similar expenditures must be prorated over a large number of potential users so that they do not combine to be prohibitive. On the other hand, luxury condominium projects are generally more successful if they are kept relatively small and exclusive while still providing the appropriate supporting facilities. The income of the potential occupants must be balanced against the monthly assessments in either case, with special attention to the inevitability of losing prestige through massiveness.

Some locations have ample drawing power in themselves without supporting recreational facilities. I recently leased a condominium site on a 99-year basis with a capitalized land value of approximately $12,000 per condominium unit. The going rate for fee land in that metropolitan area was closer to $25,000. The only common areas in that development will be the private streets, guest parking areas, utility easements, and landscaped areas. The prestige of the site in this unique metropolitan area is enough to sell the units readily without any major recreational facilities.

I normally calculate the annual cost of operating the homeowners' association in a condominium project to be between 1% and 2% of the initial cost of the units. Under 1% is rarely possible unless a complex consists of hundreds of units. Homeowners whose assessment approaches 2% will be quite demanding of complete amenities, and the assessment fee can constitute a make-or-break proposition for you, the developer. The above example carried a 2½% homeowners' fee. This assessment, however, included the land lease payments.

How to Create an Effective Design for a Condominium

The architect selected to design a condominium project must possess qualities not necessarily found in a successful designer of single-family detached residences. He must create a dwelling unit that is compatible with a wide variety of life styles, yet sufficiently customized to compensate for the fact that it is probably scaled down from the size to which its new user is accustomed. Furthermore, he must design a unit that can be repetitively reproduced on a cost-efficient basis at 20% to 25% under the going rate for detached single-family houses. As a key person in convincing the prospective purchasers that their life styles will be improved by moving into smaller, more confined units, the architect must also be an effective salesman.

In all my architectural contracts for condominium projects, I insert a clause specifying that the architect must meet at least twice with each potential purchaser. This provides the buyer with the opportunity to incorporate some individuality into his unit and will help him to visualize the results of these design modifications. By the second meeting, I consistently know whether or not I have a firm transaction, and thereafter my contracts usually call for payment of additional fees at that time for architectural consultation.

In addition to his skill in conceptualizing the units, an architect should also have a feeling for the amenities which should be incorporated into a project, relating them to the size and economic status of the families who will occupy the homes. The more demanding and costly the amenities—tennis courts, swimming pools, golf courses, clubhouses—the more talent is involved to conceive and incorporate them into the overall master plan.

How to Achieve Flexibility of Design

A key factor for the market acceptance of any condominium project, and most especially in the luxury market, is providing the flexibility of internal design. Merchandising is decidedly affected by the size of the units and by incorporating such elements as large master bedrooms and closets, formal dining rooms, patios, areas for storage, interesting and decorative entrances, and using building materials that provide for sound control between units. Complete flexibility in the site and unit plans must also exist in order that the project can be redesigned, if necessary, during the sales program, giving you, the developer, adequate time to fully understand the needs of the potential buyers and the type of product that they will purchase.

In many condominium projects, the actual unit mix and desirable characteristics will not become apparent until several of the units have been constructed or presold. It is often important to phase projects, even though they are not large in scale, to achieve this needed flexibility. By constructing the initial phase consisting perhaps of only a few furnished models, you can test the waters and redesign the balance of the project after preselling those units which prove to be most desirable and profitable to construct. You never really know, for instance, whether the one-, two-, or three-bedroom units will be the most desirable until a project is completely marketed. An educated guess can be made initially at the design and presale stage, but the condominium developer can rarely predict with any degree of accuracy the composition of his project in terms of eventual mix of the units and their sizes.

The major factor in any attempt at prediction of the market is defining the exact nature of the clientele you are trying to attract. On the whole, the needs of the lower income end of the market are the easiest to predict. The young professional people who comprise this market segment have fairly predictable life styles and purchasing patterns. The limitations of their purchasing power can be strong enough to affect even the quality of building materials used in a project.

Predicting the needs of the luxury end of the market is much more complicated. Potential buyers are accustomed to greater variations in the sizes of rooms and their design features. Furnished models have more impact on purchasers of luxury units than they do on those in lower income brackets. Buyers of luxury condominiums want to visualize the finished product, and I have found that merchandizing without offering at least one furnished model in this market is a tough and challenging experience. I usually construct two or three model units and attempt to presell the majority of the units from these furnished models. Indispensable at the upper end of the market, they can be reliable sales tools also in the lower ranges.

How to Combine and Package Interim and Permanent Financing

One of the trickiest aspects of packaging a condominium project is obtaining the appropriate interim and permanent financing. Historically, obtaining the permanent financing was almost automatic and the interim was always a challenge. In recent years the situation has reversed. Lending institutions now actively seek construction or interim financing and find permanent financing less lucrative and more difficult to commit on. Conditions are often dictated prior to obtaining interim loans requiring presale or permanent loan commitments for a vast majority of units in a given project.

Many permanent lenders are now providing interim and permanent financing as a package. Under this type of arrangement, you can normally obtain the highest loan-to-value ratio as the combined interim/permanent lending institution appraises the final product on a retail basis. Making the transition between interim and permanent loans is greatly simplified when you deal with the same institution for both commitments. Normally, these lending institutions will commit on a blanket permanent mortgage for a project in which a certain percentage of the loans will be funded at 80% of loan-to-value, another group will be 90%, and the balance will be highly leveraged 95% commitments. If you can negotiate with the greatest proportion going to the 90% to 95% category, the project involved immediately becomes more salable because of the larger market of buyers with limited down payments.

I recently arranged for interim and permanent loans on a $2.5 million condominium development in which the permanent lender, a savings and loan, required the interim loan as a prerequisite for funding the long-term takeouts. In my estimation, the yield to the lender on the interim loan was probably 4 to 5 percentage points above that achieved on the permanent commitments when one considers the duration of the loan, the up-front points, and the interest rate that floated at one point over the Chase Manhattan prime rate. By offering the permanent lender the interim construction loan, you can often package both loan commitments with the same institution, at a substantially lower cost.

Advance commitments for permanent financing are becoming increasingly important as long-term interest rates continue to fluctuate widely. Combined with rising costs of land and construction, this means that many potential buyers can be temporarily eliminated when interest rates accelerate sharply. By the same token, interim lenders are not making commitments on projects where permanent loans and realistic interest rates are not locked in for at least the duration of the development loan. The interim lender looks at the potential profitability of condominium ventures, many of which carry a maximum 15% to 20% profit margin. With the interim interest exceeding 15% per annum, not an uncommon situation recently, a lender can become quite uncomfortable if the project stalls and the appropriate permanent financing is not available. Often under these circumstances, when the projected sellout period of any given phase is past, a development can become marginal, placing the lender's highly leveraged construction mortgage in jeopardy.

How to Maximize Interim Financing

In general, the percentages of interim financing to development costs of a typical condominium project can be described as follows:

1. 3% to 5% of the total sales value of the project goes into front-end expenses. The lender usually requires that you or your investing partners advance these funds.
2. 70% to 75% of the total value of the project is normally advanced by the interim lender during construction. This is usually not sufficient to clear the up-front cost of the land, at least during the initial construction period, where releases of the various parcels are needed for construction.

3. 5% to 10% of the total value relates to the typical closing costs, sales commissions, or other expenses that are incurred when you receive your compensation.

The remainder, customarily about 15% of the sales value, is your profit. From the foregoing, it becomes clear that the developer of a typical condominium project can control sizable amounts of money with relatively little up-front cash.

The real key to obtaining maximum financing is to have the lender recognize and advance sizable sums during the early stages of the development. This can often be accomplished if the venture is in a well-recognized and desirable area or if a substantial number of presales are achieved before construction commences. I have always tried to convince interim lenders on the strength of the area in which I am developing and the excellent potential for a quick, successful sellout. As supporting documentation I submit MAI appraisals indicating the current market value of the units combined with a carefully prepared feasibility study showing the market absorption rates in the area for comparable projects.

Last year, I put together an interesting package on a $3 million condominium project, developed on leased land. The lender agreed to advance all the necessary funds for constructing the units, installing the utilities, surfacing the roads, and completing the site work if my partners and I would advance the funds for the up-front engineering, architectural drawings, financing points, and one year's land-lease payments. These up-front advances approximated $60,000, or 2% of the total value of the project, and we obtained a commitment for the balance of the financing from the interim lender.

Proven Techniques for Obtaining 100% Financing

Another way to impress a lender and obtain the highest loan-to-value on interim financing is to present the potential lender with a firm bonded construction contract covering the total cost of all the improvements that are to be incorporated into the project. Nothing frightens a lender more than the possibility of being associated with a project where cost overruns could be prevalent and can potentially erode the profit margins, leaving the lender with a mortgage far in excess of the wholesale value of the project. Diametrically, nothing impresses a lender more than a guarantee of fixed costs, supported by a qualified MAI appraisal showing the value of the project, combined with the services of a competent marketing firm to accomplish the sales goals. Using these resources in combination will maximize the interim financing you can obtain on any given development.

As a developer of a condominium project, you should rarely have to invest more than 15% of the total value of the project in up-front equity. This will normally cover the initial costs of engineering, architecture and financing, and should release the portion of the land needed for the initial construction. In a well-conceived project, this 15% figure is a maximum and can be reduced quite early in the construction period, as you should be able to draw these up-front costs out initially from the interim financing. Exceptions occur in large developments where off-site utility extensions, construction of recreational facilities, and large contractual land payments are necessary during the initial stages of the project in order to create the proper image. In such cases, your larger equity investment should be offset by the profitable economics of scale that larger ventures can generate.

I recently developed a $125,000 recreational facility, including a tennis court and a swimming pool, in a semi-luxury condominium project. The entire facility had to be funded from the interim loan on the first of two selling phases, which approximated $5 million in combination. Under these circumstances, Phase One of the project showed less than a normal profit initially. However, both the lending institution and my limited partners understood that the overall project would be more lucrative if these facilities were constructed up-front. Not only were there substantial savings effected by completing this recreational facility initially, but sales accelerated because it was in place, attractive and operational.

How to Minimize Your Equity Requirements

Because payment for the land is normally the largest cost that you, the developer, have to fund initially, it is imperative to negotiate the best possible terms for acquiring the land and releasing the desired portions. Chapter 10 outlines many of the successful techniques for negotiating with landowners.

Often, condominiums can be developed on leased land, thereby eliminating a considerable amount of the up-front costs of land acquisition. Sometimes you can obtain additional leverage by persuading the landowner to subordinate his leasehold interest to the construction loan and the permanent financing. If he will not agree to a total subordination, he may be willing to agree to a partial subordination on the land to be initially developed, or to defer lease payments for a period of time to coincide with the duration of the completion of the construction. Arrangements such as these can be an important assurance to the lender that the appropriate land-lease payments will be kept current throughout the development period of the project.

Leased land is becoming an increasingly important vehicle in condominium development, especially in highly desirable areas where land has been held by families, individuals or trusts for generations. Holding idle, non-income-producing land can be quite expensive during inflationary periods, as we have often mentioned before. Officers or financial advisors of non-income-producing trusts are particularly anxious to enter into long-term land leases. Converting non-productive holdings into an income-producing vehicle without having to sell it and pay the corresponding capital gains tax can be quite beneficial to many trust recipients.

How Subordinated Land Leases Can Produce 100% Financing

I am currently developing a 36-unit condominium project in cooperation with a well-known guest ranch in the Southwest. The basic agreement calls for acquiring the property from the ranch on a 99-year lease. The up-front payments are structured so that one-third of the land lease will be prepaid upon closing of the units, and the balance will be equally amortized over the duration of the lease. The ranch agreed to subordinate its interest in the land lease during the interim construction period. This translates into my having no outlay for the acquisition of the land and limiting my up-front costs in this $5 million development to architectural, engineering and financing costs.

Further structuring of this arrangement, which is beneficial to both parties, calls for the ranch management to provide full use of their recreational facilities to potential purchasers of my condominium units. In exchange, the ranch gets an up-front fee for the use of these facilities and a management contract to use these condominiums in their rental pool during peak seasons. The negotiated fee I arrived at as a value for the recreational facilities is also not payable until each unit is closed, so that the amount of initial equity funds required for the development was less than 1%.

The arrangement just described was quite unusual. However, a variety of mutually beneficial transactions are possible, limited only by the imagination and courage of the consenting parties. In this instance, the ranch management used another's assets to expand their facilities and increase their cash flow by incorporating these units in their rental pool.

Often, the highest leverage for developing condominium projects can be obtained by offering an equity position to the permanent lender or the interim financing institution. This vehicle inevitably produces 100% plus financing, with the lender receiving a predetermined percentage of the profits. The risks involved are always reduced when the lending institution is an equity partner, and the other advantages can entail substandard interest rates on interim loans and higher loan-to-value ratios on permanent commitments. Provided one doesn't have to sacrifice too much equity or autonomy, you can find the best of both worlds where a lending institution strictly provides the funds, and leaves the day-to-day operations to you, the developer. There are no specific guidelines for lender's equity participation; however, no more than 20% to 25% should be offered unless the circumstances and lender participation are totally unique. Under these conditions, an equal interest might have to be offered; however, you as developer should be compensated at full market value for your services during the lifetime of the development.

Proven Methods for Marketing Condominiums

The techniques for marketing condominium projects are similar to those outlined in Chapter 9 on apartment conversions. Basically, you must determine whether or not a qualified outside firm should be retained to market the project. Doing so often reduces the up-front cash requirement for organizing an in-house sales operation, and in many respects gives the project broader marketing exposure, especially if the retained firm cooperates with other brokers through the use of multiple listing services. Conversely, utilizing outside firms can cost twice as much as developing an in-house sales organization, as the standard realtors' commissions for normal-size developments are in the area of 5% to 6%.

Among the many advantages of an in-house sales organization is that individuals can be put on retainer with the overall effect, depending upon the size of the project, of reducing the total marketing costs to 2% or 3% of sales. In addition, in-house people fully understand the product, know the stage of its development and the capabilities of the developer, and provide a full-time, on-site service.

Marketing arrangements must depend upon the type of development and the area from which sales will be drawn. I have used both in-house and outside sales organizations. In general, I have found that a large project amply budgeted for television and newspaper advertising can best be promoted with an in-house sales staff. Smaller ventures should be contracted to local real estate firms, since a considerable amount of time is spent in training personnel and setting up a media campaign that can be counterproductive in a smaller development.

Unusually higher promotion and selling costs can be expected on resort condominiums. A network of outside independent brokers must be retained to furnish sales leads, and a backup on-site sales staff is necessary to show the project and close the transactions. The resultant brokerage commissions are often in excess of that which is paid on conventional condominium projects. At the furthest extreme, many time-sharing projects promoted on an international basis have sales costs running between 30% and 40% of gross sales prices. Expenses are compounded by the extensive travel, advertising, and the operation of a multitude of sales operations.

I am currently involved with a group of investors who have acquired 21 condominium units in a new resort area in Mexico called Cancun. They purchased these units from a group headed by Mexican nationals for 2,000,000 U.S. dollars, and they are reselling these units to American citizens at a considerably higher price. The cost of marketing is extremely high in relation to a conventional condominium project stateside, as not only do commissions have to be paid to the Americans selling the project in Cancun, but a considerable amount of travel and entertainment is necessary throughout the United States in order to effectively stimulate interest in this development.

Educating a Sales Staff to Sell Condominiums

The sales staff of a condominium project must be able to field the many difficult questions posed by the potential buyers. Without a staff that is well-motivated and educated to the overall ramifications of condominium development, you can develop serious problems, as often potential buyers do not understand clearly just what is included in the purchase agreement. Misunderstandings commonly arise concerning such areas as:

- defining the area or unit purchased;
- defining the interest in common areas;
- the financial responsibiity for maintenance and security;
- the responsibility for structures and mechanical equipment;

- fully explaining the restrictions regarding pets, children, and guest privileges;
- explaining the storage of recreational vehicles; and
- the nature and extent of potential capital expenditures.

Special complications can arise when owners sublet their condominiums. Over time, many projects develop a high percentage of occupants who at one time or another lease their units. In general, these tenant-occupants bring with them objectives and life styles far different from those of the owner-occupants. For this reason, many condominium complexes have incorporated tightly restrictive covenants relating to tenancy, especially limiting the number of minor children and pets that can occupy rental units.

My major managerial problem with condominium projects has been controlling renters and pets, especially large animals. During the initial sellout of a development, there is tremendous pressure to deviate from a set of stringent rules and compromise in order to obtain quicker sales. One learns very quickly that compromising early in the sales effort can create major problems later, especially when a project is developed in several phases.

In the last condominium project that I developed, the first six units were sold to one investor, who in turn leased them all. These particular condominiums also happen to overlook the swimming pool and tennis court, and the tenants, unlike the owner-occupants, did not have the same respect and feeling for the other individuals in the complex. Several had pets and children who were inadvertently allowed to roam through the recreation facilities. There were many unpleasant encounters before the situation was rectified. Often, being overly restrictive can reap large benefits when selling a condominium development.

Whatever the managerial problems with residential condominiums may entail, they are similar to those found in apartment management and usually of a much shorter duration for you, the developer. Problems with apartments persist over longer periods of time, sometimes to the point where premature disposition of the asset becomes a necessity. While disillusionment with an apartment complex may provoke or warrant its sale, such a motive is hardly sufficient to justify the alternative that we will discuss in the next chapter—converting apartments to condominiums.

9

Cashing in on Apartment Conversions

The apartment field, for the most part, attracts the small-to medium-sized developer who, with a minimal investment, can capitalize upon his managerial talents. Yet, within this field lies one of the most lucrative vehicles for real estate speculation— condominium conversion. The developer who views the apartment field from this perspective can capitalize upon the attractiveness of location, and the realization that most apartment complexes can be purchased for considerably less than their replacement value, as they are normally priced on a cash-flow-after-operating-expense basis.

Systematically, this chapter will outline for you how to locate and price converted units, how to set up and successfully operate homeowners' associations, and through the hiring of competent advisors, limit your exposure to almost zero. Many successful techniques for obtaining interim and permanent financing, converting older buildings, and increasing your leverage through leased land techniques, are supported by actual practical money-making examples.

Included are a multitude of practical tips on how to diplomatically make the transition with tenants from a rental to a for-sale project, how to inexpensively provide warrant work and individually meter utilities and how to qualify marginal buyers, that will enable you to cash in on one of the most lucrative recent trends in the real estate development field.

Five Advantages Found in Converted Apartments

Existing apartments that are converted have distinct and built-in lucrative advantages over new competing condominium projects. They are:

- Existing tenants are normallly a source for a minimum of 25% of the sales.
- Costs of the finished units are relatively fixed. Cost overruns are minimal.
- Construction/conversion time is reduced to months, not years.
- Normally, the converted units sell for 20% to 25% under the market for new condominiums.
- The location is established and mature, creating a solid image.

Successful conversions are found in areas where luxury high-rise or garden apartments prevail. Such neighborhoods are considered prestigious, and most condominium buyers want to combine connotations of affluence with the luxurious, carefree style they seek. All of this works to the converter's advantage since potential clients will have the funds necessary for sizable down payments, the income to qualify for mortgage financing, and the mental attitude to absorb changes for maintenance of common areas and recreational facilities.

Determining the Appropriate Neighborhood

Several years ago I was involved in a 200-plus-unit apartment conversion where the project was surrounded by houses that had a value of at least twice the appraised value of the converted units. Before conversion, this development had one of the lowest rental rates in the metropolitan area. These converted units were enormously attractive to first-time buyers, largely because of the relatively affluent image of the neighborhood. The sales catered to the up-and-coming young professional or couple who could hold an equity position constant until they were in a financial position to find a larger and more comfortable home. Even though they purchased at the low end of the market, the buyers were able to do so without sacrificing social prestige.

Other reasons exist to attract you, the developer, to the fashionable residential areas. During periods of tight money markets, luxury units in prime locations have a tendency to hold their value and move quickly, regardless of the financial situation. The normal down payment in luxury condominiums is in excess of 25%, whereas 90% to 95% financing prevails in moderate- to low-priced complexes.

Areas to avoid are those where rent control exists or is being contemplated. Excellent conversion opportunities are found where apartment complexes can be purchased for a fraction of their replacement value, but the pitfall lies in the prevailing hostility of the area's residents toward landlords. I have been offered many potential conversion opportunities, particularly in California. It is often appropriate to let such opportunities slip by, especially if a municipality is hostile enough to pass rent control statutes, resulting in a sizable number of apartments that potentially could be converted into for-sale condominiums. Under these circumstances, conversion moratoriums are inevitably on the way and can easily trap you in mid-stream during the conversion process.

Proven Methods for Pricing the Converted Unit

As the foregoing warning about rent-controlled areas implies, the sale price of a converted unit is determined by its rental price. Where existing rents are at a fair market level, a converted apartment should command a sales value of approximately 100 to 120 times its former gross monthly rental. In other words, if a two-bedroom luxury apartment rents for $500 a month, it can be expected to command a value of between $50,000 and $60,000 if it is sold as a condominium to a resident tenant after minor cosmetic changes have been made.

FIGURE 9-1

The foregoing generalization is applicable only when one compares the fair market rent with the various tax advantages and appreciation factors involved in the ownership. Many locations, such as the volatile California markets, do not fit these broad generalizations; only independent analysis can accurately determine the appropriate converted value. Let us assume that a sales price of $60,000 is established on a particular unit, with a 20% down payment. The mortgage interest and principal payments on that unit at an interest rate of 11% will be approximately $470 a month for 25 years. In addition, real estate taxes and insurance, depending on the municipality, will total close to $150 a month. An additional fee of $50 per month must be added for maintenance of common areas and recreational facilities. Upon totaling these figures and deducting the tax benefits derived from the interest and property tax deductions, the after-tax obligation should roughly equal the current monthly rental. In a luxury complex, sophisticated buyers will probably pay a 15% to 20% premium over and above their current rent in order to achieve ownership and the corresponding appreciation, as well as to establish relatively fixed payments over a period of years, which they could not accomplish if they continued as renters. Let us analyze and list this hypothetical situation:

$60,000 = sales price
−12,000 = down payment
$48,000 = amount to be financed
470 = monthly interest and principal payments

In addition to interest and principal payments we must add:

$ 50 = monthly maintenance and recreation
470 = facilities payment
150 = real estate taxes and insurance assessments
$ 670 = total monthly obligation

Stressing the After-Tax Benefits

From the above illustration we deduct the after-tax benefits for the payment of taxes and interest—assuming a 35% individual tax bracket, (federal taxes only) and average interest payments on a 7-year holding period:

$175.00 = $500.00 (deductions for interest and taxes) × 35%
$495.00 = net monthly payment after tax considerations

This after-tax figure is approximately equal to the $500 a month currently being charged as rent in our hypothetical situation. For presentation purposes we next include the appreciation factor that benefits the owners of a converted unit. Most presentations use a 1% per month appreciation factor.

FIGURE 9-2

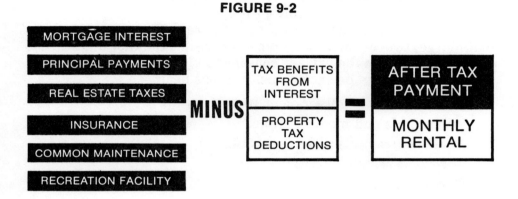

$600.00 = $60,000 value × .01 per month.

With this type of presentation, the potential purchaser can easily be convinced that the conversion is a worthwhile investment, as he actually makes money on the unit when this appreciation factor is incorporated into the formula.

The formula for selling luxury units in prime areas must be carefully translated when it relates to marginal areas, as people of moderate means are more interested in monthly payments than in long-term investments and appreciation. If the difference between renting and buying exceeds 10% in a marginal area, converted apartments may not sell and the projected conversion conceivably will not be financially feasible.

How to Effectively Analyze the Competition

Converted apartment units must compete both with newly constructed condominiums and with detached single-family housing in the same or comparable areas. New condominium projects do not look warmed over. They are specifically designed to be more functional, to have better room sizes and arrangements and recreational facilities. Adjusting for these advantages means offering converted units to the public at a minimum of 15% to 20% under the current market price obtained in newly constructed developments. To compete with detached single-family housing, converted units must be offered at a discount of 25% to 35%.

I recently turned down a conversion opportunity, as the apartment unit was fully priced before conversion for the neighborhood in which it was located. Land for construction of new condominiums was both cheap and plentiful in the area, and subsidized tax-free permanent mortgage authority funds were available on several competing projects.

For conversion purposes, the most desirable complexes are those with large, two- or three-bedroom apartments. Smaller units do not lend themselves to the privacy consonant with a luxurious life style, although there can be exceptions. In areas near:

- state and city government complexes
- hospitals and medical clinics
- affluent schools and universities
- service-oriented areas
- research parks, and
- airports

one-bedroom or efficiency units appeal to purchasers whose only other alternative, considering their income range, is something similar to a mobile home. If small converted condominiums in such areas are sold only to professional people, the development can be quite lucrative since basic rental prices and conversion values traditionally accelerate with smaller square footage. In special situations, profits on such conversions can exceed those obtained on luxury projects.

Sizing Up Potential Conversions

Many conversions are attractive because they cut the developer's exposure by selling units, in some degree at least, to occupying tenants. Taking this perspective, you must look closely at the type of tenants who occupy a complex, the vacancy factor, and the turnover rate. You must further consider that the majority of potential buyers, beyond those currently renting, will generally reside within a short distance of the existing structure.

Furthermore, you must analyze the availability of land in the immediate area. Vacant parcels that can potentially be developed as condominiums threaten your market, since newer projects are usually better conceived, designed, marketed, and promoted with more attractive financing. The availability of land adjacent to a conversion can be especially important in solving parking problems. Many apartment complexes were not designed for the convenience of parking near the individual units, which is prevalent in new built-for-sale condominium developments.

If parking is not available close to the individual units, price reductions must be made to compensate for the inconvenience involved. You must determine how many parking spaces are available for each unit, the adequacy of guest parking, and whether the parking space is covered. Open parking may require security provisions so that potential purchasers do not encounter problems of theft or vandalism during the evening hours.

Recreation areas and facilities must be considered, especially in luxury units, but other basics must be provided as well. It is important to determine if laundry facilities can be incorporated into the individual units or whether the project has ample laundry facilities closely accessible to each of the converted units. Ample storage must be available either within each unit or in certain designated areas throughout the complex.

The Importance of Metering Utilities Separately

Many developers will not even consider purchasing a complex for conversion if utilities are not or cannot be metered separately. Converters quickly learn that separate metering cannot be accomplished easily or cheaply.

Curiously, the more affluent and professional purchaser is most resistant to sharing utility costs with other owners. The logic of this situation is that busy professionals are not often home during daylight hours, and many of them travel extensively. They strongly resist paying utility bills on a pro rata basis with other family-oriented occupants of these complexes when they are not physically consuming the energy being metered.

Lending institutions also resist financing complexes where common meters prevail. They resent being involved in predicting the total consumption of energy within the complex, and many will not make loans on individual units without separate meters. If the project encounters financial difficulty and a majority of the units are neither sold nor leased, the utility bills must be prorated among existing tenants or owners. Such bills can create a major financial burden in a partially sold conversion.

During the conversion process, until a majority of the units in the project are sold, you as the converter must usually operate the homeowners' association. This fledgling association must prorate expenses, including the utility bills if units are not metered separately. Should utility rates increase substantially from the conception of the project until the time it is sold out, resisting tenants find the developer a convenient scapegoat.

How to Structure Warranties and Owners' Association Dues

The same consumerism movement which is providing the incentive for the purchase of condominiums is dictating that converted units carry the same warranties as those found on newly constructed condominiums. Standard guarantees on such items as:

- the roof
- the appliances
- heating and air conditioning units, and
- the major mechanical systems

are now mandatory. They are demanded by permanent lending institutions and especially by such secondary market lenders as FNMA, to which many permanent loans are sold.

Lenders now require that all major categories of construction be guaranteed for a minimum of one year. This means that, when prospective lenders review a conversion, they look closely at the proposed condominium association fees and the portion of those fees allocated toward maintenance and major capital improvements. An important aspect of the project's viability is the assurance that the homeowners' association need not fund major capital expenditures during the first year or two of operation.

I was recently involved in a conversion rejected by several of the prospective permanent lenders. Most of the conditions of warranty could be met, the condition of separate metering for electricity was feasible with minimal expenditure, but the impracticality of separately metering the gas eliminated many of these lenders. Other conditions imposed by the lenders were a one-year warranty on the appliances and a two-year warranty on the roof. The roof warranty was expensive and still carries an exposure factor. The other warranties—ranges, refrigerators, and other mechanical devices—are actually available to developers from many service companies for minimal fees. Offering them for one or two years eliminates the costly and time-consuming aspect of rejuvenating each separate piece of mechanical equipment.

Difficulties Found in Obtaining Permanent Financing

Unless you are extremely well connected or have proven and reliable sources of permanent financing, you will find that obtaining financing for converted units is a real challenge, second only to locating the project and analyzing the market for potential purchasers. An offer to purchase an apartment building for conversion must be made subject to obtaining permanent financing. Stipulating this condition is imperative. Lenders are increasingly putting major restrictions on presales before a conversion is funded. Many projects have a 50% to 70% presale requirement before any permanent loans are closed. This condition is prevalent especially when funding is obtained in the secondary money market.

Conversions involving a single building or a limited number of structures are especially difficult to finance. The combination of renters and owners creates an unhealthy environment when a project sells out slowly, and lenders fear that such projects might not ever fully close out as a condominium conversion. In such a situation, the interim lender must not only carry the conversion financing, but must also warehouse the permanent loans. Taking the purchaser's down payment normally involves permitting him to move into the unit, which is undesirable under a 50% to 70% presales requirement. Sometimes you can circumvent this problem by phasing the project, especially when many buildings are involved. Most interim lenders are not in the long-term lending business and take a dim view of the possibility of having to make permanent loans on the entire project.

Several years ago, I attempted to phase a conversion project in which I encountered some resistance from the lender proceeding from the fact that the underlying land, recreation, and community facilities were under one ownership, that being controlled by the homeowners' association. Even though the project was to be phased, the permanent lender took the position that the land and recreation facilities belonged to the entire project, and that 50% of the units would have to be presold before any permanent loans could be funded.

Pitfalls of Interim Financing

In many instances similar to the one described above, interim lenders recognize the complications involved in presales requirements and make conversion loans based on 75% of the total sales price of the units or the value of the project as a going apartment complex, whichever is less. Many lending institutions, including some of the larger banks and insurance companies, specialize in conversion loans and do it on a nationwide basis. Historically, conversion loans are considerably less than 75% of the sales price, and they normally will not exceed a percentage of the value of the project as a rental apartment complex.

Under normal conditions, a loan commitment at 75% of the sales value is more than sufficient to cover the total cost of acquiring and converting a project. The minimum return on sales should be 15%, and that combined with the remaining 10% for sales commissions and closing costs, which can be deferred until the actual time of closing, adds up to 100% of the project's retail value. Interim conversion loans generally command a higher interest rate than loans on newly designed and built condominium projects, and require a considerable number of up-front points. Lenders look for individuals or corporations with track records in conversion projects or those with selling and merchandising capability in for-sale residential housing. Because of the risk that a project might not be timely or totally converted, they also look for strong financial statements among the individuals involved.

Another approach to interim financing which requires a larger equity contribution by the converter is to arrange an interim loan with the seller of the complex during the conversion period and acquire an additional bridge or gap loan from a lending institution covering the cost of converting. The converter compensates both the seller and the lender by giving both parties a certain percentage of the sales proceeds from each individual unit. This procedure prevents any conflict of mortgages and takes both lending parties out simultaneously on a predetermined percentage basis as the units are sold. By the same token, both lending parties will require higher compensation. The seller will want additional consideration for carrying the interim note due to the increased risk. The bridge loan lender will require higher interest rates and more of your equity since his loan will be in second position to the seller's first mortgage.

How to Limit Your Exposure

As we mentioned earlier, you minimize your exposure by preselling the converted units to previous tenants and to others living in the vicinity of the existing complex. Sophisticated lenders also realize the advantages of conversion over new construction, since the developer is compensated for his operating costs and interest expenses during conversion by the rents generated from the project. His ability to convert at a predetermined rate—thereby cutting down lead time for construction and interest and avoiding nonproductive vacant units—will often be dictated by the existing leases in a complex.

Lenders are impressed with the stability and maturity found in older converted units with strong rental histories and established track records of occupancy. Higher loan-to-value ratios are achieved for both developer and purchaser in established older buildings. Minimal down payments are usually required of existing tenants in order to reserve their units; these are refundable if the overall complex is not successfully converted. During conversion, the developer's income from the rentable units will normally more than offset the loss of income from the units being converted. The carrying charges, especially those for maintenance of common areas and recreational facilities, will also be minimal.

Obtaining the Right Professional Expertise

Before concluding a transaction on a conversion, consult carefully with appropriate attorneys, title insurance companies, and municipal building inspection departments, seeking out those who have previously participated in conversion projects. Delineating the common areas for conversion documents requires tremendous coordination with architects, lawyers and surveyors. Legal expertise is required to draw up the condominium owners' association agreements providing for continuous operation and maintenance of the structure, and outlining specifically the fixed and joint obligations of the potential purchaser when the sale is closed. Many municipalities have separate code requirements for apartments and condominiums that must be monitored closely.

Especially in areas where many conversions are taking place, you must be assured that no moratoriums on apartment conversions exist and that none are in the offing. Municipal regulations can also require that the potential converter give specific, timely, and often costly notice to tenants vacating a converted project. Sometimes, in cities where major conversions are going on, municipalities protect tenants by requiring that the converter give them sufficient time to vacate and find new space, or, in extreme cases, by requiring that the converter make comparable space available to evicted tenants.

Making the Best of an Older Building

When competition with newly designed and constructed condominiums is a factor in deciding to undertake a conversion, a tremendous amount of rejuvenation may be required. Older floor plans with small rooms and little closet space do not serve today's modern needs well and may outdate a building to the point where you decide against purchasing the conversion. Entrances resembling hotel corridors in older apartment buildings can be especially difficult to overcome. Even if a potential buyer is not impressed by the imaginative entrances incorporated into new condominium structures, he will still want his front door to look presentable. For the most part, older complexes provide few or limited recreational facilities and even less space for developing or expanding laundry and recreational areas.

Potentially, the most catastrophic problem that can surface relates to a deficiency in soundproofing between the units and throughout ductwork systems. When the situation exists, the total marketing effort can hinge upon successfully rectifying this deficiency. Prior to acquiring an existing building for conversion, a qualified engineer should be consulted to determine the insulating characteristics of the structure.

Yet many older locations with strong drawing power do exist, and the imaginative entrepreneur will seek them out. Restructuring the interior walls of an older unit may well be economically feasible in terms of the premium sales figures generated. It is difficult to assess the part that nostalgia plays in drawing potential purchasers to converted old construction, especially when one thinks about the number of old houses in New England and on the eastern seaboard where George Washington is supposed to have slept.

Developers can gamble successfully with nostalgia, or they can gamble against it. I am currently in the process of negotiating to purchase an old hospital which is perfectly suited for conversion into residential condominiums. The location of the building is absolutely prime. Much of the 140,000 square foot, $2,500,000 building is absorbed by wide corridors, nursing stations, and cafeterias. Even after the extensive expenditures for gutting the building, the shell still could be purchased for only 40% of its replacement value.

Structuring the Management Team

If one does not have a strong marketing organization, it is imperative to retain the best real estate brokerage firm in the area for the conversion. People purchase condominiums to indulge their desire for a carefree life style, and will want reassurances about the managing agent's handling of the day-to-day affairs and about the competency of the management of the homeowners' association.

During the conversion process, a two-tier management system is essential. A professional management team must be on site to handle:

- the renting of the units;
- relocating the tenants where units are being converted;
- coordinating activities of the tenants as they vacate; and
- acting as liaison with the construction crews in rejuvenating the project.

At the same time, a sales staff must be retained to promote, sell and close the converted units. Members of the sales staff should not only be highly professional, but should also be chosen for their ability to relate to potential purchasers. Retirees and older people feel comfortable with salespeople of comparable age and mentality, just as young professionals relate to those of their own age group. The functions of the two staffs are entirely different, and they should act somewhat in isolation from each other. The renter of an apartment and the potential owner of a condominium have separate objectives, and their varied interests should be served by different personnel.

Conversion Opportunities on Leased Land

It is not uncommon for a developer either to acquire a project that is on leased land or to convert a project and keep the land as a permanent investment, leasing it back to the homeowners' association. With tight money market conditions and spiraling costs of construction for new units, land-lease conversions are becoming more prevalent.

The length of the land lease is an important factor in the salability of converted units. The permanent lender will normally require that the lease extend at least twice the duration of the mortgage, which in today's market means 50 to 60 years. More important from the marketing aspect, buyers want assurance that, if they acquire a unit and build up equity over a period of time, they will be able to profitably resell that condominium at a later date. From the marketing aspect, it is imperative that the land lease should be effective for at least 100 years, providing for additional options to renew or granting a right of first refusal to the homeowners' association if the leasehold interest is sold. From the point of view of structuring the interim and permanent financing, it is important to anticipate the potential lenders' requirements that the leasehold interest be subordinated to their loans, although this is not totally critical to making the conversion work.

In most land-lease arrangements, a prime ground lease is executed before the conversion begins. The prime ground lease is eventually phased out by a series of unit leases which are executed every time a condominium is sold. For purposes of mortgage financing, this is a necessity. If the permanent lender has to repossess a unit, he is only obligated to make lease payments on the individual condominium itself, leaving him without any responsibility for the balance of the lease payments on the other units in the complex.

Last year, I was involved in a transaction complicated by a short-term unsubordinated land lease with a major university. Since the lease was only for 68 years, it was extremely difficult to arrange for permanent financing of the project. Although the financing package was completed and the units were sold out, the permanent lender required that a major portion of the condominiums be presold before any of the permanent loans were funded. These units were on the low end of the marketing scale and appealed to first-time entrants into the equity market. If the units had been more expensive, appealing to relatively sophisticated buyers, I think that the project would have failed because of the short-term nature of the lease and lack of subordination.

Typical Assessments and Problems Encountered with Homeowners' Associations

We mentioned at the beginning of this chapter, and also in the chapter on apartments, that prime clients as tenants and condominium buyers are the older generation of "empty-nesters" and the young groups of professionals. Proverb-makers through the centuries have commented upon the incompatibility of the young and the old, and few experienced dealers in real estate cannot testify to the truisms on the subject.

Especially when older buildings are converted, a mixture of occupants can develop with a majority of the purchasers coming from outside the project. Under such circumstances, animosity can develop between the current renters who will be vacating and the management team that is trying to convert the units. The problem can become so serious that the converter often must terminate some of the leases before their expiration, sometimes vacating entire floors during the conversion process. There is usually no way to anticipate such a problem before starting the conversion and no way to alleviate the severe drain on the project's cash flow when the problem arises.

The typical monthly assessments on converted condominiums should include:

- trash removal,
- water,
- management,
- maintenance,
- taxes,
- insurance, and
- replacement reserves.

Depending upon the nature of the project, additional common monthly assessments can be:

- utilities if not metered separately,
- recreation facilities,
- security guards, and
- land lease payments.

I was associated with a conversion of a building which an older group of tenants had occupied for periods well in excess of the normal tenancy period for the area. Many of the elderly were not interested in purchasing the space, as they believed it to be overpriced and they had no intention of paying cash for the units or committing themselves to long-term, high-interest-rate mortgages. The conversion was therefore geared to attracting young professional people whose life styles were completely different. The two groups did not mix well and the animosity reached such a pitch that it was necessary to terminate many existing leases early in the conversion.

How to Handle Existing Tenants Diplomatically

If existing tenants are not given notice of an impending conversion, and especially if they are not afforded the opportunity to purchase their units or others in the complex, a conversion often will receive unwanted publicity. I know of an instance where rumors of conversion leaked out before all the conversion sales documents were formalized, and the project found its way onto the front page of the local newspaper which depicted the converter as a ruthless profiteer intent upon evicting all the existing tenants in order to make an unconscionable profit on the conversion. One of the tenants was so disgusted with the way the conversion was handled that he started a fire in his apartment. The bad publicity from the fire again set the conversion effort back several months. Here, as in all conversions, it was short-sighted not to recognize the existing renters as the most important source of potential purchasers. It is extremely foolish not to give these occupants first option to acquire their units.

Especially during the promotional stages of a conversion, it is important to keep the monthly homeowners' assessments as low and constant as possible. Both lenders and owners take a very jaundiced view of high assessments in converted projects and need assurance that a low fixed rate will prevail at least for the initial years after the conversion. Most purchasers will be conscious of the total monthly payments, not only for interest and principal, but also for the homeowners' association dues.

One way of assuring the lenders and potential purchasers that the monthly assessment will be low is to review operating expenses of the project for the three to five years preceding the conversion. The sales presentation can then categorically state that the projected assessments are based upon the previous operating history and that it is unlikely that figures will be revised upward to any large extent in the foreseeable future. Under any circumstances, you must establish absolute credibility regarding monthly assessments, and this is even more essential when you keep control of the homeowners' association for an extended period of time, as is customary when the project is large and needs to be phased.

How to Overcome Problems of Permanent Financing

During the initial phases of a conversion, lenders want to see the strongest possible buyers for converted units surface in order to assure the project's success. You as converter may not share this viewpoint. In some cases you are involved with sales to speculators who deposit small amounts of earnest money as down payments subject to deferred closings and obtaining a high degree of leveraged financing. In the interest of qualifying speculators, you should prefer, especially during periods of tight money, to help qualify marginal buyers.

I recently completed a condominium project in which many of the units were sold to speculators who did not intend to be owner-occupants. When the mortgage market tightened, many of the lenders would not commit to non-owner-occupants since their mortgages could not be sold in the secondary mortgage market. As a consequence, droves of these speculators could not qualify for their loans, and over one-half of the potential buyers backed out of their sales contracts.

Before closing on a conversion project, you might be obligated to obtain private mortgage insurance for the entire development. In many conversions, financing and leverage loom as larger problems than the conversion process itself, since many buyers must arrange financing in excess of 80% of the sales price. To provide this high leverage financing, private mortgage insurance must be obtained and a master policy issued to insure the entire project before the first unit is closed and funded.

Many of the problems associated with apartment ownership and their solutions are equally pertinent to apartment conversions. We have avoided repeating here some of the issues raised in the chapter on apartments. Adding amenities is a case in point. The best amenities are those requiring little or no upkeep or maintenance. The same is true with conversions, particularly in the choice of amenities added to common areas and recreational facilities. Maintenance of such amenities as swimming pools directly and often adversely affect the monthly assessments levied by the homeowners' association. While expensive amenities are inevitable in a luxury complex, you as a converter must have the foresight to mix those requiring more and less maintenance if you believe that inflated fees will materially affect your marketing program.

With the preceding three chapters on apartments, condominiums and conversions, we have covered the topic of multifamily housing in successive degrees of complexity. We have not concerned ourselves with the land, as such, for these developments. The speculation entailed in the development of raw land makes it a highly sophisticated and lucrative business. One of the most self-defeating myths of the twentieth century is that holding idle land is a productive form of investment. Land can be the funnel through which equity is drained, as so many individuals have found; or it can be an exciting vehicle for a high degree of leverage. With the development exposure of the preceding chapters, we are prepared to deal with the economics of fractionalizing parcels of land for speculative development.

10

Successful Techniques Of Land Acquisition and Development

Seventy-five percent of all land in the United States is classified as undeveloped, and much of it will never show any material appreciation, irrespective of how long tracts are held or how aggressively they are promoted. Most of this land will actually depreciate in value if you consider the ramifications of the excessively high cost of carrying it. In this chapter, we will outline the lucrative methods of speculating in satellite areas of rural communities that border on booming metropolitan centers where values will increase sharply, whatever the land use. Many of these techniques will be backed up by actual practical examples on residential, commercial and industrial properties. I will show you how I recently increased the value of a piece of land by subdividing 32 individual lots on paper. In this particular instance, the platting of the residential tract into single-family home sites created an instant value in excess of a quarter of a million dollars. This value was created before even having to construct the roads or install the utilities.

In many of these areas you will discover how to leverage and in the process obtain a premium for raw acreage you purchase, often regardless of the inherent value of the land, since many unsophisticated investors are more interested in having a piece of the action than in analyzing the market. Eventually, they get caught up in the general excitement created by the rapid mobility and expansion, leaving behind the profits to the knowledgeable entrepreneur. The proven techniques in this chapter will show you how a sizable profit can be made, only by subdividing on paper or rezoning a marginal piece of property purchased in the right area.

Included are ratios for pricing large and small tracts, methods for comparing and establishing raw land costs as a percentage of the final sales price, and a multitude of techniques for obtaining quick return on equity that will enable you to accumulate sizable amounts of equity by developing real estate subdivisions.

Structuring Advantageous Owner Financing

Since most land transactions are leveraged with the seller's money and the equity positions are normally thin, the rewards are exciting. The reason for the high multiple of profit on equity is that the purchaser usually recoups his initial investment quite early. In typical agreements, the seller of the land, who carries the financing, must release certain portions free and clear as payments are made, commencing with the original down payment, over the duration of the contract. By liquidating small portions of the tract, you can quickly recoup your down payment as well as the annual carrying costs, retaining most of the land intact in order to capitalize on the potential profits to be assumed at a later date. This is an attractive vehicle for real estate investors, especially for people who syndicate with associates or friends, as the land investment concept is easier to sell than any other real estate investment, especially where the group can accumulate a relatively large asset with a correspondingly small down payment. Unsophisticated investors without the managerial talents required for income-producing properties can easily see the exciting rewards in syndication for land purchase.

One method I have successfully used in several subdivisions is giving the seller an "equity participation" in lieu of a cash down payment. I recently offered a seller a substantial interest in the net profits of a subdivision for his subordination of the entire 45-acre tract to the development loan. The seller jumped at the opportunity, as did the lending institution, where their entire development loan was only 30% of the total appraised value of the finished subdivision. The seller received payment for his land as the lots were sold, making this virtually a risk-free approach to developing the subdivision. This approach is especially effective during periods of tight mortgage financing.

Pricing Large and Small Tracts

An often used and somewhat misleading rule of thumb is that, given the excessive cost of carrying a highly leveraged tract of raw land, the value of the raw acreage must double every six to eight years in order to justify the acquisition. The average small tract averages between 10 and 25 acres. When purchasing a larger holding, anything in excess of 100 acres, a rule of thumb is that the larger parcel should sell for approximately two-thirds the price of the smaller tract. When you invest in even larger tracts of 200 to 300 acres, you can purchase these for 50% of the small tract price and can normally expect a 20- to 25-fold increase in your equity over an eight- or ten-year period.

Undeveloped land far exceeds the number of knowledgeable land developers, giving you, as a sophisticated developer, the opportunity of purchasing land far below its fully developed value. If this were not prevalent, very little land development would take place. I am always pleasantly surprised at the number of people who approach me with land they own, wanting me to participate in subdividing their land for an equity position. The majority of these people own the land outright free and clear, which makes it a shoo-in for packaging the financing and doing the development work.

Quick Return on Equity Techniques

The ability to structure a land acquisition and partial release provision is considerably more important than being concerned about the total value of the raw acreage. The actual criterion of success is return on equity and the amount of time that your equity is tied up, as well as the actual out-of-pocket cost of carrying the interest and principal balance remaining on the land. The potential for large profits lies in:

- the near term appreciation of the land;
- the structuring of the purchase contract;

- the ability to merchandise small segments of the land initially; and
- preserving the major portion of the tract for future profits.

Unlike structures such as apartments, commercial buildings, and shopping centers, land offers you the ability to concentrate your limited capital resources in a given area. Land investment avoids the highly leveraged situations that sometimes do not succeed because of a lack of sophisticated management. A large commercial investment improperly structured and managed can put a sizable financial burden on the investor if the project does not fully materialize. On a preliminary basis at least, land speculation is easier to analyze, especially the elements of downside risk or exposure. The preferences of many investors to diffuse their risk among several different types of investments is open to land investors through purchase of land in several geographic or suburban areas.

Advantageously Timing the Resale

The greatest misconception in land speculation is that the longer one holds a piece of property, the more it will appreciate. This is completely contrary to reality. The cost of interest, combined with uncertainty about future municipal ordinances, environmental restrictions, availability of utilities, and increasing taxes, works against the land subdivider, building in a larger and more explosive risk factor than the normal investment in stocks or bonds. The timing for resale and development is critical, as most developers create values in a tract by adding the minimal improvements necessary to attract prospective buyers. Most developers speculate on land that can be carved into subdivisions within a couple of years, looking strictly at the value of the land and not necessarily at the physical terrain of the parcel in its unimproved state without grading, streets, or utilities. In other words, when an area is right for resale or development, the developer who acquires at the lowest cost and resells with the most favorable terms will dispose of your land the quickest, and will, therefore, achieve the greatest advantage over your competitors in the area. I recently sold a portion of a 100+-lot subdivision by initially installing the roads and offering a 10% discount under the appraised value of the lots if the purchasers would close within 30 days. I was successful enough to have obtained the right number of buyers initially, as many people cannot pass up a bargain. I completely paid off the cost of rough grading the roads and the land contract payment that was coming due at the time for which the quick closings were scheduled.

This is not to say that speculators should purchase raw acreage with title defects or major physical difficulties of drainage, subsoil, access, or unusual grading problems which would prevent full development of the tract. The largest single mistake made in purchasing raw land lies in paying a premium for the raw acreage only in order to obtain terms and conditions of financing that are considered favorable. Undeveloped land is normally sold with a minimal down payment and carried on a deed of trust at interest rates considerably lower than those offered by conventional lending institutions. What might initially seem like an attractive financing package can turn out to be, after thorough investigation, nothing more than the standard within the industry. Offsetting income from recreational use, grazing, or growing of crops should not even be considered in analyzing the cost of carrying raw acreage, as it is generally such a small fraction of the investment in the overall project that the lease-back arrangement with the seller is not worth making concessions over.

Pricing Raw Land as a Percentage of a Fully Improved Subdivision

Rules for analyzing the potential purchase price of land as it finally relates to the improved and subdivided tract are based upon the same kind of analysis used in most investment real estate ventures. The value of the final product is projected and analyzed in relation to the cost of carrying and developing the tract, thus working backwards to a realistic figure of worth for the land in its raw state. Two formulas are generally used: the "Rule of Five" and the "Rule of Three." Under the Rule of Five, one-fifth or 20% of the final value of the subdivided and improved land should be allocated to the cost of raw acreage. This is more conservative than the Rule of Three, which applies the same concept with the effect of increasing the value of the acquired land from 20% to 33%. Those who use the Rule of Three normally do not completely understand the full cost of development and promotion of land sales.

Twenty Percent of Subdivision Costs Allocated to Raw Land

The more accurate Rule of Five generally works this way:

- One-fifth or 20% of the final value of the completed subdivided tract should be allocated to the cost of acquiring the raw acreage, excluding all costs of carrying the project throughout the holding and selling periods.

- An additional two-fifths or 40% should be allocated to the developer's profit, his advertising and marketing, and the sales commissions. This is called an administrative 40% and additionally covers the developer's overhead during the entire holding period.
- An additional one-fifth or 20% of the value of the subdivision is allocated for engineering, installation of the streets, curbs, sidewalks, gutters, electric, water, gas, and other utilities.
- The remaining 20% is allocated to the financial cost of carrying the project, the construction cost overruns, and miscellaneous factors of misjudgment.

Many subdivisions look so attractive on paper that the developers allocate certain prices for tracts within that subdivision. Since most subdividers do not physically walk and examine each potential lot, unpleasant surprises occur at the end of the sale of the subdivision when several lots emerge as less than desirable, and the paper analysis of the value of the lots has to be reduced substantially. Most developers overlook the need to allow one-fifth or 20% as a margin for this almost inevitable error.

The Rule of Five can be modified depending on the local circumstances and the developer's expertise. For instance, the cost of acquiring a certain tract should be adjusted if you are forced to pay exorbitant bank interest rates, note renewal, or escrow fees. Standard sales commissions of 10% for selling land can be reduced to

FIGURE 10-1

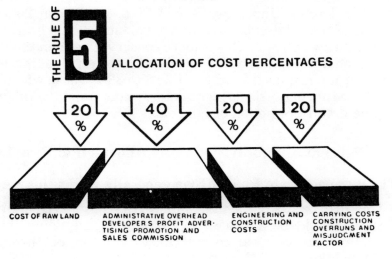

THE RULE OF 5 — ALLOCATION OF COST PERCENTAGES

20%	40%	20%	20%
COST OF RAW LAND	ADMINISTRATIVE OVERHEAD DEVELOPER'S PROFIT ADVERTISING PROMOTION AND SALES COMMISSION	ENGINEERING AND CONSTRUCTION COSTS	CARRYING COSTS CONSTRUCTION OVERRUNS AND MISJUDGMENT FACTOR

about 3% for a large tract if you are in a competitive marketing area or have an in-house sales organization. In areas where I have this in-house sales capability, I normally stay in the 3% to 4% range. I recently went up to 5% on a subdivision in which I felt it was necessary to utilize an outside brokerage firm. In the past, I have gone as high as 6%, utilizing outside brokerage firms, where they had offered to co-broker the property within the local multiple listing service.

Creative Methods of Acquiring Raw Acreage

The actual way land is physically acquired most affects the Rule of Five. If you purchase the land on a rolling option basis, where you initially commit yourself to a small portion of the overall tract and have the option to acquire, subdivide, and sell various portions of additional land at a later date, you can reduce your potential exposure and afford to reduce the Rule of Five somewhat, justifying a larger value on the raw acreage. Under this approach, if things do not fully materialize, the developer can financially abandon the project.

Land Contracts/Rolling Options

Most land contracts or deeds of trust are structured so that the land only stands as collateral and developers will not receive deficiency judgments against them personally in the event of default. On a rolling option approach you have the right to purchase various tracts at deferred periods of time. Here you cannot generally obtain the lowest price, and will normally assume a higher land basis upon exercising the options. If the rolling options are spread over a long period of time and you can accurately predict a rapid increase in the value of the tract over the option period, this approach and the corresponding cost of obtaining the land is not as detrimental as it initially sounds.

Declining Credit Options

Several other approaches can be used with a seller. One is called the declining credit option, which differs somewhat from the rolling option in that option money is applied toward the purchase price on a declining scale. The longer the option is extended, the less option money is applied toward the sale price. If you exercise early in the term, a large portion of the option money is applied toward the purchase price; the longer the option extends, the lesser the amount of option money applies. Utilizing this method, both the buyer and the seller have more flexibility since the seller, in effect, obtains a higher price for the land the longer the transaction is extended. Sometimes this approach works to everyone's benefit. Both the rolling and declining options have favorable tax benefits to the seller, as they permit him to tie up his land contractually, and in the meantime be compensated. If the options are exercised, the seller can defer the capital gains through the use of installment sale. I used this tactic on a project I developed as a mobile home park, in which I exercised the option early, and applied a sizable portion of the option money towards the purchase price. This approach had the effect of giving me the necessary time to structure the financing, and had additional time been necessary, it would have been a relatively inexpensive way to have acquired it.

Installment Sales

The most common practice is to utilize a combination of options and installment sale purchases in which the land is conveyed to you, the developer, in stages. Under this arrangement, you exercise your option on a schedule of fixed dates. This permits you to develop the improvements on the entire tract if desired, without putting substantial money into the cost of the unimproved land itself. Normally, the developer works these arrangements on a deed of trust basis, in which the collateral is the land itself and not the personal guarantee of the purchaser, permitting you to walk away from the contractual obligation to buy the land if the projected sales do not materialize. If the transaction is structured correctly, you can obtain the proper releases from the land contract encumbrances for various desirable pieces of property when you make the initial down payment. If the annual installments of unencumbered and released parcels are structured correctly, the developer will not lose any money on the transaction except for the out-of-pocket expenses and promotion. The advantage in using this approach is that you can cut your losses early if the project fails, and still own free and clear a portion of the contracted land to sell at a later date in order to recover your costs.

Under this system a developer can do a minimal amount of advertising, provide some initial amenities, and subsequently sell off the optioned parts without ever actually getting into the development of the land itself. You can tie up a large amount of acreage with a small investment, selling off the options to potential investors without ever actually having to physically build a street or install a utility line or a curb or gutter. The only substantial expenditure might be fees paid to an engineer or land planner.

Release Concepts

The key to advantageous structuring often lies in the sequence and location of areas released. It is extremely important to be able to take title to the most desirable tracts free and clear early in the development, so as to obtain the necessary momentum for a project and have the flexibility of annually selling off small tracts to cover the costs of carrying the entire parcel. In some instances, you can choose the appropriate area to be released, not only at the time of down payment and initial closing, but also over a period of years as the annual installments are made. You, the developer, with the help of your engineer, will be in a position to design the subdivision in a way that is beneficial to you, based upon the prenegotiated release pattern. Sometimes the seller has preconceived ideas as to which areas of his land are most valuable and will not agree to let you unilaterally determine the release pattern. However, if the seller wishes to retain certain areas until the final payment, this does not necessarily work to the detriment of the developer. You can still design your subdivision, access, and commercial areas around the area of land released initially. An associate of mine recently optioned a site subject to rezoning, in which he committed to buy 25 acres of a 145-acre site irrespective of the outcome of the zoning and annexation. Since the 25 acres he committed to purchase was the prime piece, worth several times the overall value of the raw land cost, even if the rezoning fails he will recoup all his expenses and make a handsome profit by selling off that small tract.

The original owners seldom comprehend a total development and the value of each individual subdivided lot. Until a firm agreement covering the release provisions of the contract has been reached, it is to the buyer's advantage to divulge as little as possible of his plans for layout, project composition, access, etc. By the same token, you may decide only to sell your options and not to fully develop the land. Here you should not make any representations to potential buyers of the options regarding what zoning and subdivision ordinances can or might be obtained for the tracts they are acquiring.

Principal or Interest Only Arrangements

I have, from time to time, favorably structured interest-only payments, thus reducing the Rule of Five. The obvious approach has the effect of keeping the interest factor as low as possible. Many sophisticated developers use the reverse interest approach, which works if the seller has owned the acreage for a long time and will show large capital gain on the sale. Here the purchaser's down payment is treated as an installment sale and no interest is initially paid on the outstanding principal balance. That balance is reduced by fully amortizing the loan over a period of, for example, 20 years. In other words, if the principal balance is equally reduced over a 20-year period—5% a year to amortize the loan fully over 20 years—the overall effect is to substantially cut the cost of holding the project to only 5% annually in contrast to other methods of paying interest only at a rate of probably twice that amount.

To sell this concept to the owner, explain that the 5% he receives annually is taxed as capital gains, or at only 50%. He is, therefore, receiving a more favorable treatment, and receives, after tax dollars, about the same as the rate of interest the purchaser would have to pay on a conventional deed of trust note. Then you, the purchaser, pay him the accrued interest on the principal amount when the project is approaching the point of being completely sold out. This permits the seller to declare the higher-taxed ordinary income or interest when he actually, physically receives the money in one lump sum.

Alternatively, you can arrange to pay the interest only with no reduction of principal for the initial years. Here the seller must be convinced that considerable monies are being advanced to promote and develop the tract which will work to his benefit and that these construction and promotional activities will directly accrue to him in the event that you default on the land payment.

Reducing Up-Front Equity Requirements

Sometimes it is helpful to guarantee a certain amount of up-front money for the development in order to satisfy the seller that improvements will actually be made. A bank letter of credit, stating that a certain amount of money will be advanced over a period of time to improve the tract, reassures the seller of your legitimate intentions and guarantees that, if the money is not spent within a predetermined period of time, the balance must be used to reduce the outstanding principal amount owed on the land contract. When you as purchaser make overtures for development or commitments to improve the land, you must carefully restrict obligating yourself only to the land that is physically released by deed. Otherwise, you may improve the wrong segments of the land only to find that the entire project has little or no merit and that you have made a charitable contribution to the seller.

Quite recently, I was brought into a 104-lot subdivision by the developers, in which a seller had two short-term balloon payments due on his land contracts, one of which was not subordinated to the development loan. This type of situation can be extremely dangerous for the developer if the sellout period of the project does not meet its intended projections. This is especially critical in periods of tight financing. The short-term balloon payment on this development meant that we could not offer a realistic market rate, terms, and conditions in selling the improved lots when the conventional financing sources evaporated. Under these circumstances, the developers were given the unpleasant option either to collateralize the land with other unrelated investment properties, or to pay an exorbitant increased rate of interest on the two remaining tracts of land. This, combined, with a floating interest rate tied to the New York prime on part of the development loan, would substantially cut into the overall profit margin on that subdivision.

A close examination of the nature and extent of the improvements required by the local municipality may lead to further reductions in allocations of the Rule of Five. The 20% allocated to engineering and site improvements can be reduced and the value of the land increased accordingly, depending on the nature of the improvements. I have, from time to time, joint-ventured land subdivisions with engineering firms in which they participate in a percentage of the profits for providing the up-front and later the complete engineering work. I occasionally use this method when rezoning or annexation is involved, as it considerably cuts my up-front exposure. In some areas where municipalities do not require the standard city sidewalks, streets, curbs, gutters, and underground utilities, or where local municipal ordinances do not make it mandatory that extensive improvements of the subdivision infrastructure be installed, an upward adjustment on the raw land can be completely justified.

Making Allowances for Misjudgments and Assessing Appraisals

More difficult to analyze until the subdivision is partially sold, is the misjudgment allowance for the less desirable lots that will remain unsold at retail levels when a subdivision is completed. A competent real estate appraiser, realtor, or engineer will have to evaluate the percentage of loss in any given development. Sometimes it is possible to acquire an almost perfect piece of land where the views are exceptional and the loss of acreage is minimal. Here, the streets and lots can be designed in a fashion to maximize sales efforts. If this is the case, the Rule of Five can be modified to include a higher value of the raw land. Reliance on this particular exception must be directly proportionate to the sophistication of the developer and his advisors in analyzing the actual market value of the developed units within the subdivision.

The major stumbling block in purchasing raw land is that it is almost impossible to determine the actual fair market value for the proposed acreage at any given point in time. This applies not only to the value of the land when it is acquired, but also to the eventual price that the land will command at a future date. The massiveness and dissimilarity of undeveloped rural land, combined with the fact that most appraisers of rural real estate are less than qualified to determine and evaluate its true potential for a major subdivision, severely restrict you, the investor.

Most rural appraisers analyze raw land for its agrarian value, which is normally determined by its suitability for crops or grazing, or on its current value based upon a comparable sales approach, which for all practical purposes places a strong emphasis on land as an agrarian parcel. Many times, you, the investor, cannot call upon the expertise of an appraiser who views it as a typical income-producing property and can set a fixed value based on the current cash flow and reproduction value of a similar income-producing investment in the marketplace. Even a qualified income-property appraiser is limited by working with local or rural appraisers whose information is normally not suitable for his purposes.

The art of appraising raw speculative land is less than sophisticated. Many times, the appraisal of raw land does not reflect the fact that land transactions, when used as comparables, are so structured that the owner carries the financing. On several occasions, I have made offers on properties where the eventual value of the sales or joint venture price is to be contingent upon an independent appraiser setting a value. Often, this has permitted me the flexibility of acquiring the land if it is appraised right, or if not, going on to another project. The appraisal process often takes months, permitting me to control the property for the inconsequential price of an appraisal. Most rural appraisals show a value per acre without regard to the financing techniques that were used in arriving at comparable sales. These factors distort the appraised valuation of raw land and mislead an unsophisticated purchaser, who thinks he is getting a bargain on interest and carrying charges, and is therefore willing to pay a higher price for the land.

Spotting Excessively Priced Speculative Land

Most raw acreage being actively promoted in the marketplace has not been held by the same family for generations, but has been sold several times within a relatively short period, with the profit at each sale subsequently inflating its value. In some parts of the country, second, third, and fourth mortgages identify tracts of land that have changed hands often within a few years and obscure the true value of the property, especially in rapidly growing areas where unsophisticated people are purchasing land for quick resale, not development. There are several ways to spot excessively priced property:

- Researching records at the tax assessor's office will reveal how often the tract has been resold.
- Determining whether buyers were local people alert to local values, or out-of-state speculators.
- Determining who recorded mortgages, recognized lenders using appraisals, or owners carrying back inflated mortgages and values.

Several years ago, I was presented with an opportunity to purchase a 53-acre tract of land which, after careful review, I found had had seven different owners over a 3-year period. Several of the transactions involved down payments of approximately 10%, with the balance of the interest and equity deferred for many years. I declined to purchase the tract because of the inflated price. Subsequently, a soft market developed and many of these paper transactions collapsed, with the properties reverting to their original owners when the balloon payments became due.

When mortgages are held by established lending institutions that frequently make appraisals of the property, the land price might very well be realistic. When mortgage loans are held by

existing owners and prior sellers, it is usually an indication that
values have been inflated and that thin and speculative equities were
involved in these prior transactions.

Accepted Loan-to-Value Ratios

Most established financial institutions do not make a practice of
lending on raw land unless the tract is actually located within an
area that will be developed immediately. They prefer commercial or
income-producing property where an immediate cash flow is
assured by sophisticated evaluation and appraisal. An exception
occurs when a lending institution can obtain additional short-term,
interim loans for improving the subdivision and permanent loans on
the completed houses. During the recent periods of inflation and
unstable long-term bond and mortgage markets, fully developed
projects that cannot provide long-term permanent commitments at
competitive rates to prospective purchasers will not be viable.

Raw land has a tendency to be merchandised on a wholesale
basis when the developer or the local economy gets into trouble,
which is not normally the case with income-producing real estate on
which a lending institution can take assignment of rents. This
wholesale pricing factor and the lack of liquidity make conventional
lending sources very low loan-to-value ratio lenders on speculative
land and, consequently, conventional financing sources should only
be used for borrowing money for the on-site development
improvements.

Pitfalls of Moratoriums and Annexation

In addition to familiarizing yourself with local ordinances, you
should establish rapport with the appropriate municipalities to
determine their long-term objectives. The easiest approach is to
retain a respected engineer or land planner from the area, even if
this means contracting with an engineering consultant to develop
and design the plans. Only a local person knows the mechanics and
politics of the zoning and planning commissions and how best to get
preliminary plat approvals or a written set of guidelines from the
appropriate governing bodies. An engineer who has completed
several subdivisions within the local municipality can generally
analyze the pitfalls and time factors involved, has the necessary
contacts with general contractors to estimate the cost of the
improvements to meet local code requirements, and has the ability to

anticipate upward cost trends in construction and predict annexation trends.

The economic feasibility of the project may hinge on the availability and cost of utilities. With the help of local contractors or engineers, the developer should check with various utility companies in both the private and public sectors to determine what the actual capacity is for extending those lines into the proposed subdivision at a future date.

How to Equitably Distribute Utility Extension Costs

It is also important to determine who will bear the cost of the utility extension and to establish a proposed time frame for bringing utilities to the site. Recent trends have required that the developer pay for the utility extensions; however, it is sometimes possible for you to be reimbursed on a prorated basis as additional developments tie into the utility systems. A formula for reimbursement, usually on a per-acre, per-lot, or per-household basis, must be established before starting the project. Local officials must agree to issue building permits to people who connect to the trunk lines only if they agree to reimburse the developer who extended the utilities. All agreements regarding utilities and availability of future municipal bonding capacity should be covered in writing before closing the transaction. It is important to contact adjoining landowners to determine if they have any immediate development plans. I recently did this on a 43-acre subdivision, and I got the adjoining landowner to participate in the cost of extending the sewer line, as he had fairly immediate plans for developing his land. This saved the project almost $30,000 in offsite improvement costs.

A commitment from a city for services and utilities normally involves annexation of the property when these services are provided. In such instances, differences between the city and county real estate taxes and municipal services should be explored. You must also analyze carefully the differences between city and county ordinances regarding:

- ability of the municipality to provide future services,
- paved streets, sidewalks and gutters,
- sanitary and sometimes storm sewers,
- allocation of portions of the subdivisions for parks,
- dedication of land for green belts, and
- allocation of acreage for future school sites.

If county ordinances provide for busing and adequate transportation to schools and have adequate trash removal and police and fire protection, you, the developer, should consider the possibility that it may be more efficient to deal with the county rather than with the urban governing bodies. Many cities are now passing ordinances to extend their jurisdiction beyond current city limits into outlying counties in an attempt to regulate new subdivisions that they may eventually annex. Several years ago, I advised an associate to draw up and file a preliminary plat in a county which had no formal planning and zoning commission. He did so, and now has a valuable "grandfathered" subdivision, as the county has since established a strong and restrictive planning and zoning ordinance. Even where cities have not adopted such ordinances to extend jurisdiction to your proposed development, it is worthwhile to get preliminary plat approval from the county even if the plat is not used as the final subdivision document. Doing so, in anticipation of constantly changing annexation policies, can give you more leverage when the time comes for you to subdivide the acreage.

Countering No-Growth Attitudes

Having preliminary approval on a high-density subdivision and later shifting to one with less density can put you in a better position to deal with environmentalists, city officials, urban land planners, and surrounding landowners if the rules are suddenly tightened or changed.

Moratoriums on sewer, water, and gas services are only too common. If you as a developer have platted a subdivision, however incompletely and imperfectly, and have tentative commitments from the local utility companies, you are in a position to force their respective hands by requesting the city planning commission to halt authorization of additional new subdivisions until the utilities are provided to your own. This not only assures top preference and priority, but facilitates the marketing of lots where shortages exist, often at premium prices.

Providing Protection, Utilizing Rezoning Contingencies

In many instances it is appropriate, if not imperative, that you the developer, make your offer to purchase contingent upon preliminary plat approval, even at the expense of depositing more than the anticipated earnest money and risking its forfeiture.

Because of the rapidly changing municipal regulatory bodies and policies, you need to anticipate any resistance you may encounter long before closing.

Several years ago I agreed to acquire a 19-acre tract of land subject to obtaining rezoning for a 216-unit condominium project with an overall density of 12 units per acre. Initially, the rezoning appeared to be almost automatic, as the property had been zoned for 21 units to the acre several years prior to my involvement. In the interim ownership it had reverted back to the original 5 units per acre density as the rezoning had a reversionary clause in the event the rezoned project was not under construction within a predetermined period of time. During that interim period the political climate shifted to favor the anti-development forces, and the best compromise I could obtain was 7 units per acre. The city, staff and the anti-development groups tried to force me to make concessions for dedicated public roads, open areas, traffic signals, and parks, making the entire cost of the land and proposed concessions prohibitive for this particular low-end development. The "subject to rezoning" clause enabled me to cut my losses early in the project and proceed to other more lucrative developments.

Using Plat Approval as a Hedge

Obtaining preliminary approval of a subdivision plat is not nearly as expensive as obtaining final approval. Normally, the finished product requires submission of:

- Contour maps,
- Dedicated easements,
- Road cross sections,
- Utility drawings,
- Elevations,
- Required municipal fees,
- Staked boundaries of the lots,
- Drainage and flood plain reports, and
- Impact of traffic studies.

For preliminary plat approval, you can usually purchase existing air photos mapping the contours of the tract and the surrounding areas with which a qualified engineer can lay out the general areas, proposed roads, and rough lots. This rudimentary document, together with some minor subsoil testing, is frequently enough to obtain preliminary approval from a city within 90 to 120 days after an offer to purchase is signed.

Spotting the Hidden Carrying and Development Costs

Additionally, a good land-planning firm can set up a marketing and merchandising approach for the subdivision and can easily identify some of the hidden costs even sophisticated developers are likely to overlook. A qualified firm can also help structure the overall financial success of the project by determining the amount of land that should be released on an annual basis to maintain the momentum of the project and to cover the carrying costs, and by scheduling the deferred sale of the major and most valuable portion. After the subdivision is established, you will realize the maximum economic benefits on your development.

An additional area of extreme importance in land speculation is the ratio of local real estate taxes to the total value of the land. Taxes on raw land should be between 1% and 2% of the total value of the property per year, not exceeding 2% of the total value by any large margin. Taxes in excess of 2% have a detrimental effect on the cost of carrying the land during the development.

Selecting the Most Lucrative Markets

As many communities continue to expand and develop, they become their own centers for commerce and industry within a network of cities, a megapolis, making them less and less dependent upon any one supporting major city. They create their own unique employment and educational facilities, and can become a stratified market for development of high-density commercial, industrial, retail, and office complexes once concentrated in downtown sections of our major cities. Attractive as they are for speculation, many such growth areas must strain to provide adequate municipal services and to acquire or annex other existing municipalities or utilities. Moratoriums on services and growth are signals that rezoning—for industry, hospitals, schools—is in the offing. The developer who is insensitive to current suburban trends can too easily get trapped, especially where buffer zones do not exist to reconcile incompatible needs for his subdivisions.

The most attractive areas for land development are those substantially lacking in building and zoning codes. You, as a developer who enters such an area on the ground floor, set trends to your own advantage, of course. By precedent and with the tendency of a rapidly growing community to pass "look-alike" ordinances, a sophisticated developer who enters an emergent area can direct legislation and taxation to eliminate future competition.

For at least the next several decades, the urban shuffle will continue, accompanied by an inflationary trend in housing. The cost of subdividing acreage will increase as empty fields and unproductive farmlands give way to subdivisions, shopping centers, distribution and industrial centers, medical facilities, office complexes, and apartments. The fatigue created by this turnover has created the escapism of the past decade or more and a burgeoning new direction for speculation in suburban subdivisions.

Raw land offers the investor more leverage, and if structured properly, more liquidity than any other type of real estate investment. Though equities are normally quite thin, structuring releases properly makes it possible to retrieve your equity within days or months of purchase. Land acquisition offers an ease of entry not found in many other areas, as we will see in the chapters on shopping centers and office complexes.

11

Building Equity Through Shopping Center Developments

The shopping center appeals to the conservative, long-range investor who wishes to minimize the problems connected with day-to-day management. The combination of sophistication, industry contacts and capital required to develop a major center is beyond the capabilities of many individuals. However, this chapter will outline the concepts and principles necessary to structure a successful tenant mix that eventually leads to overage or percentage rents that are the true profit of any center, large or small.

You will find many proven techniques permitting you to analyze and successfully leverage both the structures within the centers and the tenant improvements. Included are the keys to break-even rental analysis and the unique tax advantages of short-term leasehold improvements. Step by step, this chapter will show you how to determine the scope of the market, size up the competition, attract the key tenants, profitably structure their rents, and leverage your way to a long-term, lucrative investment holding.

Important Shopping Center Trends

Over the next decade, approximately a thousand new shopping centers will be created annually in the United States. Within the next decade and a half, the number of shopping centers will have doubled from the present approximation of 20,000, which have currently more than a quarter of a million tenants.

Originally, the shopping center was a small neighborhood complex built around a dime store, a supermarket, and a limited merchandise or department store where the major concentration of large-volume shopping took place. The shifting movement to the suburbs from the major metropolitan areas created new markets for major discount, general merchandise, drug, and specialty stores. In most cases, competing major retailers served as anchor tenants for dozens of small retail outlets. As the initial instigators of these centers, only they had the knowledge and expertise to conduct the basic feasibility studies necessary to develop and finance these large shopping complexes. Initially, these major retailers were the only groups with the staying power to design, develop, and construct these centers, as the role of the local developer was limited to accumulating and assembling the land and, in some cases, providing local management once the major part of the center was leased and operational.

Many opportunities still exist for the small- to medium-sized developer. An associate and I acquired several sites for a well-known retailer who had saturated most of the major marketing areas and was looking for locations in cities of less than a quarter of a million population. This was being done in an attempt to be the first and eliminate future competition, creating fast-moving opportunities for the local real estate entrepreneur. Although I did not physically construct and retain ownership of the buildings, members of my staff brokered several sites.

How to Attract the Majors

Newer shopping center developments still revolve around the major sophisticated retailers. Many of the newer regional centers are being developed on a condominium basis in which the developer sells the land to the major retailers who construct their own buildings, leaving the enclosed mall areas to the developer to own, construct, and lease. Normally, you, as a developer, have to subsidize that land payment on the majors' space to a certain degree, and provide a cross easement on the common and parking areas within the complex. Customarily, the majors make no contribution to the interior mall common maintenance. Their total effort is usually limited to a prorated portion of the expenses for improving and maintaining the parking areas. Many large companies are not currently considering locating in major centers unless they own their structure and are given a minimum of 25% equity in the remaining space within the center. They often require this equity interest even though they put little time, effort, or capital into the development of the mall areas. They contend that they are such a major drawing power in any new sizable center, that their presence virtually assures the success of the development. If the project is not developed on a condominium basis, retailers normally obtain sizable and often ridiculous concessions in rent from the developers. Their presence, they contend, lends enough credibility to the developer's efforts so that you can obtain financing not only for the major stores, but also for the enclosed mall areas where your rents are truly maximized.

Obtaining the Profitable Diversified Tenant Mix

The major retailers in a center often pay as little as $3 to $4 a square foot, triple net, whereas the smaller local tenants can pay anywhere from $15 to $40 a square foot, thus profiting from the volume generated by the majors which is so vital for the specialty stores to remain operational.

Normally, the leases of the major retailers, who account for some 50% of the gross rentable area, run 20 to 25 years, which generally parallels the amortization of the mortgage and leaves the developer only half of the space to lease and manage over the duration of the mortgage. The leases on smaller spaces normally run three to five years. If the major tenants are successful, the shopping center can, over a period of time, increase the sales volume and percentage rents of the smaller tenants considerably. As most leases have escalation clauses, the rent being tied to a percentage of the gross sales, the base lease in many cases is only a break-even proposition for the developer. I have an associate who has opened food-related stores in many of the newer regional malls. These shops are quite small, and he is paying in excess of $20 a square foot when his percentage overage rents are taken into account. This is probably three to four times the square-foot rental he would have to pay in a non-regional center. However, he insists that the traffic generated by the major tenants in the center makes these locations some of his most lucrative operations.

A successful shopping center contains a diversified tenant mix, providing several stores which generally compete with each other without destroying each other in the process. Most customers want four or five stores that carry similar merchandise within a center, knowing that they can find the exact items they need without having to drive to several locations. These competing stores are usually located at opposite ends of the center, in order that customers comparing merchandise and prices will have to walk past the other stores in the process. A major achievement is to coordinate and enforce a plan for uniform hours agreeable to all the tenants, since nothing is more annoying to a prospective customer than to find that some stores in the center are open and others are closed.

Converting Older Centers to Enclosed Malls

Many of the old strip centers that were poorly conceived and designed are potentially the most exciting projects for the small developer to convert into enclosed malls, as they offer the following advantages:

- They are located in areas of high concentration of population.
- They have stabilized and predictable purchasing power.
- They limit future competition, as large commercial tracts are nonexistent.
- They have established existing retailers.

Enclosed malls, it has been proven, considerably increase retail sales. One of the most lucrative aspects of shopping center development can be the purchasing of older centers with proven sales records, renovating them with enclosed malls, and renegotiating leases based only upon a larger sales volume. The conversion cost for the enclosed mall area need not be considered excessive in a prime marketing area, where most of the tenants would be willing to renegotiate their leases upward to reflect the cost of the improvements necessary to create a pleasant and lucrative environment. If the tenants resist increases in base rents to cover the enclosure, a percentage of increased sales will accomplish the same goal. I saw this happen in three instances where existing centers in areas of high population and purchasing power were converted to enclosed malls by their owners. In each case they raised the square-foot cost to the tenants by readjusting the rental based upon a percentage of gross sales. One of these centers needed to renovate to stay competitive; the other two did it strictly to increase their cash flow, and all three have been profitable from the day they converted to enclosed malls.

Pitfalls Found in Granting Exclusives

A problem for developers is often the demand of many major tenants for exclusive rights to merchandise their products. The majors want some competition, as competition increases volume, but not in an excessive amount. It becomes increasingly difficult to grant or even to define exclusives as specialization of products increases. I have two buildings which have leases that restrict competitors from locating in the same complex. They are not controversial or competitive tenants; however, I believe that if legal action were initiated, these clauses might very well be found in violation of the antitrust statutes.

Exclusive rights to sell merchandise or to eliminate competition are also regulated under the restraint of trade acts and antitrust laws, and many of these exclusive arrangements are being challenged in the courts. Not only do these noncompetitive arrangements affect the immediate center, but sometimes the smaller local stores are prohibited from opening satellite operations within a certain radius of the existing center. Adverse restraint of trade decisions can be ruinous to the developer, since major retailers often force these terms and restrictive conditions upon him.

Complications Found in Subleasing

Another potential problem relates to the right of a major tenant to sublease his space. A national chain department store might continue to pay rent for a store after vacating the premises and subsequently sublet the space to be relieved of its lease obligation, to a tenant who will not create the volume or prestige that the center thrives upon. This can permanently affect the smaller tenants. The majors' low base rent permits them to have tremendous mobility, and the developer's profits, dependent as they are on the rents from smaller tenants, evaporate when the majors vacate. In other words, if a prestigious major tenant should sublet to a discount chain, for example, that is incompatible with the other occupants, the satellite tenants on short-term leases with percentage overrides would lose the mandatory drawing power of these prestigious tenants. The percentage leases would no longer be profitable to the developer and the smaller stores, at the end of their leases, would most likely not renew.

I owned a small building in which my tenant, a flower shop, was considered to be the prime florist in the metropolitan area. Fortunately, I had the right to approve the florist's activities in subleasing. When the business and the lease were sold to an unproven and at that time marginal operator, I successfully vetoed the transaction, preserving the value of the lease and building. One must be extremely careful in interpreting the language on these sublease provisions, as most major tenants have the ability to make the sublease provisions difficult to live with. In percentage leases, the developer must choose tenants strong enough to absorb the potential increases of escalation clauses. A tenant who cannot absorb additional overhead might force the developer to negotiate his lease downward or abandon the center entirely.

Proven Cross-Merchandising and Leasing Techniques

Cross-merchandising is probably the most difficult aspect of developing and leasing a shopping center and, in some respects, the most critical aspect if the project is to have any long-term viability and potential. The profitability generally depends upon the gross volume created by the center, which reflects directly on the merchandise mix. This is especially prevalent where small specialty stores compete with larger chains within the shopping complex itself, who must also be competitive with other stores in the general vicinity and throughout the metropolitan area. In most cases, the specialty stores provide the initial profit in a center and are the major vehicle for the developer to increase his cash flow during the initial years of operation. The wrong allocation of merchandise within a center can, over a period of time, prevent any major increases in the square foot rentals. The complex must be large enough to accommodate a healthy mix, which should be analyzed by full-time professional shopping center developers and leasing agents. Only seasoned individuals understand the complex interrelationships between the various merchants necessary to create a successful center.

Generally speaking, a competent leasing firm can be obtained in a larger center for $1 per square foot of net rentable space, excluding common and mall areas, as a one-time fee. A knowledgeable leasing agent can structure the major components and attract those individual merchants whose stores have the drawing power to create a pedestrian flow needed by the small retailers in the enclosed mall areas. Heavy traffic generates sales, and stores that create it are more attractive to the developer, who correspondingly charges them lower rent per square foot than you obtain from stores of low sales volume who profit from high markups. Normally the high volume, low markup sales generators are located on the extreme ends of the complex, with the lower volume, high markup tenants in between paying a considerably higher rent per square foot.

How to Analyze a Center's Long-Term Value

As a shopping center in a growing area ages, the market penetration usually increases. However, even though long-term leases exist, the value of a shopping center sometimes becomes speculative as it matures, since most buildings within a shopping center complex are single-purpose structures with large areas of retail space not flexible enough for subdivision into offices or other special use commercial space at a later date. Rarely is an entire shopping center developed in an area where it is not at least partially successful—this is certainly true of the major centers. I have acquired for clients some vacated, free-standing, smaller buildings in which a major food chain has relocated in a more prosperous area. I have purchased several of these stores for considerably less than reproduction value, and converted them to alternative uses which have been quite lucrative for the second-time user.

However, where a center has stabilized or declining income and the average or percentage rents are doing likewise, the value of the structure is lessened considerably since most of the value in excess of the mortgage in a shopping center lies in the overage rents paid by the tenants. In many cases, prime tenants of an aging or mature complex are hesitant to renew their leases if other opportunities showing more potential become available in the immediate area. This is particularly true of the major tenants who command the lowest rents and can sublease or absorb rent losses if they find more desirable locations.

How to Profitably Structure the Rents

The best publication for analyzing shopping center rentals, *The Dollars and Cents of Shopping Centers*, published by the Urban Land

Institute, Washington, D.C., outlines the amounts of rent that each and every type of retail or service operation can afford to pay. In addition, the percentage override on gross sales is calculated to represent what each one of these services or retail establishments can realistically absorb. I use this directory religiously in every center that I have either analyzed or have been involved in. It is not only helpful in planning, but gives me a well-documented sales tool to use with tenants when asking them for overage participation rents. Several years ago I encountered a retailer who strenuously objected to the concept of percentage overage rents. After I showed him this publication, he was convinced that this was a widely accepted standard in the industry, and promptly executed a percentage-of-gross-sales lease. By cross-referencing various types of firms in this publication, determining the overall square footage to be constructed in the complex, and allocating the total amount of square footage per retail entity, you can determine the base or minimum rent the shopping center will have to generate.

While percentage override rents normally do not take effect in the initial years and are difficult to predict, they generally reflect the true profit picture within the shopping center. Operating expenses are relatively fixed and minor in nature, and are calculated into the base year's rent, with the escalation clauses protecting the owner. In effect, the tenants absorb any increases in operating costs over the base year for the duration of the initial lease and subsequent periods. The base year's rents and the initial escalation clauses for operating expenses are the critical factors in designing and developing the center. If they are not calculated properly, the center will show an operating loss from the day it opens.

How to Lucratively Use Percentage of Sales Leases

Some developers structure lower rents during the early years of operation in order to expedite the leasing and occupation. Some lease on a very short term, six months to one year, on a percentage of gross sales only, with the fixed long-term rent taking effect after that initial rent-up period. Generally speaking, leases are structured so as to provide predetermined break-even fixed payments for the center covering:

- insurance,
- common area assessments,
- taxes,

- mortgage payments,
- maintenance, and
- management,

the concept being that percentage leases will become effective as the center makes a larger penetration into the marketing area, thereby enhancing its overall value. In other words, the developer will analyze his break-even point allocating a certain portion of those costs to each tenant, and set the rents at a break-even level until the center starts to achieve maturity status. As soon as each tenant reaches his break-even sales figure, the shopping center reaps the benefits from the increased volume and takes a percentage of the gross income over and above this break-even point.

Many years ago, I executed a lease at a less than break-even level on a property that was extremely difficult to keep occupied. However, the product was right for the neighborhood, and I knew that once I put the tenant into the location he would be successful and I would eventually profit from the overage rents. I was disappointed initially because of his lack of advertising and market acceptance; however, as it turned out, this was one of the most lucrative percentage of sales leases that I have ever negotiated.

With operating expenses fixed in the base rent and increases covered by escalation clauses, percentage rent increases are pure profit. If the marketing center is one with a long-term potential, a shopping center becomes extremely lucrative.

The Importance of Understanding National, Regional, and Local Centers

The "neighborhood shopping center," which generally has the supermarket as its only major tenant and is backed up by several small stores, usually occupies between 4 and 10 acres. Such centers offer convenience goods such as food and drugs, and not a wide variety of merchandise and services. The neighborhood center rents are 10% to 15% per square foot higher than those in the "community center," with comparable operating expenses.

The tenant most effective in establishing a break-even point in a community center where convenience goods are promoted is normally a supermarket. Supporting it are usually an apparel store, a bank, and limited professional facilities. This type of center usually sits on 10 to 30 acres. The major tenants pay between $4 and $5 a square foot triple net.

"Regional shopping centers," generally, have a minimum site of 30 acres and will range in size from 250,000 to 1,000,000 square feet of rentable space. Most average between 500,000 and 750,000 square feet. Major tenants usually pay between $3 and $4 a square foot as a base rent plus $1.50 to $2.00 per square foot for operating expenses. The rents tend to be higher in these larger complexes even though tenants absorb larger blocks of space because the developer and retailer can predict with a greater degree of certainty the volume that any given center will generate. Supermarket rents are generally in the $4 to $5 per square foot range, and rents for drug chains, like those for general merchandise stores, tend to be a little higher. The specialty stores in these large complexes pay upwards of $6 to $8 per square foot, especially those with national status who follow the major food and retail chains from one shopping complex to another. The locally oriented specialty stores, restaurants, and service facilities, which do not command the prestige that the national firms bring, normally pay from $10 to $40 per square foot.

How to Accurately Categorize Operating Expenses of Major Tenants

Generally speaking, the expenses in a larger center will run about $1 a square foot. This includes:

- promotion,
- advertising,
- real estate taxes,
- administrative costs,
- parking, and
- insurance.

The balance of the expenses vary and consist of:

- utilities,
- maintenance, and
- common area charges.

These are approximate figures for a large center with an enclosed mall area; a 10% to 15% reduction can be applied to large shopping centers without enclosed malls.

Figures in gross space for the composition of a large regional shopping center are: major department, drug, and food stores,

FIGURE 11-1

ALLOTMENTS OF SPACE IN A LARGE SHOPPING CENTER

approximately 50%; apparel stores, about 20%; variety stores, generally, between 5% and 10%; all other stores, financial institutions, and service facilities within the complex, approximately 20% to 25%.

Since the majors usually occupy about half the space and pay the lowest rental of all the tenants in a large complex, it can become expedient for you, the developer, to convert these large blocks of space into condominiums and sell them to the major retailers, keeping for yourself the inside mall areas where the smaller tenants absorb the higher rents. The majors tend to be more permanent and spend more on promotion if they actually own the space instead of renting it. To reiterate, the break-even point is normally reached only through the base rents, which allow the developer to cover his fixed overhead expenses, and through built-in sales escalation clauses you are protected against increased operating expenses.

Establishing a Value by Determining the Degree of Market Saturation

Make certain, when purchasing an existing center, that it has not fully penetrated or saturated the market area. Analyze the total rental picture as it relates to the base and overage rents. An unusually high percentage of overage rents in a shopping center might mean trouble later if the market share is split by a competing center, and it may also indicate that the developers initially had a difficult time leasing the center, settling for a low base rent. A combination of low base rents and high fluctuating overage income might not cover the operating expenses of the center under conditions of market saturation. The key to the actual value of a center is the correct analysis and interpretation of rents as they relate to base leases and escalation clauses. Another factor to examine in the existing leases is whether escalation of the operating expenses can be offset by the overage rent clauses.

To illustrate this point, I recently had the option to acquire an interest in a community shopping center which one of my close associates had owned for years. A chain supermarket was one of the major tenants, and it had occupied the 25,000 square-foot building for approximately eight years. The company had an option to expand an additional 19,000 square feet at a very low base rent, almost equal to the combined base and overage rent on the initial lease. The overage rents were extremely high in relation to the existing square footage, due to their successful market penetration, which led me to believe that they would eventually exercise their option for the additional space. A closer analysis of the lease indicated that the overage rents could be applied to the base lease payment obligation on the expansion space. I concluded that, if I purchased the complex, I would most likely have to construct the additional space for the supermarket and forfeit the overage rents on the initial space. In effect, I would have to build the additional space for them and correspondingly not receive any additional rent based upon the way the original lease was structured.

Analyzing the Trade Area

The analysis of a shopping center is complicated, sophisticated, and time-consuming; a process requiring special talent for interpretation of the local marketing area and for combining a desirable tenant mix in the complex. General analysis of a center starts with a given trade area for the complex drawing from a population radius to the proposed center. The local supermarket chain, which is oriented toward convenience, has a smaller and more predictable trading area than high fashion specialty apparel stores, which must draw from large suburban or metropolitan areas. Most developers talk in terms of driving time or distance to a given area. A small neighborhood center will require some 2,000 or more households within a half-mile radius in order to justify its existence. The large regional centers with 500,000 to 1,000,000 square feet will generally have to serve a trade area with a quarter of a million people. Some of these large regional centers can extend their trading area over 10 to 15 miles in either direction of the site. In rare instances, they can draw from up to 20 to 25 miles, where unusual circumstances prevail. However, the prime marketing area is normally considered to be from 4 to 8 miles. These distances will vary according to existing competition, the pattern of retail expenditures within a delineated area, and the type and variety of merchandise to be promoted at the center.

The Importance of Determining Potential Sales Volume And Analyzing Competition

In analyzing the size, nature, and feasibility of the market, you must obtain pertinent figures relating to the population, income, and its distribution for a given area, from which you then approximate the expenditures a family allocates to general merchandise, clothing, food, drugs, etc. The percentage and category of expenditures for each of these items will fluctuate considerably, depending on the level of income. Obviously, a family making $10,000 a year will spend more on food and less on clothing and luxury goods than a family generating an income of $25,000. The quickest way to analyze this data is with the standard metropolitan statistical area abstract for each urbanized area, which can be obtained from the Bureau of the Census. This abstract categorizes the different marketing areas as to:

- race,
- employment,
- sex,
- housing, and
- income levels,

and provides other information needed to analyze a specific marketing area. Income figures obtained from these statistical area abstracts can then be cross-referenced against a publication called the *Sales Management Annual Survey of Buying Power*, which gives a comprehensive picture of the percentage of income allocated toward specific merchandise. In other words, deducting the 15% that a family with an annual income of $20,000 will spend on food, the *Survey of Buying Power* analyzes the percentages of other expenditures, thus providing an outline of categories or merchandise that the shopping center can rely upon selling in the given market area.

Local expertise is important in the interpretation of these figures, since they are geared to the census published every decade and become increasingly out of date. You, the developer, will have to analyze population growth patterns in the appropriate municipalities and make the corresponding adjustment. After determining the number of households and adjusting the purchasing power to current standards, you take the number of family or dwelling units in the immediate marketing area and calculate the existing and potential market for retail sales. Then, by using the *Survey of Buying Power*, you come up with a figure of total consumption for the marketing area in each merchandise category.

> Number of households in the marketing area
> × purchasing power of each household
> ÷ average amount spent for
> > (1) food
> > (2) drugs
> > (3) apparel
> > (4) other items
> = categorized figures for the area's purchasing power.

How to Determine a Center's Break-Even Point

The Dollars and Cents of Shopping Centers mentioned previously will determine what the break-even point is for any given type of retail business within the complex. A generally accepted principle, for example, is that a supermarket has to generate $150 per square foot of gross sales initially for the operation to be profitable. In the most recent supermarket locations that I have packaged for the major chains I find that they require a minimum of 30,000 square feet of space to be initially profitable. They normally look for a minimum sales volume of five million dollars out of these stores. These at least are the current requirements for two chains I have been involved with. As a norm, most developers aim at a combined average for the entire shopping center complex of about $100 per square foot in sales. A center with 250,000 square feet of leasable space will probably have to average in excess of $25 million in annual sales in order to be profitable. After you complete your study of the percentages of income spent on such things as men's and boys' wear, shoes, drugs, and apparel, you will allocate a certain amount of space in the complex to each different category of merchandise. Once total purchasing power for the given marketing or drawing area in each merchandise category is calculated, the existing market competition must be assessed and the drawing power of the voids in the market must be directly related to square footage in the proposed shopping center development.

As an example, I recently did an analysis on a supermarket location that indicated the following: There was $50,000,000 in potential food sales within the marketing or drawing area, based upon income and population analysis, and there were currently 200,000 square feet of leased space devoted to supermarket sales. By dividing the existing space into the $50,000,000 I determined that the existing stores are generating $250 a square foot in volume. By comparing figures in the appropriate publications, I determined that a supermarket could break even at $150 a square foot. I then took the $50,000,000 and divided it by $150 per square foot, giving me a total of 333,000 square feet of space which theoretically could break even in the marketing or drawing area. Subtracting the 200,000 square feet currently devoted to food sales from the 333,000, I determined that there could be a need for 133,000 additional square feet of supermarket space, a portion of which could constitute a feasible allotment in my shopping center.

You can do this for every category of retail sales within the area, finding the voids in the market, and structure your tenant mix to allocate a certain portion of square footage in a shopping center. In summary:

> $50,000,000 potential food sales
> ÷ 200,000 existing square footage
> = $250 per square foot actual food sales;
> $50,000,000 potential food sales
> ÷ $150 per square foot break-even point
> = 333,000 potential square feet that could break even;
>   333,000 square feet (market potential)
> – 200,000 square feet (existing)
> = 133,000 square feet potential additional space.

Determining Tenant Mix, Rent Concessions, and Tenant Improvements

Specialty stores generally average around $75 a square foot in sales; major food and department stores, well in excess of $100 a square foot. Sometimes it is difficult to analyze and allocate a given percentage of square footage in each category of retail sales, as specialty stores often duplicate sales of the major department stores. This is the toughest part of structuring a center—allocating different square footage to the various types of closely related products that are to be merchandised. The ultimate objective is to match space allotments with voids in the existing market and projected needs of the immediate trade or marketing area in such a way as to reflect the incomes and spending habits of the local population. A rough rule of thumb is that a major portion of the market for daily essentials, such as food and drugs, easily falls within a two- to three-mile radius of the center. Department stores, specifically, draw from a larger area, usually ten to twelve miles, and specialty stores, depending upon their nature and merchandise, can draw from an almost unlimited distance.

Most centers are located in middle-class marketing areas and should not be considered either in areas of extremely high purchasing power or where low income prevails unless the tenants are specifically selling this level of merchandise. Within this basic framework, internal needs must also be balanced.

I am currently developing a small shopping mall in an arts and crafts community in the Rocky Mountain area of the Southwest, with mainly seasonal tenants. This can be a risky venture unless one completely understands the market, as high tenant turnover can be readily expected in these types of complexes, especially where sales per square foot will be considerably under the $150 normally predicted for conventional shopping centers. On the other hand, the profit margin on merchandise sold in these specialty centers is extremely high, and can be quite lucrative to the owner if one can develop a well-balanced and long-term viable group of retailers. The square foot rents can be extremely high, as margins of profit are three to four times those found in most other retail volume-oriented businesses.

When to Grant Exclusive Rights to Merchandise

Major tenants usually demand rights to exclusive operations or exclusive types of sales within a complex before a leasing agreement is reached. If a developer plans to add land and additional buildings to the complex at a later date, exclusive leases granted to major tenants should not bind the additional phases of the shopping center. Several other major anchor tenants may be needed to make the later phases of the complex viable. An exclusive on the entire project may often inhibit development of the balance of the center.

Where the developer usually improves the rental space completely for the major tenants, he normally gives the smaller tenants fixed and incomplete allowances for their improvements and extends the services of the project's architect and contractor to complete the spaces. The developer normally provides the shell space; minor tenants pay for interior improvements such as wall and floor coverings, ceilings and lighting fixtures, partitions, electrical, and plumbing. Improvements and concessions are geared toward the strength and drawing power of the tenant, the duration of the lease, and the completion or rental stage of the complex. It is not uncommon for moratoriums or percentage-only leases to be signed for the initial months of occupancy in order to make it easier for the tenants to pay for their shell improvements.

An associate of mine recently acquired the management contract on a newer shopping center that had developed leasing problems in the mall areas. The location of the development was ideal, but the major tenants did not have the initial drawing power that the developer anticipated. The mall areas were leased out, giving the tenants one-year leases on a percentage of sales only, with no minimum fixed obligation, which turned out to be the only way he could initially attract tenants into this particular shopping mall. The technique worked quite well, and a large majority of the percentage-only tenants are still occupying that space.

How Lenders Analyze and Commit Funds for Centers

Shopping centers, generally, command a high loan-to-value ratio and offer sizable allowances for depreciation, not only on the shell of the structure, but also on the improvements specifically installed for the tenants. Most lending institutions require a rental achievement clause calculated on the base rents from the operation before funding a permanent mortgage. If the base rents are sufficient to carry a large first mortgage and the developer has ample staying power during the rent-up period and through the initial years of market penetration, the developer can normally achieve close to 100% financing on the center.

Most developers look to insurance companies when financing shopping centers, as they do not have the same government-related restrictions on high loan-to-value ratio financing as conventional lending institutions. Insurance companies are primarily interested in coverage of their debt service by the base rents and do not concern themselves with lending on the percentage of appraised value traditionally used by the banks and savings and loan associations.

Furthermore, insurance companies are enthusiastic about these centers, since the large sums of money necessary to finance them mean that investments can be consolidated in fewer and larger ventures. An associate of mine recently financed a shopping center during the tightest money market in the last century, through a life insurance company. This was accomplished primarily because these companies have a constant inflow of funds from life insurance premiums, somewhat subject to policyholder borrowing on cash value, and are not as susceptible to the peaks and troughs in deposits that banks and savings and loans encounter.

Normally the first-mortgage financing is eight to nine times the annual base rents after operating expenses, depending on the nature and stability of the tenants and the current interest rates. In some cases, the initial overall cash return on a center is less than the amount necessary to amortize the mortgage. In other words, it is not uncommon to find a 9% cash return on a shopping center where the annual interest and principal amortization factor is 11% or higher. The return will vary with the size and age of the project, whether it is regional, neighborhood, or community, with the quality and nature of the tenants, and with the degree of market penetration reflected in percentage leases.

The depreciation schedules on a shopping center are fairly attractive if the land does not have a value disproportionate to the buildings, which is not generally the case, especially in larger developments. Under the 1981 Economic Recovery Tax Act, all structures can be uniformly depreciated over a 15-year basis. Tax benefits are substantial to the developer who converts into condominiums the large stores with long-term leases to major tenants, retaining the balance of the short-term inside mall space.

Tax Benefits; Ratios of Building to Land

Analysis of the overall depreciation of cost recovery schedules becomes important, as the cash flow can balloon when the percentage override leases take effect. Under the old method short-term depreciable improvements such as:

- parking lots,
- mall area improvements,
- landscaping,
- mechanical equipment, and
- leasehold improvements

could be amortized quickly, showing a considerable loss in the initial years of the project. However, taking sizable depreciation deductions early in the venture was often a mistake. Accurate prediction of the potential cash flow from percentage leases is difficult and the developer may be forced for tax reasons to sell the center before it reaches full potential and market saturation. Since the Economic Recovery Tax Act of 1981, I have generally established a policy of talking straight-line depreciation on all investment property that I own, rarely making an exception for properties that generate large amounts of cash, where accelerated depreciation can shelter it.

A rule of thumb used in the industry is that one acre of land can support approximately 10,000 square feet of retail building space or approximately a 25% building coverage ratio. This provides for ample access and on-site parking. Most suburban communities require a 3-to-1 ratio of parking to building, as customers are more dependent upon automobiles for access. This ratio can be adjusted in high-density areas where potential purchasers can walk to the center. The developer normally attempts to find a tract of land that is relatively level, having a maximum 3% to 5% grade. Excessive grades complicate the drainage and construction for parking, adding considerably to costs.

Where the Opportunities Exist

Development of the major shopping centers is being monopolized by several large specialized development firms in combination with sophisticated insurance companies and a handful of major retail tenants, due to the complexity of development, the large sums of initial equity money needed, and the expertise involved. An interesting opportunity still exists in some of the smaller cities that have been at least initially overlooked by the major retailers. For instance, I recently located two variety store centers in two small cities. This variety store is one of the most successful and rapidly expanding retail chains. Their current policy is to locate in small towns with populations of 15,000 or more, with the hope that if they are the first to locate, they will eliminate all future competition. This is not to say that areas of smaller development do not exist and that strong local retailers cannot be attracted and used as anchor tenants for development of neighborhood centers. Many reputable local retailers do not care to be in large developments where their hours are dictated, their rents are excessive, and their identity is stripped from them in the mass merchandising approach. The sophisticated locals know that they are doing nothing more than subsidizing major national tenants in exchange for the drawing power that they, in many cases, generate themselves. Thinking small is not necessarily unprofitable.

Shopping centers are prime examples of the principle of fractionalization in real estate development. With many small tenants paying premium rents, profits are generated in the aggregate by these retailers. The management problems inherent in creating the right tenant mix and restricting competition without eliminating it can be compounded by the size of the center. The movement back to the inner cities, expected during the 1980's, may well encourage the construction of smaller shopping centers in less than proven locations. Many investors are going to face difficult decisions in contemplating development within these urban areas during the next decade. In order to make optimal use of existing land, many will construct or revamp existing office complexes, the subject of our next chapter, which lend themselves to higher-rise construction and land conservation, unlike the shopping center designs with which consumers have become so familiar.

12

Opportunities in Acquiring and Developing Office Complexes

The office building continues to be one of the most important vehicles in the development of investment real estate properties. The increasing demand for more service-oriented businesses, the tendency to computerize, and the paperwork and staff necessary to handle the work load are constantly creating new demands for office space. This chapter will show you why many of the major corporations are shifting their personnel into new geographic areas of the United States, creating regional marketing areas that can easily be capitalized on. Included in this chapter are proven methods for capitalizing on suburban office complexes in which you will discover how to spot overbuilt markets, how to determine absorption rates and vacancy factors, how to obtain premium rents, and determine realistic operating expenses. In many of these areas you will discover how a commitment from a major national tenant for a limited amount of space can be a springboard for developing and leveraging a major office complex, as I recently did when I constructed a building for a major American corporation in which they occupied less than 15% of the structure. Their name and drawing power was enough to obtain the right financing in order for me to commence construction on the balance of the development. Their prestigious name enabled me to prelease the building prior to completion.

How to Attract Prime Tenants

Major tenants locate in new structures for several reasons. Many may have outgrown their original space or had to lease additional areas, either adjoining or isolated, at considerably higher rates than they initially contracted for. Subsequently, they often find that by shifting to new and larger space, redesigning the layout and obtaining more efficiency, they can reduce their overall rental budget considerably. This, combined with the fact that many large prestigious space-users are in a position to command options on additional areas, makes the move less expensive than one might initially think. Because of the efficiency of newly designed space, you will find that newer buildings command a higher occupancy and higher rent per square foot than do older structures, which usually generate lesser rents and have larger vacancy factors.

An important consideration is that today's new office complexes will become tomorrow's older buildings, as most major tenants shift from one building to another on the average of about every eight to ten years. This, however, is not necessarily a detrimental factor. If one designs a building and leases it in such a fashion that several strong local tenants occupy the building, these individuals will probably stay in the building for long periods of time and, through the normal expansionary process, will absorb the space that is vacated by the major national tenants who traditionally shift from one area to another. Recently, I constructed a building for another major corporation, that I kept as a personal investment. Although they occupy 35% of the structure, no major concessions were necessary in order to attract them. With no lease subsidy involved, their presence made the complex into one of the most prestigious and high-rent structures in the community, always showing 100% occupancy. If lease subsidies are necessary, they should be short in duration and for less than 20% of the structure.

Office complexes are without peers when it comes to hedging against inflation. Unlike apartments, the traditional inflation hedge, office investments will not be subject to rent control or restricted by the declining inflationary or after-tax spendable dollars of the tenants.

Providing Flexibility for Expansion

Flexibility in providing additional space at a later date is paramount with both major national and strong local tenants, as service-oriented industries have a tendency to expand. Generally, if adequate additional room can be provided at a later date, these service industries will renew their leases in a recognized location. I recently provided flexibility to a tenant by personally subleasing 1500 square feet adjoining his prime rental space. I sublet the balance to two local tenants, paralleling their leases to expire at the same time that the major tenant had the option to expand. This gave me the flexibility to retain the major tenant who had already indicated that he would exercise his option. Many service-oriented companies are locally owned by groups of professional people not affiliated with large companies having pension funds, profit-sharing plans, and other forms of retirement benefits. In some instances, such individuals can be sold on the condominium concept, where they own and occupy their own space.

Capitalizing on Suburban Office Complexes

Most recent office development is in the suburbs of the United States, in what are called suburban office parks. Generally, such locations appeal to service and sales industries that do not require as close a contact with the downtown community as do financially oriented firms and governmental agencies. This is especially true in some of the new regional centers for commerce, finance and marketing such as Denver, Atlanta, Minneapolis, Dallas, and Salt Lake City, to mention a few. The telephone has, in many respects, depersonalized business operations, eliminating the need for close contact with the historical downtown office occupants. While suburban communities still have large tracts of land that can easily be developed and controlled by relatively small developers, acquiring an office complex is rapidly becoming impossible in the downtown sections of some major metropolitan areas. Multiple ownership, high land costs, complicated assemblage, and providing ample and expensive parking for the commuting occupants are among the inherent problems in these downtown locations.

An additional point to remember is that many large manufacturing facilities are moving to the suburbs not only because of the convenience of suburban parks, but also because downtown locations are no longer readily accessible to airports and other rapidly growing transportation facilities. Employees in many of the service industries, as well as their clients, travel extensively, and the suburban project located near an airport has considerable appeal to these mobile people.

Downtown office complexes are economically feasible only for decision-makers who must have personal contact with one another on a daily basis. The most obvious candidates for these structures are:

- the banking industry,
- lawyers and accountants,
- financial service institutions,
- insurance and commercial real estate companies, and
- government employees.

These locations also provide stronger supporting labor markets, large backup pools of secretarial and professional middle management personnel who want access to noontime shopping, closer ties to public transportation, and more sophisticated and exciting dining and evening entertainment facilities.

Advantages Offered in Suburban Parks

For most businesses, however, the advantages of the suburban locations usually outweigh those in the downtown sectors. In addition to offering lower rent and more identity, suburban office complexes can be designed and structured to serve the tenants' needs, and usually provide accessibility to surrounding residential neighborhoods, especially those areas where the top executives live. Spacious and open areas can be created within those complexes, providing an attractive, residential atmosphere in which to conduct business activities. Often when dining and shopping facilities are not readily available, they can be designed into the office complex. The management and risk factors of including such amenities are not usually worth the developer's time and effort unless you are developing a self-contained office park with a sizable amount of rentable space. However unprofitable these amenities may be to the

FIGURE 12-1

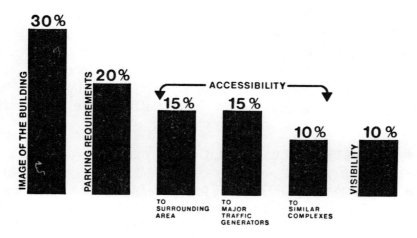

FACTORS INVOLVED IN LOCATING A SUBURBAN OFFICE

developer, they are an important factor in the success of a suburban office facility. At the least, such facilities should be located within walking distance of a suburban park and near public transportation in order to attract and retain clerical personnel. Since business transactions in the downtown area will probably be required once or twice a week, a good rule of thumb is to locate suburban office parks within twenty to twenty-five minutes of the central business district.

Among the salient factors involved in locating a suburban office complex is accessibility. The major executives and their top supervisory people who decide where to locate offices prefer minimal driving time from their own residences, not necessarily from those of the clerical staff. Recruitment of middle-management people within the area can be a problem, obviously minimized when the office force is sales-oriented or has a high ratio of sales and executive personnel to clerical workers. You, as the developer, should be aware of this problem in choosing your tenants and in designing and locating the structure. I recently developed a medium-sized office complex, built almost exclusively for governmental tenants. I located this development in a rapidly expanding middle-income section, knowing full well that many parts of this metropolitan area were too expensive for government employees to reside in. The majority of the occupants in the building commute very short distances, including the upper level administrative personnel. By choosing this location, I feel that I have assured myself of a long-term occupancy rate with these governmental employees, even though the leases are rather short-term in nature.

Determining the Fair Market Rental

To arrive at the approximate rental figures for space in a moderately priced suburban low-density office complex, you start with:

- $40 to $45 per square foot, the approximate cost of the shell building, adding
- $15 to $25 per square foot for non-construction costs, which include land, financing, architectural fees, interest during construction, leasing commissions, and management overhead; plus
- $15 to $20 per square foot for tenant improvements needed to put the space in a condition for general occupancy.

With these cost figures, it becomes apparent that, depending upon the length of the lease and the amount of time you wish to amortize tenant improvements, approximately $12 to $15 per square foot rent plus utilities will be required annually in order to cover the normal operating expenses and debt service in a suburban office complex.

These construction and rental figures are based on a building I developed several years ago, consisting of 26,000 square feet, and are adjusted upwards to reflect approximate current development costs. These figures can often double in high-rise structures, where extremely high land and construction costs prevail. Rentals also might have to be adjusted upward, depending on the local property taxes. If taxes in the community are running $1 per square foot or thereabouts and the structure is leased to major tenants for a minimum five-year term, $12 to $15 per square foot will provide a fairly lucrative return on equity, assuming the net leasable space is 90% of the gross space or greater. Utility expense figures can be adjusted to larger and/or higher buildings through the standard practice in the industry of prorating the cost of utilities among the tenants. When this approach is used, the only major variables in the operating expense statement are the local real estate taxes, janitorial services, and maintenance.

How to Determine the Nature of the Market

Such things as local employment, absorption rates, market feasibility, income, and purchasing power, that we discussed as desirable for preliminary market and site analysis in the chapter on apartments, can easily be shifted to apply to the demand for new office structures. As reflected in the fact that office development represents less than 10% of the total of all construction in the United States, the office market is considerably smaller and less predictable than the apartment market. It also has a tendency to become overbuilt in any given area, as these projects are considerably larger and take more time and expertise to develop than the traditional diversified apartment complexes. Office structures are acquired or constructed by sophisticated investors operating with high leverage and tremendous financial staying power, who can normally develop them and, if required, carry them for long periods of time. Frequently, banks, insurance companies, or financial institutions joint-venture such projects so that they can partially occupy these prestigious buildings themselves.

The element of speculation lies in the ability to outride a soft market in which price cutting is a way of life. Many massive office buildings are designed around a small percentage of occupancy. One or two major tenants are enough for you, the developer, to obtain a sizable financial commitment for the balance of the building. Large blocks of office space have a way of surfacing on the market for lengthy periods awaiting occupancy. The philosophy is that the larger and more impressive the office complex, the more its image will appeal to major tenants and correspondingly the larger the square foot rental the complex will generate. Since major tenants take large blocks and utilize the open-space concept more than the smaller ones, they are obviously the most desirable. Even though their rental commitments are at lower figures, prestigious occupants have a tendency to make the entire project a viable one in the same way that major retailers affect shopping centers. I developed a twin tower office complex in which I was having difficulty in obtaining lease commitments prior to commencing construction. I started the first building without any commitments for the space. Shortly after breaking ground, I obtained leases from two major tenants to occupy the new complex, as any project instantly develops credibility when it is under construction. It wasn't long after the word circulated that these major tenants would occupy the complex, that a multitude of local and regional tenants appeared. From there on the leasing aspect was considerably simplified.

Determining Absorption and Vacancy Factors

To avoid the hazards of overbuilding, the developer of an office complex should analyze the space requirements within a given community before deciding to invest. A ballpark figure allows between 7 and 10 square feet of office space per capita. This figure could be low in areas of heavy manufacturing, service-oriented firms, and seats of government. The objective is to establish a traditional square foot per capita ratio for the particular area, determining historically the office space the general area can absorb. As the population base expands, the future demand for office space can be predicted with great accuracy. A 5% to 8% vacancy factor for comparable space you are acquiring or developing is usually considered a danger signal in the office market. In the apartment sector the vacancy factor is not quite as critical as it is in the office field, where large blocks of space tend to glut the market at unpredictable intervals. The existing vacancy factor should be compared with the market absorption rate and the amount of new or anticipated space coming on the market as vacancy factors in the office rental market have a tendency to fluctuate considerably.

Designing a Building to Obtain Premium Rents

Office buildings must combine exterior attractiveness and interior flexibility. Some of the concepts for providing flexibility are:

- Interior partitions and load-bearing walls and columns must be laid out so that initial subdivision and later conversion can be achieved economically.
- Heating and ventilation are critical, as new office complexes tend to have larger areas for permanent fixed glass windows that will not open.
- Large, glass-enclosed complexes are the most prestigious and the corner suites in these buildings always command premium rents.
- By designing long and narrow buildings, one increases the total amount of glass or view-oriented suites within a structure and achieves the massive look necessary to command premium rents.

- By designing an almost overpowering structure you create a strong demand for building rentals which serves the economics of development as well, in that it permits you to prorate the costs of elevators, amenities, management staff, and overhead.

Furthermore, prestigious tenants seek massive structures since they can negotiate for options on additional square footage, permitting them a longer and more flexible term of occupancy than they would find if they moved into smaller, single-purpose structures which they could conceivably outgrow before the expiration of their leases.

Rent Concessions and Determining Rentable Area

I had an experience familiar to most developers when I built a complex for a major corporation. In order to commence construction on the building, I needed a major tenant. In order to attract them, I had to initially subsidize and make concessions on their lease similar to what the major retailers dictate in shopping centers. Fortunately, they only required less than 15% of the space and, based upon their commitment, I felt comfortable proceeding with the balance of the building, knowing that other tenants would soon want to occupy space in a structure having a prestigious tenant. My assumptions were correct in that the balance of the space, some 22,000 square feet, was leased in a matter of months.

Analyzing the net rentable area in office structures is complicated. Generally, one measures from the inside surface of the outer wall, or windows, to the middle of the finished surface of the inside partitions; or, in the case of an entire floor, from the inside surface of the exterior wall to the inside surface of the opposite exterior wall. Such things as elevators, lavatories, utility and janitorial closets, stairways, and hallways that are not exclusively for the use of the tenant are excluded from the net rentable figure. Precise control of "unrentable" space is extremely important in designing a new building whose interior layout and use will not be determined until space is actually leased. The more common or unrentable space, the higher the overall rental will have to be in order to make economics work. Sometimes you must make rental commitments early in the leasing stage, not knowing the exact amount of space that will be designated to the common areas. This is one reason the large national tenants become so attractive, as they occupy entire floors, and the net rentable area can sometimes be almost 100% of the building.

How to Maximize Building Efficiency

A well-utilized, efficient building will have between 88% and 90% of the inside occupied dimensions as net rentable space. This percentage will vary with the number of tenants and the amount of space that each occupies. The gross rentable area that is found on a seller's presentation is not necessarily a reliable working figure when purchasing an existing building. Only a complete set of floor plans for the structure and consultation with an architect or engineer can serve to determine the exact rentable square footage and its potential flexibility for later subdivision into suites. It is important, of course, to know where the load-bearing walls, columns, and partitions are, and to determine other structural limitations of flexibility in order to know what areas of the building can be expanded into and how they can be opened up or subdivided at a later date.

Tenant turnover is always costly, even if the incoming occupant pays a higher rental rate. As a rule of thumb, specialized tenant improvements involving new construction or major remodeling will probably be equivalent to one year's rent. These improvements will include such things as erecting partitions, reworking the electrical and plumbing, finishing walls and ceilings, and changing floor and window coverings. These items can be expensive and the interior design should be flexible and open enough so that, if one tenant vacates, another can utilize many of the existing improvements.

Some years ago, I constructed a building for a state governmental agency which was leased on a short-term, two-year obligation, in which they occupied an entire floor of approximately 10,000 square feet. Even though they gave me repeated assurances that they would continue to occupy the building when the two-year lease expired, I improved the space so that three-quarters of the partitions were five feet high and movable. After the lease expired, the agency outgrew the space and relocated. Had the partitions not been of a movable nature, my expenses in remodeling the space could have been considerable. Subsequently I was successful in re-leasing the space to longer-term occupants, and my only out-of-pocket expense was for physical relocation or removal of the partitions, many of which I resold at a later date, commanding a price equal to or exceeding their original cost.

The complete renovation sometimes necessary to attract new tenants often involves some form of refinancing, which raises another important point. In raising primary or secondary financing on existing buildings for which you have a ground lease, it is important to determine, as we have stressed before, that the balance of the lease be at least twice the term of the mortgage that you are attempting to get for the improvements, a requirement of most lenders. Should the lender repossess the property and have to resell it at a later date, he will have to provide the new owner sufficient time to amortize the mortgage on the improvements. Also, prohibitive refinance clauses in first mortgages should be scrutinized carefully, in lieu of tenant remodeling.

Pitfalls in Speculative Building

When constructing an office complex without having prior lease commitments, it is important to proceed only with the shell of the structure. On each floor, one should rough in only for:

- plumbing and electric,
- mechanical, and
- lavatory facilities.

It is not advisable to install *any* of the following initially:

- heating duct system,
- ceilings,
- light fixtures,
- partitions,
- corridor walls, or
- any other fixed improvements.

The actual designing and construction should accompany leasing. Different tenants and the degree of congestion or equipment in an area particularly affect the requirements for heat and air conditioning. In some cases, even within a given suite, such areas as conference and demonstration rooms will require special duct work, increased air flows, and extra electrical installations. Leaving each individual floor open initially permits you the flexibility of catering either to large or small tenants and maximizing the utilization of space in common or congested areas.

Structuring the Tenant Mix and Length of the Lease

Normally, leases run from five to ten years, with an attached escalation clause revised annually on a retroactive basis to reflect increases in operating expenses such as utilities, parking, insurance, maintenance, taxes and janitorial services. The long-term leases so common in the past are now giving way to shorter commitments which take advantage of inflation. An exception occurs when a single-purpose building is specifically designed for an individual tenant. Lending institutions are becoming more sophisticated in reviewing the strength of the leases and the timing of their expiration in order to support the loan-to-value ratio on a given project. A number of vacancies coming due at the same time, which constitutes 15% to 20% of the total leasable area, creates a problem with most lending institutions and developers. Obviously, the financial strength of the proposed tenants becomes significant, as the leases are an important element of the lender's collateral.

Escalation clauses must be structured carefully, as the nature of any long-term leases on office buildings can work against you, the owner, if the increase in expenses is not properly covered. The normal procedure is to start with the base year of the lease and freeze the owner's responsibility for increased expense obligations from that point on. In other words, any additional taxes, insurance, parking, maintenance, janitorial services, or utilities are calculated on an annual basis and the square-foot costs are prorated back to the tenant. This approach, in effect, provides you with a fixed and predetermined return on your project, based upon the year you make the lease, maintaining the same equal return on your investment regardless of the inflationary factors that enter into long-term leases. By using this method, you insure that your position will not deteriorate substantially when entering into long-term lease commitments. I am currently using full cost-of-living escalator clauses in all my short-term leases, and the only actual out-of-pocket or pass-through escalation commitments I am making are for long-term prime national tenants who normally dictate these terms. As operating expenses normally run between 30% and 40% of the gross income, a full cost-of-living clause on the entire gross rent really means that escalation increases are extremely lucrative, as they average about two and one-half times the actual expenses of the building. I find that most of my tenants on short-term leases give me very little resistance on full cost-of-living escalation clauses.

How to Creatively Structure the Lease

The lease payments can be structured in several ways:

1. A *stepped-up lease* can be made with a tenant either starting out in business in a particular area or attempting

to penetrate a new market where he can afford an increase in rent as his market absorption increases. It provides for a gradual increase in the amount of the base rent at a given date or at a specified interval of time.

2. An *expense-participation lease* is one containing an escalation clause, which we discussed earlier. The tenant pays a fixed amount of base rent plus a percentage of the increase in operating expenses.

3. A lease tied to the *cost of living index* obliges the tenant to accept increases in his rent based upon a predetermined index that measures the inflationary factor. This usually parallels the wholesale or retail cost of living index published by the U.S. Department of Labor. I have several leases in the private and public sectors where the full cost of living clause increases the rent upward annually. These leases are structured in such a fashion that most of the increase goes to the bottom line, especially where all utilities are metered or prorated separately.

4. A *renegotiated, appraised value lease,* common in long-term commitments, permits you the option of having the property appraised periodically, with the tenant paying a fixed percentage of the appraised value as his specified rent.

Many times, sophisticated national tenants put ceilings on the amount that escalation clauses can rise in any given year, or on a cumulative basis over the length of the lease. This insures, among other things, that owners do not take advantage of tenants by concealing and inflating their costs of operation. If these actual costs exceed the ceiling rate by a large amount, you can fully protect yourself by having the option of cancelling the lease or renegotiating it based upon the current market rental conditions. A provision for an independent arbitrator in the language of the lease can also protect you in catastrophic situations.

Mobility Factors: Analyzing the Tenant's Motivation for Renting

The prospective purchaser of an existing office building should carefully analyze the rent rolls to determine whether the tenants are potential users of additional space. You should determine what tenants you want to maintain on a long-term basis and structure the occupancy and length of the renewed leases on the adjoining spaces to coincide with the expansion plans of the larger, more desirable occupants. Existing tenants in an office building should be assessed as to how they relate to the general neighborhood. For instance, if the complex is in a financial center, near a hospital, or in an industrial area, and the tenants are not oriented toward these supporting facilities or sectors, a potential problem exists, since it is not mandatory that they remain in the immediate area, and they may potentially become mobile at the end of their lease periods.

Several years ago I was offered a medical office complex near an old existing hospital. After analyzing the market, it became evident to me that the new hospital which was under construction would attract many of the existing medical people occupying this office complex, and that a majority would relocate closer to the new facility. I declined to purchase the property, and as it turned out, this is exactly what happened.

The Importance of Finding the Right Location

Analyzing the operating expenses of an office complex is probably the easiest aspect of the investment decision, irrespective of whether one purchases or builds. Many of the nationally associated management organizations compile annual expense figures for buildings ranging from 5,000 to 1,000,000 square feet and interpolate them to local or regional conditions. Square-foot rentals are also fairly easy to analyze. They are not as diverse and complicated as found in apartment buildings, where you have to balance the amenities and different room sizes in order to arrive at a comparable rental figure. The difficulty arises when the market softens and the owners make rent concessions in order to achieve full occupancy.

After the site is chosen, the quality of the tenant becomes the second most important aspect in structuring or analyzing an office investment. If the site is in a "100% area," you normally will be in a position to attract tenants with a high degree of financial stability, as rents in these areas command a premium over those in other parts of town. Many ill-advised investors tend to locate in an area where rents and land costs are somewhat lower, reasoning that, in the event the market softens, they will be in a position to offer lower, more competitive rents. This is not normally the case, strange as it might seem, as we saw in the analysis of apartments. Certain individuals and corporations are willing to pay a premium to be in the right building and location. This is prevalent especially in office complexes and shopping centers, as companies want the prestige of an appropriate location. This concept applies in most circumstances as rentals increase at a faster rate in high rent areas than in marginal ones, augmenting the attractiveness of prestigious sites. The concept is no different from acquiring a home in a plush area in contrast to a mediocre neighborhood. History has experienced and will continue to experience higher appreciation in desirable areas.

Determining Realistic Operating Expenses

Operating expenses for office complexes are considerably higher than those for apartments because of such ongoing expenses as janitorial service, elevator and routine maintenance, and larger budgets for tenant redecoration. Most operating expenses run between 30% and 40% of the gross income on a building for suburban complexes, exclusive of parking and utilities. The approximate breakdown on low-rise suburban office expenses as a percentage of gross income generally falls into these categories:

Janitorial	7%
Electricity: Common Areas	4
Air-conditioning/heating maintenance	2
Reserve for replacement	2
Elevators	2
General building maintenance	4
Administrative costs/management	2
Energy	15
Redecorating	1
Insurance	1
Real estate taxes	10
% of income/year	50%

FIGURE 12-2

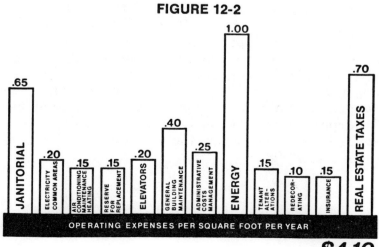

$4.10

The resultant figure for operating expenses is about 50% of the gross income. When subtracted, this gives an approximate amount of income available for debt service and return on equity.

Interrelationship of Income, Expenses, and Debt Service Coverage

Here again, as we discussed in the analysis of apartments, we arrive at a net income after operating expenses and multiply this by our constant loan factor, or the amount of money it takes to amortize the interest and principal over the life of the mortgage, to determine a realistic mortgage amount that the building can support. Depending on the strength of the tenants and the length of leases, lending institutions require coverage over and above the cash flow ranging from 1.2 to 1.3 times. These preceding operating figures are national averages, not always applicable to local situations. For older structures, operating expenses are considerably higher.

Income and operating figures are relatively easy to assemble, as most local management firms can determine or estimate the gross rents and expenses. In many of the large metropolitan areas, rental figures for high-rise buildings in the right location can run in excess of $25 per square foot per year. The operating expense figures have to be adjusted depending on the size of the structure, as larger buildings are considerably more efficient than smaller ones. As an example, the national average for utilities on a building of 1 to 5 stories is approximately $1.50 per square foot; the same is true for 5- to 10-story buildings. After that, as the buildings get larger, the cost increases. It is not uncommon in a 50-story building for utility costs to be 25% to 30% in excess of those in smaller buildings. The same geometric concept applies to the age of a structure since, generally speaking, as the building ages, the cost of operating it increases.

One of the important expense factors, the real estate taxes, can range from as low as 50¢ per square foot in the southern parts of the United States to $2 or more in the Northeast. Regardless of the regional average, real estate taxes should not exceed 15% of gross income on any structure. These average expense figures generally relate to conventional office complexes and must be adjusted for special purpose buildings, such as those housing medical or computerized operations, where the cost of interior improvements can be excessively high.

Unique Opportunities in Executive Office Suites

Any form of development, as we have discovered, is inseparable from the managerial ability of the developer. Your investment of entrepreneurial talent and time is the key to success. By developing a condominium—of apartments or offices—you minimize managerial demands, but you can still utilize your capabilities lucratively by a controlled investment in the creative time required to run an executive suite in your own complex. Establishing your own office with a full-time staff, you can additionally create a full-service package for tenants, including:

- fully furnished offices;
- complete telephone answering;
- conference and meeting rooms;
- receptionist and secretarial services;
- Xerox, telex, and reservation services.

Semiretired executives or young professionals moving into an area usually are not in a position to utilize or justify a full-time receptionist or secretary. They can more easily invest in twice the going rent per square foot plus a monthly billing for the typing and phone answering services they require in order to establish themselves as more than shoestring operators when they start out. Once they are established, they can obtain cheaper space and justify the supporting personnel. In the meantime, a continuing market exists for the developer who is willing to pit his managerial ability against the high turnover of such occupancy.

Several years ago I successfully converted an 85-year-old 6,000 square foot hotel into 21 executive office suites, using the lobby with its massive fireplace and cathedral ceilings as a showpiece and reception area for the project. Utilizing this concept, I obtained a 30% rental increase over and above the existing market rents that were then prevalent within that metropolitan area, with little additional management input, as my office staff ran the building. These renovated projects often have huge tax-sheltered benefits in relation to the capital invested, especially if they are located in historic preservation areas, as my hotel was, where special legislation for accelerated depreciation or cost recovery is available.

Why Offices Are the Most Lucrative Long-Term Investments

Among the many advantages unique to developing office complexes is the facility of obtaining prime national and local tenants. A well-designed building with the proper image can attract these quality tenants. I have found in the office complexes that I have developed over the years that I can attract major tenants without having to deal with other development companies or real estate brokers, as the prestigious occupants of office space are normally in the area, where I can easily isolate and contact them myself. Many find out that a new complex is being developed, and often will seek me out in order to upgrade their current facilities. Financing is facilitated by long-term leases, which in turn minimize management problems and financial exposure. The healthy expansionary trend of most national corporations, especially service-oriented industries, coupled with the fact that office rents historically have not been subject to rent control ordinances, makes the acquisition and development of office complexes one of the most lucrative and inflation-proof long-term investments in the real estate field.

Office complexes, probably to a greater extent than any other type of commercial property, have a tendency to project successful images. We have already mentioned that massive structures project the gilt-edged stability so important to many tenants, but this is the simplistic end of the equation. Factors of location, architectural design and competent management can combine to create auras conducive to successful business transactions or competent professional service. Small corporations or professional associations, in particular, associate so comfortably in certain environments that they are prime candidates for condominium conversion of office or industrial space which we will discuss in the next chapter.

13

Opportunities in Selling Commercial Condominiums

From the developer's standpoint, a condominium is a condominium is a condominium. Regardless of who occupies the space and for what purpose, the concepts are identical.

Converting a residential unit, as we have discussed previously in this book, is within the capability of a developer of even modest financial means and talents. Limitations lie more in the size of the project than in its nature. Much the same is true of converting commercial property, with the difference that both management and salesmanship are refined. You, as a developer who converts business property, must be in a position to monitor the economic pulse of a community more precisely in order to deal with these sophisticated buyers.

This chapter will show you the important factors in location, how to select the market and locate the buyers. We will outline for you the proven methods for structuring low down payments and high leverage. You will learn how to price commercial condominiums lucratively by stressing the after-tax advantages of ownership. We will demonstrate to you through practical examples how the pros capitalize on large office projects and point out some of the unique advantages characteristic of industrial condominiums.

253

How to Select the Market

Perhaps the largest and surest market for business condominiums consists of professional people. With established practices
lucrative to them as individuals or small groups, they are
particularly vulnerable to the pride of owning a segment or a floor of
a prestigious building which they do not have the financial capability
to construct for themselves. Furthermore, many professionals,
especially those in the health sciences, have acquired little if any
sophistication in tax matters.

Neither pride of ownership nor lack of sophistication in
specialized areas of economics is peculiar to professional individuals.
Small business firms are equally attracted to occupying space which
they own. I recently sold a small suite of 2,500 square feet to a real
estate firm well established in its successful merchandising of
residential housing. Without expertise in commercial development,
they fully appreciated how much the value of real estate is contingent
upon its location. With this awareness, they were the natural
purchasers for my space.

Professional people are often even more dependent upon
supporting facilities in immediate areas or convenience of access to
other business people. Many doctors, for example, must locate near
hospitals or medical centers. Lawyers, to a somewhat lesser extent,
benefit from access to the courts and full-service law libraries.

A few years ago, I attempted to structure a $2,500,000 medical
condominium near a new hospital then under construction. I was
ahead of time and met with some resistance from the medical
community. Many practitioners were not completely convinced that
they wanted to leave the old hospital area permanently, and many
did not want to pay the higher rent required to cover the cost of my
new space. Realizing my mistiming early, I switched my approach
prior to completing the shell of the building, gearing it toward
conventional office rental units with conversion as my ultimate goal.
Several years passed between the time I approached the medical
community regarding relocation and the time it actually did.
However well I had formulated my concept, I would have incurred a
prohibitively expensive holding period if I had waited for these
individuals to decide. When they finally did make the move,
comparable space was selling at 40% higher than I had offered it.

The Important Factors in Location

The most obvious clients for commercial or professional condominiums are those who can project and visualize their operations predicting the need for a specific location for a fixed period of years. Some professional groups will be permanent occupants of an area irrespective of how the community evolves, and will have little interest in whether the suburbs prosper or how many of their clients relocate there. By contrast, relatively few businesses are quite this independent of location.

Businessmen and professionals alike are sensitive to the accessibility of their location. Proximity to major thoroughfares is usually an important factor in choosing a business condominium. Just as doctors favor proximity to hospitals, some service-oriented businesses must consider accessibility to airports or other frequented places as a factor of location. Industrial parks are in the same category, with traveling executive personnel.

As present economic trends continue, location will increase in importance to business and industry. The in-fill policies of many metropolitan areas which we mentioned in Chapter 8 will affect business condominiums, just as they will greatly increase the development of residential condominiums. Energy shortages and rising fuel costs affect business and industry directly, and it is a fallacy to assume that these costs will be completely absorbed by consumers, and that this absorption can be accomplished quickly.

Conversion of a building's use can be an important factor in the logic of establishing condominiums. We have mentioned renovation of older office buildings that can be and often are converted to capitalize on special aspects of location. Investment, legal and accounting firms, for example, may be attracted to converted, reconditioned office space near the banking and lending institutions with which they deal.

How to Structure the Sale and Locate the Buyers

Prospective buyers of business condominiums have in common their ability to project their needs for space over long periods of time. Most are substantial members of the community who probably have had some experience in syndications or limited partnerships involving passive investments in real estate. The most obvious purchasers for office condominiums are:

- doctors,
- lawyers,
- accountants,
- investment advisors, and
- real estate entrepreneurs.

These professional people are conditioned to purchasing only a fraction or a small percentage of investment properties. They can relate to the concept of the space they will physically occupy in their professional activities, and can readily see that buying a business condominium achieves the same objectives as their other types of real estate investment.

The risks of condominium ownership are considerably less than those found in limited partnerships, since the purchaser actually holds title to his space and has an active say in the managment. If a complex develops financial problems or goes into foreclosure, the individual condominium owner can protect his investment by remaining current with the first mortgage lender and paying his prorated share of the common charges. Transfer of shares in a limited partnership is complicated by the requirement that the general partner must approve the transfer, whereas the owner of a condominium who outgrows his space or no longer occupies it is free to sell at any time the market is right.

I am currently developing a $3 million residential condominium project in which the limited partners are given an option to exchange their partnership equity and the profits derived from the venture tax-free for one of the finished condominium units. This concept is being applied to commercial condominiums as well, and is an extremely strong inducement for potential investors.

How to Analyze the Typical Space Requirements

The largest potential market for office condominiums, as we have mentioned before, consists of professional people. The typical office condominium suite runs in the area of 1,000 to 1,500 square feet (excluding common areas), about what is needed for a small professional operation. Often, these individuals acquire space over their current needs for investment purposes. In addition to assuring flexibility as their requirements change, this space can be subdivided, leased or resold at a later date.

Any small- to medium-sized businessman who examines his rent receipts over a period of time realizes that he has had to share a percentage of his profits with his landlord as escalation clauses were implemented. Purchasing a business condominium means greater independence of operation without the usual proration of profits going to the landlord. Furthermore, condominium projects can be structured to insure that well-established local firms have room for expanding their operations later. Like the professionals, these firms often buy in excess of their needs and sublease.

Several years ago I sold part of a ground floor office complex to a retail user, who in turn subleased 800 square feet of the space to a hairdresser. The special tenant improvements that he incorporated into the suite were quite extensive and were depreciable on a short-term basis. The corresponding cash flow that the owner received from renting the improved space was phenomenal. He found that the rent combined with the unusual tax advantages made this an extremely lucrative investment.

How the Buyers Profit from Inflation

Early in the 1970's, when inflation was not a major factor, long-term leases were executed with direct pass-through costs only, and not tied to the cost of living indexes that are now prevalent. Newer accounting practices require that long-term leases be footnoted on corporate balance sheets, and many progressive companies find that the long-term mortgages associated with condominium ownership provide a better hedge against inflation than do the more traditional long-term leases. Property has a tendency to appreciate in value the longer one holds it, as we often mentioned, while a lease commitment often depreciates the closer one gets to the end of that fixed obligation. Despite the validity of these concepts, the seller of condominiums often meets resistance from potential buyers who cling to the concept that leasing provides more flexibility.

In every commercial condominium project with which I have been associated, the key selling point has been the potential for long-term occupancy at a relatively low and stable cost. While the tax factors and appreciation can be important, the bottom line seems to be the sum total of the annualized payments. Curiously, the major national corporations have been the slowest in appreciating this new dimension of cost stability. Because of the rent concessions they can command in office complexes, they continue to abide by the theory that they can obtain more flexibility by shifting operations as their leases expire. Without question, such firms are less susceptible to the pride of ownership concept which we have mentioned previously as a characteristic of the local professional market.

One of the strongest selling features is the relative constancy of the monthly mortgage payment that one can expect over the duration of a 25- to 30-year obligation. This payment normally accounts for close to 50% of the monthly commitment, and the variable expenses for janitorial services, utilities, taxes, maintenance, and insurance make up the balance. This combination permits a fairly accurate prediction when compared to dealing with landlords who lock into predetermined rent escalation clauses with their leases. As any tenant knows, the relationship between rent increases and a landlord's actual cash outlay is usually arbitrary at best. I recently structured a 20,000 square-foot office condominium where the stabilized rent over a 25-year period was so low that the presentation had to be carefully explained to gain credibility. A detailed analysis of the Southwest Plaza project is found at the end of the chapter.

The After-Tax Advantages of Condominium Ownership

Assuring a long-term 50% constancy of monthly payments through the mortgage vehicle may not be a strong enough selling point for some potential purchasers of business condominiums. The interest, property tax, and depreciation or cost recovery deductions that one derives from direct ownership are a more important advantage. Often these exceed the normal rent that one would receive, and can be used to offset other ordinary individual or corporate income. This factor increases in importance as you deal with individuals or corporations in the higher tax brackets. That is why I gear my projections and developments toward purchasers in the 50% tax bracket. This is the maximum that corporations are obligated for, as well as a close approximation of the range at which individual purchasers are attracted.

The potential purchasers of professional condominiums plan to occupy space for considerable periods of time, and normally they have preconceived ideas on how to utilize their space. The earlier you contact potential purchasers, the easier it is to determine the space utilization in anticipation of the semi-permanent tenant improve-ments. Although these improvements can be quite costly, especially in the professional market, they can be depreciated quickly, especially under the Tax Act of 1981, often in as little as five years. (This is the current situation with professional equipment.) Other advantages to the potential purchasers consist of:

- depreciation of the shell space and improvements;
- the deduction of the interest on the mortgage;
- deductions for operating expenses; and
- the potential for long-term appreciation taxed at capital gains rates.

With depreciation representing a large factor in the overall picture, the purchaser of a condominium gains another advantage in not having to acquire a major piece of land. His percentage of this undepreciable asset is linked to his percentage of ownership of the building. Constructing a condominium on leased land eliminates even more of a purchaser's up-front costs and allows him to deduct land lease payments in much the same way he would expense rent on a conventional office complex.

FIGURE 13-1

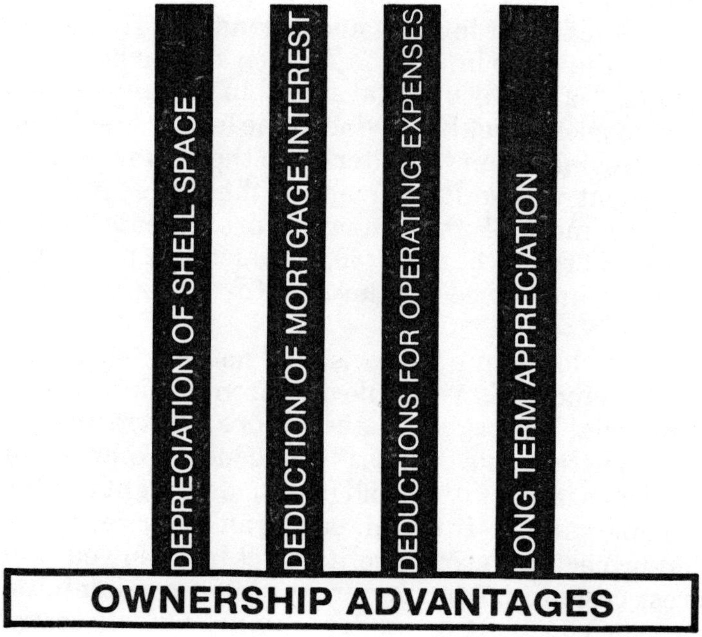

DEPRECIATION OF SHELL SPACE
DEDUCTION OF MORTGAGE INTEREST
DEDUCTIONS FOR OPERATING EXPENSES
LONG TERM APPRECIATION

OWNERSHIP ADVANTAGES

Several years ago, I developed a condominium office complex on land leased from a lending institution. The land under the buildings was packaged on a prepaid lease, and the parking lot was constructed by and leased for 99 years from the savings and loan. The value of the parking lot and improvements was subordinated by the lending institution to the first mortgage. Because of this unique provision, I was able to obtain an appraisal of $2,600,000, encompassing both the buildings and the parking lot. The inflated appraisal enabled the potential buyers of the condominium units to receive financing that averaged 85% to 90% of the purchase price, a great attraction to those interested in maximizing their leverage.

Structuring Low Down Payments in Highly Leveraged Situations

Among the categories of potential buyers of business condominiums, professionals are particularly attracted by the degree of leverage they can often attain. When down payments range in the area of 20% to 25% and appreciation is predictable at 10% to 15% per annum, a purchaser's equity can potentially be returned in a two-year period, through the inflationary process.

Several years ago, I arranged the financing for the purchaser of a condominium unit that I had developed. The same lending institution handled both interim and permanent financing, with a fixed rate on the interim and a higher at-market rate on the permanent loan—a highly unusual situation. An upward movement in the money market quickly convinced the lender to shift as much of his funds as possible from the interim to the permanent financing. The arrangement was so lucrative that the lender included in the purchase price most of the tenant improvements and financed approximately $115,000 of the $130,000 purchase price. My excited buyer was duly impressed by the 90% financing which had been achieved.

Business condominium projects tend not to be successful unless prearranged financing is available at reasonable interest rates. The range of financial packages is much more limited than those for residential condominiums because the secondary market for selling commercial loans is less liquid, and in periods of tight funding can be virtually nonexistent. Interim carrying charges on a newly constructed project can erode profits quickly when you cannot shift your interest costs to potential purchasers of condominium space. For this reason, construction lenders require presale commitments during periods of tight money which can often be detrimental.

These presale requirements are particularly restrictive to the developer whose commitments are often contingent upon loose arrangements with potential purchasers obtained during the conceiving stage of his project. If the presales requirement is not met in a timely fashion, those purchasers the developer thinks he has pocketed are likely to drift off and find alternative space.

The condominium office complex I recently developed with a lending institution certainly optimized my efforts and equity position. As a partner, the lender could not maintain the detachment traditional to the normal lending role. In this instance, the lender had the incentive to provide permanent financing and close it quickly in order to make the project viable.

How to Maximize the Salable Space

Allocation of common areas is not a major factor in the development of residential condominiums; however, it generally plays a critical role in the development of the professional condominium. A well-designed project will provide flexibility and maximum utilization of space without excessive costs in providing and maintaining common areas. This is often not the case in converting older office buildings, especially those built in the early part of the century. The massive corridors, atriums, elevator shafts and large open stairwells which contribute so much to their atmosphere are all common areas which must be maintained by owner-occupants when these buildings are converted to condominiums. Even though common area expenses are normally built into standard tenant leases, the concept of paying a percentage of the cost of common areas can be difficult for the potential purchaser of an office condominium to understand. Professional people, in particular, resent the additional 10% to 15% they must invest in order to cover their prorated share of hallways, lavatories, entryways, and other common facilities.

I recently developed an office condominium in which a preconceived number of restroom facilities were a part of the preliminary plans. I had initially thought that the building would appeal to sales-oriented people who would be spending most of their time out of the office. As the project progressed, it became apparent that more clerical people would physically be occupying the space. Due to the change in composition, the building inspection department of the municipality required that I install an additional set of toilet facilities. This change in plans increased the costs which had to be passed on and allocated to the purchasers. While justifying this cost increase was relatively simple because of the building inspection requirements, the incident is typical of the cost aggrandizements a developer must face and defend in his selling process.

Experiences such as the one I have just related indicate the extreme care you must take in selecting an older downtown building for conversion into office condominiums. I have found that such structures must be purchased at substantial discounts if they are to be profitable. Advantages of location in the older buildings are not outweighed by the costs of maintaining common areas, together with the limited flexibility of redesigning floor plans for expansion and the additional difficulties one may encounter in providing ample and accessible parking.

What older buildings do obviate is the long lead time required for new construction. We will elaborate later on the combined effects of lead time and presale requirements. By comparison with converted downtown buildings, most new condominium construction is in suburban areas where less expensive land permits low-rise, less costly construction.

How to Price Professional Condominiums Profitably

The cost of the land and construction of the shell of any condominium building can be determined early in the development stage. This base sales price can easily be refined by incorporating the costs of such standard items as:

- walls,
- partitions,
- doors,
- floor and window coverings,
- acoustical ceilings, and
- standard electrical outlets.

With a general idea of the market you intend to research, you as the developer can then project costs of the owner improvements with reasonable accuracy. Your major exposure from the development standpoint is the element which we stressed early in this chapter, the allocation of the development costs for the common areas.

Until one specific floor, or in remote instances, even the entire building is sold out, the developer does not know what percentage of the building (corridors, entryways, restrooms) will be allocated to common areas. The guesswork involved in prorating common costs among a multitude of occupants is obviously minimized as the total number is reduced. Space must be reserved and sold at prices contingent upon allocation of common costs when the building is fully occupied. Sometimes this final determination results in raising the overall purchase price considerably. When this happens without strong evidence of justification, you can lose your credibility and your potential buyers to other projects quickly. In the last office condominium project I developed, I quoted a base price for the shell and a $10 per-square-foot allowance for interior improvements. Many purchasers had special requirements and exceeded the allowable figure; however, this approach permitted me to successfully correlate and monitor my costs and sales prices throughout the project.

How to Effectively Manage a Professional Condominium

Early in this chapter we discussed conversion as a concept which minimizes the demands on a developer's managerial talents. Obviously, you must have the ability to conceive a project in the first place and bring it to a conclusion, but sometimes you cannot bow out as quickly as you would like.

People acquiring quality condominium space expect first-rate management. A great deal of diplomacy is often involved in convincing them that they must pay for the high level of services they demand. You, as the developer, normally have to subsidize the condominium management during the construction and sellout phases. You must also structure the bylaws and covenants, conditions and restrictions of the owner's association so that the eventual management can be turned over to a representative of the owners when a project reaches approximately 80% to 90% of completed sales.

The beginnings of management are in the covenants, conditions and restrictions. They must specify that you will continue to manage the project until a certain predetermined percentage of sales is achieved. This is normally accomplished with a combination of Class A and Class B stock, one owned by you, the developing entity, and the other owned by the purchasers. The developer's stock entitles you to a disproportionate number of votes per share. When the number of votes is equalized through sales, the developer relinquishes the management to a professional group hired by the owners' association.

This method of stock distribution permits you to retain control over the project from its inception to its completion. It gives you complete flexibility over the type of people to whom you wish to sell and over those to whom a buyer can initially sublet. Midway through the sales of an office condominium complex that I developed, I acquired a tenant for 7,000 square feet on the condition that no other occupant in this building could offer the services and products specific to this major national firm. Because I had reserved control through weighted stock, I was able to insert an exclusionary clause into the condominium documents even after a sale had been achieved. Because the tenant was so prestigious, I purchased the space myself.

Management of a professional condominium can be both lucrative and extremely complicated. It can be so profitable that statutes in many states regulate the period of time a developer can lock himself into a management contract. Complications of management most often arise when highly technical and expensive equipment is jointly used by a number of the owners within the structure. The X-ray rooms and clinical laboratories of medical and dental condominium structures, for instance, pose special management problems beyond the expertise of most developers.

Controlling the Occupant Mix by Restrictive Covenants

Occupants of professional condominiums sometimes demand exclusivity which can constitute a sales deterrent within a project. To overcome this, you can segment a portion of your structure, restricting the purchase of certain designated floors or areas. Within a complex, you may also designate certain buildings for specific uses. Some percentage of the restricted space is usually designed "for general office use" or "for limited commercial or retail usage." This accomplishes the goal of giving you some flexibility in your sales. Exclusivity clauses are particularly prevalent in first-rate condominium projects where sales efforts are geared to assure potential purchasers that a building will be sold and maintained in relative conformity to the uses of the occupants.

I draft my condominium documents carefully, with special consideration given to two factors:

1. to assure conformity of occupancy with existing zoning regulations and potential clients; and
2. to define the limited categories of usage, such as retail, office, industrial, commercial, etc.

Doing this gives me the initial flexibility of selling to individuals I find desirable, and also permits me to tighten up the restrictions toward the latter part of the project so that I can assure harmonious occupancy by all owners.

In addition to exclusivity clauses, the documents for many business condominiums also restrict leasing of excess space. Tight restrictions on subleasing can create major problems at a later date, particularly after the developer relinquishes the management of the project. Without his weighted vote, amending the bylaws and declarations requires a majority vote of the owners, which can be very difficult and time-consuming to obtain.

To assure some degree of harmonious coexistence among the purchasers of my condominium units, I insert a clause in my covenants, conditions and restrictions giving the owners within the complex the right of first refusal to purchase any space being sold by one of the unit owners. This permits members of the existing owners' association either to utilize the space themselves for expansion or to purchase it and resell to a congenial buyer with interests similar to their own.

How to Handle Utility Prorations and Reserves for Replacement

Unless the problem of utility proration is addressed during the initial sales period of a business condominium, this issue will inevitably surface when utility prices rise, and perpetuate itself at each increase. With a mixed tenancy encompassing, for example, a computer-oriented firm with an extremely high load factor and a conventional type of office operation with a limited amount of use, the proration of utilities in a condominium operation can become extremely complicated. If high consumers cannot be metered separately and the general office users cannot be prorated on a square-foot basis, it is essential to have some initial understanding about prorating and submetering. I encountered such a problem in an office complex with mixed occupancy. A governmental agency occupied a sizable share of the structure which housed the computer system for its entire operation of 4,000 employees. The cost of the electrical prorations became so disproportionate to the other occupants of the structure that separate meters had to be installed for the computer operation in order to keep harmony within the building.

In commercial structures, unlike residential units where much of the mechanical equipment is owned by individual occupants, the failure of a major piece of equipment, such as a heating or air conditioning unit, can be quite expensive to all the condominium owners. For that reason, a portion of the monthly assessment to the owners' association should be allocated as a cushion or reserve for replacement to be augmented over the years. Establishing an emergency fund is simpler than raising the thousands of dollars that may be needed to replace a major piece of mechanical equipment by a one-time assessment. This fund should commence with the initial occupancy and be funded at a minimum, in my judgment, of 1% of the annual gross income generated from the building. Calculating this can be difficult when you are selling, not leasing, the units, but a pro forma projection of potential rents is normally adequate to establish the needed basis.

Exciting Profit Opportunities in Industrial Condominiums

A substantial market for condominiums exists among industrial firms, but the market is small by comparison with that for office or residential developments, and requires a sophisticated analysis. The prototype buyer is normally a light manufacturing company, such as an electronics firm, without large capital investment in equipment or inventory. For such firms, recycling profits by purchasing condominiums in attractive industrial parks makes economic sense.

One of the reasons for distinguishing between office or professional condominiums and those sold to industrial firms is the space requirement. While the normal professional or business operation can be conducted in 1,000 to 1,500 square feet, industrial operations usually require substantially more space. Many users of industrial condominiums occupy as much as 10,000 to 15,000 square feet.

On the one hand, constructing an industrial condominium for sale in a developing area involves relatively few buyers who purchase proportionately more space than in the office or professional market. On the other hand, selling industrial condominiums is a sophisticated business requiring detailed knowledge of the industrial base of a community. The developer who enters this field without previous experience may well have to revert to real estate brokers specializing in industrial listings who maintain close contact with these clients.

More appropriate to the developer seeking diversity of operation is a new concept emerging all over the country. Shell space for manufacturing or industrial warehousing is combined with a proportionally small more visual office or clerical area. These developments offer space considerably smaller than that found in conventional industrial condominiums, and it is not uncommon for occupants to require only 2,000 to 3,000 square feet. Meeting these special requirements through proper merchandising enables you to obtain an extremely high sales price per square foot by comparison with that charged for the average industrial condominium building.

An associate of mine is developing such complexes in a half-dozen major cities. He initially contemplates rental units, taking the appropriate depreciation during the early years and retaining the option to convert to condominiums when the initial leases expire. His lenders generally take an equity position in these complexes and are following him from project to project.

In relation to residential condominiums, industrial developments can be quite speculative. Demand and available financing can vary considerably. These projects must be planned, timed, and merchandised during economic upswings, since they can conceivably stand unoccupied for extended periods if they are developed during recessionary times.

A close working relationship with the interim lender is indispensable for a successful development of industrial condominiums. The precision with which sales must be timed, especially during down markets, often requires that the space be leased on a temporary basis to tenants who are given a purchase option when the economic picture brightens. This flexible arrangement has been the salvation of many industrial condominium projects, and should be built into any developer's plan.

On the whole, the demand for industrial space cannot be projected as accurately as that for office use. To compound the difficulties in selling industrial condominiums, the resale market for them is not as broad as one finds in the office segment. Skillful salesmanship and detailed market knowledge are necessary to convince the potential purchasers that appreciation will work to their advantage even if the resale process is slow.

Capitalizing on Large Condominium Projects

We introduced this chapter by commenting on the similarities of all condominium projects, be they residential or commercial. Just as developing a small business condominium requires somewhat more sophistication than its residential counterpart, so the need for experience and financial staying power increases with the size of the development. The economics of scale prevail in any project, with larger projects producing wider profit margins.

The complexities of developing a major condominium venture can extend its completion through an entire economic cycle, sometimes leaving a surplus and expensive inventory at the wrong end of the cycle. The disastrous effect of such timing can be compounded when presale requirements are attached to the interim financing. Sales evaporate as interest rates rise, and, additionally, the developer's costs have a way of being uncontrollable when the inflationary spiral nears its peak. Under these circumstances, what initially seemed an interesting and lucrative project can often turn into a long-term unproductive holding, cancelling out the initial profitability of the development.

When you anticipate entering the business or professional condominium market, you must fully comprehend the risks. With the full understanding that the domino effect works both ways, you must decide whether the 10% or 15% in additional profits that you can achieve in a larger project are worth the substantial risks entailed in the increased economics of scale. One of the methods I use to circumvent a lender's presale requirements is to locate an investor who will purchase a block of the space when I deliver executed leases at predetermined and profitable levels. This leaves me the option to cancel the arrangement if the prevailing circumstances warrant selling the space to an owner-user at a higher price. As an additional hedge, I attempt to obtain a long-term commitment on a portion of the condominium space for myself, either as a means of providing a vehicle for occupancy if sales do not materialize, or as a long-term investment should the appropriate tenant surface. In a recent building that I was converting to condominiums, a major national corporation offered to lease approximately one-third of the structure on a five-year basis with options to renew. Given the valuable nature of this lease, I immediately executed it and closed on the space.

How to Tailor the Investment Package

Although developers seek out investors for in-and-out sales like the one just described, the vast majority of purchasers of business condominiums have a long-term vested interest in what they are acquiring and occupying. They opt for permanence of location rather than mobility, and are understandably selective about their physical requirements. Just as you, the developer, must project their needs into your building and help them visualize and refine their preconceptions, you must similarly zero in on the financial position of your prospective client in order to understand his investment requirements. As we have so often mentioned before, no two investors have exactly the same needs, and the after-tax ramifications must be projected on an individual basis.

The format following in Figure 13-2 was prepared for my use on a recent condominium project by a certified public accountant. The basic guidelines utilize a typical suite of 1,000 square feet with a 25-year life of the asset. The depreciable life of this asset could be shortened to 15 years under the Economic Recovery Tax Act of 1981, showing substantially more after-tax benefits. With this presentation, it becomes readily apparent how a high degree of leverage combines with relatively fixed and constant operating costs to work to the advantage of an owner as compared to a renter. Adding an annual 5% appreciation factor over a 25-year holding period is frosting on the cake.

For purposes of brevity, year 1, years 1 through 5, and years 21 through 25 are illustrated.

The bottom line represents an after-tax per-square-foot rental of $7.33 at the end of 25 years. This building is approximately 4 years old, and the current rentals on the non-owner-occupied space already considerably exceed that projected 25-year rental figure. Operating expenses were adjusted upward to reflect the then current conditions.

I literally found this presentation irresistible. The longer I studied the figures as I started to convert the building to condominiums, the more attractive they became. After selling a relatively small portion, I decided to keep the balance of the structure myself as a rental unit. I knew that my sense for a lucrative investment had not failed me when I obtained a major American corporation as one of the prime tenants in the rental space I had reserved.

Most successful projects are conceived through careful market analysis. What often stands out in the prospectus on projects that don't materialize is the lack of depth of the market analysis or the developer's overly optimistic thinking. Some faultily conceived projects do find their way into the mainstream of development, and many of those that are well-conceived still fall victim to catastrophes that could not have been easily predicted. These combine to create a category of "distressed" holdings which are particularly attractive to the most speculative and sophisticated of developers. We will discuss the opportunities and risks in the following chapter.

FIGURE 13-2
Southwest Plaza
Pro Forma Twenty-Five Year Cash Forecast
Cost of Ownership and Operation—1000 Square Feet of Office Space

	YEAR 1	YEARS 1 thru 5	YEARS 21 thru 25
CASH FLOW			
Assuming $50,000.00 purchase price; 20% down payment; 9½% interest rate; 25 year financing:			
Mortgage payments	$ 4,194.00	$20,969.00	$20,969.00
Management fee	210.00	1,160.00	3,078.00
Real estate taxes	350.00	1,934.00	5,130.00
Insurance	76.00	420.00	1,114.00
Janitorial service	450.00	2,486.00	6,598.00
Parking lease	390.00	2,155.00	5,719.00
Elevator maintenance	10.00	56.00	146.00
Utilities	1,050.00	5,802.00	15,394.00
Exterior maintenance	100.00	552.00	1,466.00
Total Cash Flow	6,830.00	35,534.00	59,614.00
CASH SAVINGS— TAX DEDUCTIONS	(5,099.00)	(24,020.00)	(22,951.00)
Net Cash Cost	$1,731.00	$11,514.00	$36,663.00
TAX DEDUCTIONS			
Mortgage interest	$3,782.00	$18,460.00	$ 4,326.00
Depreciation – building	2,280.00	10,110.00	2,931.00
Depreciation – improvements	1,500.00	4,905.00	–
Expenses	2,636.00	14,565.00	38,645.00
Total	10,198.00	48,040.00	45,902.00
Cash savings (assuming 50% tax brackets)	$5,099.00	$24,020.00	$22,951.00
AVERAGE SQUARE FOOT COST PER YEAR			
Investor's rental cost per year after tax	$ 1.73	$ 2.30	$ 7.33
After tax cost per square foot adjusted for equity buildup – 5% per year	$ 1.32	$ 1.80	$ 4.01
Investor's square foot rental cost based on 12% return on $10,000.00 investment (assuming 50% tax bracket)	$ 1.92	$ 2.40	$ 4.61
Equity – land, buildings, improvements	$10,411.42	$12,508.00	$ 50,000.00
Replacement cost increase	$52,500.00	$63,814.00	$169,318.00

14

Profiting from Distressed Property

Any property experiencing financial difficulty is said to be "distressed," and almost all distressed properties look like bargains, whatever little else they may have in common. A developer who steps into an existing project and rescues it from financial oblivion is said to achieve a turnaround. Most of these workouts are lucrative and memorable, but not every troubled project is a candidate for the legerdemain that a turnaround requires.

Like any other industry, real estate has its fund of Horatio Alger stories. The majority of these involve workouts. Much has been written about rescuing distressed properties and the quick return to be gained. As tempting as it is to repeat these success stories, this chapter is precautionary. Some properties are sows' ears that, for various reasons, won't be turned into silk purses.

This chapter will stress the underlying reasons for distressed properties, how to analyze them, and why timing and financial staying power are so important. Step by step the chapter will show you how to locate, acquire and successfully negotiate favorable prices on financially troubled investments. You will learn how to overcome management problems, how to cope with the intricate legal ramifications commonly found in foreclosures, and how and when to profitably dispose of distressed merchandise.

271

The Underlying Reasons for Distressed Properties

A small percentage of properties were eccentrically conceived and will always remain unmarketable white elephants. Many others came into being as the result of faulty market analyses. Their developers did not properly analyze the amount of rent they could generate, the potential market absorption rates, or the competitiveness of the marketplace. An error in any one level can spell potential failure in an overbuilt area, especially when a product comes on the market toward the end of the upward aspect of an economic cycle.

I recently purchased a defunct 50-unit condominium project in which the original developer's costs for construction, land, and holding were far in excess of the total achievable sales value of the units. After a long-drawn-out foreclosure procedure lasting three years, I purchased the property for approximately thirty cents on the dollar. Since I acquired the complex at a reasonable level as a second owner, the inflation factor over the long foreclosure period added about 25% to the value of the units, and, on this basis, the condominium project eventually proved to be feasible.

You, as a prospective buyer of a distressed project, normally can learn a great deal about its long-term viability from the initial market feasibility study. These studies can help you determine whether the property has a realistic value in the current marketplace, and, given the current amount and nature of financing, whether it should be completed according to the original concept or converted to a higher and more lucrative use.

When the original market feasibility study is obviously defective, it is extremely important not simply to update it or to cover it over. Some years ago I was involved with a 200+ unit apartment complex that was being offered for sale by an REIT after foreclosure. An MAI appraisal and feasibility study were presented to me prior to my involvement. These documents did not reflect the local market conditions accurately. Even though the MAI appraiser was recognized nationally, he failed to fully understand that this project was located in a second-rate area, and could not achieve the rentals and occupancy levels that would justify his appraised value. This particular appraisal indicated an artificial value in excess of 25% of the actual fair market value, based upon this basic oversight. As a new or potential owner of a distressed property, you should bring in an independent consultant to determine if the market for your product still exists. For those people initially involved in a development which failed, many such ventures have acquired and retain the image of being perennial losers. A new projection of success is often essential to convince the existing lender and/or potential investors that the project has a bright future.

Conversely, more often than you might imagine, lenders refuse to admit that they are taking a financial loss on a given loan subsequently termed an investment. I discovered this recently in five houses that a savings and loan acquired after foreclosure, when the contractor went bankrupt. For purposes of audit, the lending institution did not want to show a loss on these units. By providing ample funds at less than market interest rates, the lender in effect subsidized the project in order to show a break-even situation, at least on its books.

Why Proper Timing is So Important

Many distressed properties are the victims of poor timing. As we mentioned previously, they come on the market toward the end of the upward swing of an economic cycle and are paralyzed in mid-occupancy or prior to completion by adverse economic conditions. Poor timing can result from various delays in construction or sales, but sophisticated developers can normally maneuver to minimize these untimely incidents. What even sophisticated developers frequently cannot outmaneuver is the insensitivity of their mortgage lenders during difficult times.

Financial institutions continue to operate by making profits for their stockholders and depositors. While their analyses of economic cycles may be sophisticated, they are often selective about the areas in which they continue to financially support a developer during periods of economic decline. As we mentioned earlier in this book, an entrepreneur backed by limited partners normally has more flexibility than one supported by most financial institutions. Too many well-conceived projects become distressed because of nervous bank auditors taking the short-range view of highly leveraged developments. At the other extreme, the real estate investment trust industry has a tendency to go through the wringer every time interest rates reach excessive levels. As a consequence, many of the larger distressed properties have fallen victim to the unwarranted panic of REITs and lending institution auditors.

It is also conceivable that lenders as well as developers can enter into bankruptcy. I acquired a condominium project on such a basis, where the original developer had presold 50% of the units in what was a viable project until the REIT that provided the interim financing went into reorganization. The initial developer was not in a position to refinance and salvage the project, and he himself went into bankruptcy. This gave me the opportunity, after long foreclosure proceedings, to acquire the assets of this condominium development at a level that was considerably less than their replacement value.

How to Overcome Management Problems

A third characteristic of distressed property is poor management, often the consequence of inexperience. Overcoming a project's reputation for second rate management can be a major challenge requiring both financial and psychological expertise. Two years ago, I offered to purchase an apartment complex consisting of 216 units that had been foreclosed on. My offer contained a contingency for obtaining interim financing and provided for the necessary exploratory time to analyze the project's operating expenses and tenant profiles. I found that a majority of the occupants were totally disenchanted with the complex and its management, to the point where the tenant turnover was three or four times that found at comparable units within the area. I initially intended to convert this apartment complex into a condominium; however, the past management's reputation would have outlived any conversion and would have been seriously detrimental to the eventual results of the conversion. I did not exercise my option to purchase this property, based solely on this factor.

It is not uncommon to acquire a distressed property that has been operational for extended periods of time under substandard management. The major reasons for defaults on existing properties often relate to:

- high maintenance expenses;
- financing in excess of the cash flow of the project;
- high vacancy rates;
- extreme tenant turnover;
- rentals considerably below market value;
- increasing costs of real estate taxes;
- utilities expenses that cannot be passed on to the tenants;
- excessive management turnover; and
- an overbuilt or highly competitive market.

Major Factors Contributing to Property Foreclosures

Many distressed properties are frequently offered for sale before they become completely operational. Among some reasons for their distress are the following:

- overextension by the developer;
- disagreement among the partners in a development;
- fraudulent acts by the developers where mortgage funds are diverted from the project;
- construction defects, and cost overruns;
- costly delays occasioned by actions of environmental and ecological groups; and
- lack of permanent financing commitments for either rental or for-sale projects.

The first of the items on the preceding list, financial overextension by the developer, is especially noteworthy. I recently looked at an apartment project in which the interest on the construction loan was based on a floating rate over the New York prime. At the apex, this rate was carrying an interest factor of 23%. The developer's projections assumed a maximum of 12% to 13% on his interim interest, and the extra 10% interest expense was the difference between the success or failure of the venture. Working on thin profit margins, as was the case in this project, is characteristic of many developers, who often do not account for the unknown contingencies which can lead to a disaster in a highly leveraged speculative situation.

How to Analyze a Turnaround Situation

Poor market analysis, faulty timing of economic cycles, financial overextension, and substandard management are all factors characterizing distressed projects. One or more of these characteristics can be expected when acquiring any troubled development. The decision to purchase must be preceded by close analysis of four critical areas:

1. The cash flow which the project generates must be adequate. In rental properties, positive rental income must be projected after operating expenses and debt service. In for-sale properties, the potential sales price must exceed the cost of acquiring and

completing the structure to allow for a realistic contingency and profit margin.

2. The potential for obtaining loans against a distressed property must be analyzed carefully against the reputation the property has acquired. Both interim loans for acquistion and completion and permanent funding must be considered.

3. As a potential purchaser, you must accurately predict your deficiency of income during the turnaround process. This can be the most complicated aspect to project and can play the biggest role in whether a potential acquisition will be profitable from the developer's standpoint.

4. The wholesale value of the project must be determined and fully substantiated, permitting you, the potential purchaser, to cut your losses in the event that you are not successful in turning around the distressed investment. This often takes either the form of minimal rentals that will assure a respectable level of occupancy, or the value of the brick and mortar reproduction cost that could be obtained on the wholesale market should the project have to be aborted. In this connection, it is also imperative to determine the most advantageous time to dispose of a property, should this be necessary. We will consider the timing of the resale in detail later in this chapter.

How to Spot Turnover and Maintenance Problems

Various means exist by which the extent of a property's distress can be measured. One barometer, for example, is tenant turnover in rental units, which can sometimes be as high as 30% or 40% per annum. This factor must be analyzed in relation to existing income in the project and competing rents in the immediate area. Rentals must then be weighed against the current occupancy rate to determine what the upside potential actually is.

An on-site inspection is always a prerequisite to determine the quality of a project's physical condition and, even more important, the extent to which maintenance has been deferred for such items as:

- mechanical equipment;
- faulty electrical systems;
- interior and exterior painting;
- structural defects;
- substandard plumbing; and
- parking lots and landscaping.

All such factors and a multitude of other one-time expenditures can contribute to the major expense of bringing a substandard building up to a level that is lucrative and operational.

Finally, it is critical not to underestimate the cost of establishing effective management for a formerly distressed property and budgeting ample funds for the necessary promotion and advertising, especially during the sellout or lease-up stages. Management and advertising costs in turning around a distressed development can sometimes be four to five times those normally expensed for viable operating real estate projects. I have found that every time I have acquired a distressed property, a completely new management team must be brought in, including on-site managers, in order for the project to be successful. In all my experience I have never been convinced that an existing management, which normally is incapable and underfinanced, has the ability to create the new image that will be necessary to turn a project around. Most financially troubled developments, especially those run by lending institutions during periods of foreclosure, install minimal management people, strictly as a holding pattern.

When to Advantageously Acquire Distressed Properties

Troubled properties must be acquired in downward economic cycles, when interest rates are high and demand is so low that few individuals or corporations are in a position to acquire property. These properties then must be disposed of during upward cycles, when mortgage financing is plentiful and optimism prevails. Most distressed developments surface in the marketplace during the lower part of the downward cycle, many months or even years after they fall into delinquency, foreclosure or bankruptcy. Obviously, dealing in distressed property is highly speculative. Not the least of the demands upon you, the developer, is analyzing economic cycles carefully in order to determine whether you have the capabilities to weather these cyclic storms. In addition, turning a distressed property around means weighing your overall commitments to determine that other investments will not suffer or deteriorate during the critical periods when a distressed project demands your undivided attention.

Distressed properties require an extraordinary commitment of time—through the processes of acquisition, redevelopment, and eventual disposition. They are simply difficult to manage and merchandise. In addition to having the background and expertise, you must have ample risk capital or be in a position to syndicate if you wish to speculate in distressed property, as what might look like an initial short-term commitment can often turn into an extended nightmare of construction and management headaches.

Many lenders require additional equity funds for hidden contingencies when committing on turnaround properties, especially if the project has been unoccupied for long periods of time. I recently acquired a distressed condominium development in which the interim lender required that I syndicate $250,000 before making a construction loan in the amount of $1,300,000. In addition, the bank dictated that a certificate of deposit for an additional $200,000 be placed in escrow in the event that there were any cost overruns that could not be covered by the construction loan. With those two conditions met, the lender financed the balance of the project. The limited partners and I showed a sizable profit even with this unusually restrictive equity requirement, by acquiring the property at a bargain price.

Maintaining Credibility with Lenders During the Workout Period

Close coordination and updated briefings with either the limited partners or lending institutions are a requirement with distressed projects. Those contributing to the financing must understand that they can be potentially committed on a contingency basis if the development materializes slowly, and that they might be obligated for the additional funding required for completion. I have had to return to lending institutions from time to time to obtain additional funding because of underestimation of construction costs, sales, or construction time. Rarely have I encountered problems in obtaining the additional funds because I have kept the lenders abreast of the problems and have informed them of the development's progress.

When speculating in distressed property, you must take extraordinary pains to preserve your credibility, not only with lenders and investors, but also with your tenants or potential buyers. If concrete positive results are not quickly produced with distressed property, the developer's reputation can also shrink quite rapidly.

Some time ago, I encountered a minor cash-flow problem on a foreclosed condominium project that I purchased from the interim lender. I initially set up a predetermined release schedule with the lending institution where 90% of the proceeds from the sale of the units would be applied against the interim loan. This unique release provision corresponded to an extremely leveraged interim loan on the project. Some minor cost overrruns developed, which meant that more of the initial sales prices of the units had to be allocated towards the construction costs and less to the interim lender. The overruns were not sizable, and the interim lender fully understood that by restructuring his repayment schedule he still retained ample protection on his construction mortgage. He quite willingly adjusted his per-unit release figure to facilitate paying for those additional construction expenses.

Locating Distressed Real Estate

Bad news travels fast in an industry looking for bargains, and locating distressed property is usually the easiest part of the process. A well-recognized summary source, for instance, which analyzes and categorizes all distressed property held by the real estate investment trust industry is published by Audit Investment Research, Inc. of New York. Additional sources are banks which are holding substandard loans; local management companies which are operating properties under limited budgets and are seeking potential purchasers in order to perpetuate their management contracts; local tax assessors who have lists of properties not current on the municipal tax rolls; architects and engineers who have not been paid for their services; and contractors who have liened projects and are looking for substitute owners in order to receive full compensation. Qualified real estate brokers are often finely tuned to the market and can keep you, as a potential investor, fully aware of all the interesting opportunities.

Some of my most interesting and rewarding projects involved considerable new construction and were brought to me by architects and contractors anxious to recoup the time and funds that they had invested in these initially shaky developments. I recently took over a defunct condominium project where I advanced no compensation to the architectural firm initially, but paid a fee of $750 as each unit was sold. When the entire venture was completed, the architect received 100% of his original contract amount through this mutually beneficial arrangement.

How to Negotiate for Distressed Properties

Owners of troubled developments, quite naturally, are optimistic about their efforts to salvage as much as possible, and seldom evaluate their holdings realistically. Unwilling to sustain major equity losses, they tend to play several investors, many of them marginal, against each other. For these reasons, negotiations with banks or lending institutions holding first liens are usually more fruitful than those with the owners directly. Rather than foreclose, most lending institutions prefer to find a substantial replacement investor with the financial resources, managerial ability, and turnaround expertise to protect their interests.

When a financial institution locates the right individual, it will often subsidize him by placing a moratorium on interest and principal payments for its loan or by advancing him the appropriate funds for completion of the project until sales or rentals make it viable. In many instances, the combination of these moratoriums and the additional capital injected by the lending institution are sufficient to generate profits larger than the average conventional developer even dreams of. Lucrative alternative arrangements can take the form of management or consulting fees, exclusive brokerage or marketing commissions, with an option to participate in either the cash flow from the project or the profits from the eventual sale. The workout specialist can often obtain an option to purchase the entire project or an equity position in it once the turnaround process has been successfully initiated, without investing any up-front equity.

A bank recently approached me on acquiring a 16-unit first phase of a condominium project which was going through foreclosure. Because I had worked with this institution previously on one other distressed property, they felt comfortable giving me the funds to complete the development in a fashion that would permit them to recoup a substantial portion of their investment. The bank had ample protection, as a tract of land adjacent to the condominium project was subordinated to their first mortgage. I could not come to terms with the landowner for the remaining phases at a price I considered appropriate to achieve a respectable profit on the full completion of the development. Nonetheless, the lending institution was satisfied that a sophisticated developer had examined the project and concluded that the value of the first mortgage was amply protected. The landowner eventually acquired the project in order to protect his equity.

The Legal Aspects of Acquiring Distressed Properties

Reviewing the legal problems accompanying the acquisition of a distressed property can be a major undertaking. The number of liens, their dollar value, and the rights of these lienholders must obviously be explored, as well as the stage which the foreclosure is in and the rights of redemption of the current owners. If a bankruptcy or reorganization of the owner is involved, a review of the appropriate laws is in order, since transfer of title can be complicated under such circumstances. Both foreclosure actions and bankruptcy proceedings consume considerable time, and such delays will affect the eventual closing and timing of the completion. I recently went through a three-way asset swap on a bankrupt development in which five legal firms were handling the various interests of the buying and selling parties. Several of the attorneys practiced exclusively in states outside of where the property was located. It took in excess of 60 days just to coordinate the closing activities and complications that arose through the foreclosure, bankruptcy and asset swap proceedings on this particular project.

Other elements can force costly and time-consuming delays such as reobtaining:

- building permits;
- ecological and environmental approvals;
- permanent or interim financing commitments;
- renegotiating with the various contractors;
- restructuring leases with major tenants;
- commitments from utilities companies;
- the renewability of title insurance policies.

A distressed project must be reviewed for these and a multitude of other problems contingent upon the time required for full satisfaction of these necessary legal obstacles.

How to Effectively Use Original Contractors on Foreclosed Property

One way of overcoming some of the delays and potential financial hazards is to check with the original general contractor or his subcontractors to determine if they are interested in and capable of completing the development. They will have a feel for the overall scope of the project and, with proper assurance of adequate funds, can expedite construction to completion more quickly than a newly retained firm not familiar with the project. They should, of course, be asked to provide warranties for completion of the work, which cannot generally be obtained when a new contractor is to take over and complete the work.

Some time back, I purchased out of foreclosure a property in which the list of the general and his subcontractor defendants was almost two pages long, encompassing 25 to 30 different lienholders. Of the many subcontractors I contacted relative to returning and finishing the work, most were so disenchanted with the initial developer and contractor that they refused even to discuss the matter. I considered myself very fortunate to obtain the services of two of the key subcontractors, the electrician and the plumber, who were able to complete the work on a more than satisfactory basis.

Taking Advantage of Asset Swaps

The real estate investment trust industry has experienced extraordinary difficulties because of marginal developers, the inflationary cycle, and extremely high and unprofitable—to the developer—short-term interest rates. No matter how strongly the real estate market continues to rebound, many of these trusts increasingly find that they do not have sufficient assets to fully repay their outstanding loans. Many lending institutions have made short-term loans to these trusts for construction purposes, and in the process have neglected to tie their first mortgages directly to the properties under construction. Normally the REITs assign shares of their common stock to collateralize these loans. In effect, many of the banks involved with these trusts are left holding worthless stock and invalid first liens when the REIT's construction loans go into foreclosure and they subsequently enter into three-way swap or debt forgiveness arrangements with developers who buy these properties at bargain prices.

I recently purchased a partially completed 126-unit condominium project located in the Southwest, which was originally financed through a commercial bank in California, and a real estate investment trust located in Florida. I offered the REIT 30 cents on the dollar for the property, and they negotiated with the California institution for debt foregiveness of the other 70%. I acquired the property for a bargain price, and the REIT negotiated its way out of loan indebtedness which, given its current insolvency, it could never repay. The bank, which was the eventual loser, got 30 cents on the dollar for what was considered totally worthless stock.

The foregoing example is typical of the swap and mortgage forgiveness arrangements by which distressed properties are being acquired from REITs. Lists of such available properties are easy to acquire, as mentioned previously.

Analyzing the Risk-Reward Aspects of Distressed Properties

Imagination, a good track record in marketing and management, and a financial statement showing stability and staying power are the key ingredients to purchasing distressed real estate. Rather than extracting the last drop of blood, offers for the acquisition of troubled properties are basically structured so that all those who survive can profit from the venture. The only losers are those who were washed out long before the restructured transaction closed.

Turning distressed real estate around is an art requiring a unique person or organization. A successful developer or contractor is not necessarily a successful workout specialist. The process requires special talents, primarily in marketing, advertising and promotion, since most distressed properties have already acquired poor reputations. Alternative budgets must be structured, incorporating various contingency plans in case more time and funding need to be available in order to improve a project's image. Underestimating a development's marketability and underbudgeting to compensate for deferred maintenance are the two primary areas of vulnerability.

Some time ago, I was involved in acquiring a foreclosed apartment complex in which deferred maintenance was primarily evident in the heating and air conditioning units, the recreation facilities, and the basic roof structure. The roof was the most glaring problem, on which it was literally impossible to obtain a realistic estimate of the replacement cost unless the contractor physically removed the top layer in order to estimate the damage that had been done to the supporting structure. There were 8 buildings in this complex, and all potentially needed to have their roof structures completely redone. My estimates on total replacement ranged from $75,000 to $200,000. These variations in ranges are not uncommon in major projects, and alternative budgets must be set up to cover these potentially catastrophic contingencies.

Both the owners of distressed properties and the lending institutions holding the financing are eager to minimize their losses, and it is often feasible to restructure the debt on a distressed property with the owner or the lending institution serving as the major interim or permanent lender. With a little imagination you can defer or waive amortization or interest, or discount the purchase price. Alternatives for restructuring the financing are shown in Figure 14-1.

FIGURE 14-1

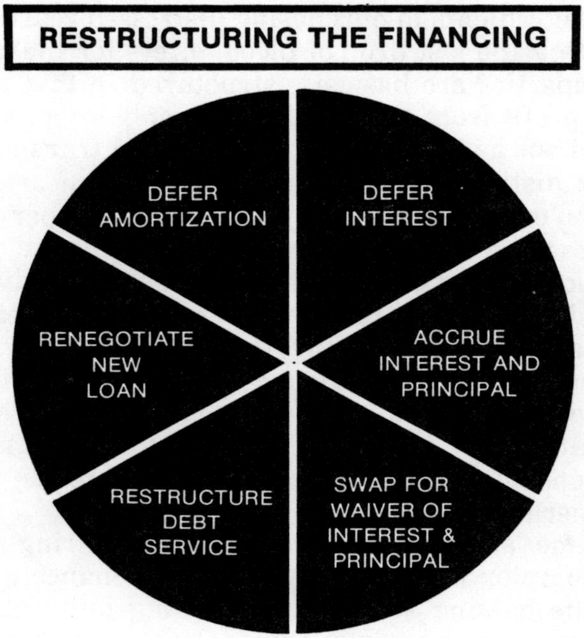

RESTRUCTURING THE FINANCING

DEFER AMORTIZATION

DEFER INTEREST

RENEGOTIATE NEW LOAN

ACCRUE INTEREST AND PRINCIPAL

RESTRUCTURE DEBT SERVICE

SWAP FOR WAIVER OF INTEREST & PRINCIPAL

How to Profitably Resell Distressed Properties

Troubled property attracts bargain hunters all the way down the line, not just at the development level. Pricing these properties for resale involves intricate market timing. Just as properties are profitably acquired when markets are weak during downturns in the economic cycle, so they should be sold when market conditions improve and higher prices prevail. Improving the tarnished images of distressed properties requires financial staying power, and often sizable funds to correct costly structural, mechanical, and electrical problems. When for-sale housing is involved, you, as the developer, must often give extensive and costly warranties to potential purchasers in order to attract them. These warranties can be quite tricky, and if not properly structured, costly. As an example, I acquired a defunct condominium project in which the warranties for the appliances, the roof, and the heating and air conditioning systems had expired due to the lengthy foreclosure proceedings. I found it virtually impossible to merchandise these units unless I provided the purchasers with the normal warranty, which I could not obtain from the initial manufacturers or the general contractor. I had to provide that complete warranty in order to facilitate the sales. Fortunately, during the foreclosure proceedings the project was well maintained by the interim lender, and my out-of-pocket expenses were nominal. However, this can be an extremely risky proposition, which needs to be thoroughly examined prior to standing behind these extensive warranties.

A condominium project which I purchased several years ago had been vacant for several years during foreclosure and litigation. During this idle period much vandalism had taken place, tarnishing the image of the venture to the point of public embarrassment. Under these circumstances I was able to acquire for $860,000 a development in which the lending institution had a $2,500,000 investment. Even though I anticipated that the sellout and project acceptance would be time-consuming, I had ample cushion in my purchase price in the event that I had been overly optimistic in my initial expectations.

In the final analysis, the best properties for turning around are those located in prime areas, geared toward specific markets broad enough to overcome previously detrimental images. Many prospective renters and purchasers will not even consider distressed projects unless generous concessions are made in the initial pricing.

When and How Much You Should Discount Distressed Property

Some potential turnarounds are irresistible, even to a developer with the skepticism I have taken no pains to hide in this chapter. I recently acquired and completed a $2,500,000 condominium project which I resold in 48 hours. Prior to closing, I had it appraised to determine the sales value to be expected on completion. Knowing that completing the project would take me approximately nine months due to the complications of construction and financing, I instructed the brokerage firm to market the project at lower than appraised value in order to initially stimulate sales. When I acquired the project, its image was not first rate, and the appraisal reflected this, proving to be approximately 15% below the prevailing market value.

Many of the initial sales were not closed, since the units were optioned by speculators who never intended to take occupancy of the units and who could not obtain financing without being owner-occupants. I had anticipated this, and it gave me the opportunity to rescind these sales contracts and subsequently resell the remaining condominiums at higher prices.

Distressed property never fully commands a resale price comparable to what you can obtain from a property you develop from its inception. The stigma of distress can be attached to a development for many years. I have found that offering a small discount to potential purchasers two-thirds or three-quarters of the way through the upgrading process is probably the most lucrative way to merchandise these properties. Not only are purchasers attracted by the added value that they are receiving for their money, but you, the developer, are likewise spared much of the time and effort required to achieve that last 25% to 30% of the development's upside potential. This approach, which was the thrust of my 48-hour sellout, created the impression in the minds of potential buyers that tremendous bargains could be had. You, as a developer with a successful image, can reinforce this concept with the implication that the final aspect of your turnaround is occupying a disproportionate amount of your time and effort which could be better devoted to other projects. You can, with a carefully conceived strategy, create a maddening rush of potential buyers eager to get in on what they contemplate as bargain-basement prices.

The extent to which you, as a developer are successful in turning distressed properties around may be a measure of your theatrical abilities. However carefully a presentation is prepared for the potential buyers or lenders, you must sell yourself as well as your projections. The developer who can anticipate his customers' needs and desires and project these into his development preferences has the greatest chance for success.

In the next chapter we will be concerned with the "discretionary dollars" of investors who are cognizant of life styles and investment appreciation. Resort developments, second homes, and time-shared projects require special ability and ingenuity in advertising and promotion and, due to their speculative nature, also contribute liberally to the distressed real estate market. In fact, the turnaround artists who succeed in the resort and second-home market may well be the Oscar and Emmy winners of the real estate industry.

15

Creating Quick Value in Resort Developments And Time-Sharing Markets

Analyzing the market for resort properties is one of the most difficult aspects of real estate development. Not only does this specialized activity require larger amounts of equity than any other type of investment, but sophisticated planning is a necessity to attract the "discretionary dollars" of purchasers in these distinct markets. Tagged for recreation, discretionary dollars are particularly vulnerable to the shifting whims of the consuming public, especially when inexpensive package tours and deregulated discount air fares have opened most parts of the world to at least moderate vacation traveling, causing second-home developers to compete on a worldwide basis, particularly at the upper end of the market.

This chapter will analyze this complex market in terms of expected drawing radius and the amenities necessary to attract the potential purchasers. You will learn how the pros determine the economics of major developments, how they overcome initial cash-flow problems and maximize their financing by discounting land contracts, and how they acquire, with little equity, major holdings already existing in lucrative developments. You will learn the inside details for budgeting for advertising and promotion and how to use newspaper, television, and the direct mail media effectively. We will also outline in this chapter the opportunities in resort time-sharing: where to find the projects, how to structure and merchandise them, and how to make them profitable.

How To Successfully Capture the Discretionary Dollar

Since the successful developer of a second-home project is often competing with the organized recreational programs of major resorts, you must immediately concern yourself with the year-round potential your project has to offer. Water-oriented locations in warm climates can readily be developed for year-round use with the addition of limited amenities. In less temperate areas—the Rocky Mountains, the upper Midwest, and New England, where 75% of the skiers migrate during the winter months—large-scale investments must be made in facilities to accommodate and capitalize on the seasonal varieties of recreation.

Whatever the precise limitations may be in some areas, second-home development accounted for approximately 10% of all residential construction in the United States in the last two decades, and the value of acquired acreage far exceeded these in-place construction figures. Most development actually took place in areas no more than a two- to four-hour drive from major metropolitan centers. Second-home communities are being developed surprisingly close to major metropolitan areas, thereby substantially increasing the cost of acquiring the land. This additional land cost can be justified when supporting recreational facilities exist or local conditions can be easily adapted to cater to the recreational needs of the buying public. (See Figure 15-1.)

FIGURE 15-1

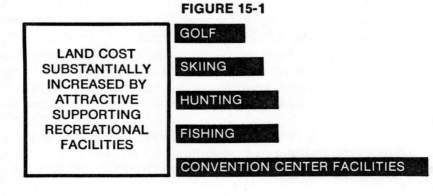

LAND COST SUBSTANTIALLY INCREASED BY ATTRACTIVE SUPPORTING RECREATIONAL FACILITIES	GOLF
	SKIING
	HUNTING
	FISHING
	CONVENTION CENTER FACILITIES

How to Analyze the Resort Market

Sometimes, over short periods of time, properly located second-home developments can become primary-home projects, creating additional value in the raw acreage. I saw this happen over a period of a decade in a major Midwestern metropolitan area of some five million people. Initially, many prominent families had second homes surrounding a large lake within an hour's drive of this city. Within a relatively short period of time, and after the interstate highway system was completed, these large estates were subdivided and converted into suburban areas consisting of primary homes.

The first step in locating a second-home development is to pinpoint an area having the most potential natural recreational facilities and then determining the radius of drawing power that the area might command. The major factors affecting this potential market are:

- existing competition,
- established travel patterns,
- the potential purchasing power of prospective buyers, and
- the established work week of your clientele.

The first two are subject to wide variation dependent upon specific location. The third, buyer affluence, is intrinsic to marketing any real estate development, and the established work week or occupational classifications of the potential purchasers are, in many instances, the key to isolating the market.

Zeroing in on the Weekend Market

The fact that most major companies now recognize ten paid federal holidays, many of them entailing three-day weekends, has created a submarket in the resort development field. In addition, the trend within the last two decades for major employers to provide three or four weeks of paid vacations has opened the second-home market to the blue-collar worker. Shorter work weeks, longer weekends, and paid holidays have combined to encourage the do-it-yourself projects beginning initially with the purchase of a second-home lot.

At this end of the market, the standard approach is for the developer to offer an improved lot, often combined with an option to acquire a prefabricated house without substantial interior improvements. Not having the financial means to acquire a fully completed product, many potential purchasers prefer to finish the interiors themselves. Understandably, the delinquency and foreclosure rates on such developments are often high, certainly much higher than those in more prestigious resort projects, but this is a market growing almost as astronomically as blue-collar wages.

From time to time I have been associated with two resort developments in the Southwest, located approximately 100 miles apart. The smaller project appeals almost exclusively to blue-collar families, and unlike the larger venture, provides extremely limited year-round recreational facilities, with the exception of a mediocre 18-hole golf course. The only visible attraction to the lesser project is the relatively inexpensive value of the lots; in many cases they are being sold for 50% of the value of the improved lots in the larger amenity-oriented development. I am totally convinced that the only attraction or reason for this development's existence is price.

The Lucrative Retiree Market

Many people have spent most of their adult lives in major metropolitan areas and have cultivated an instinct to retreat from these cities during weekends, perhaps purchasing lots in second-home developments on which they plan to build in anticipation of retirement. This line of reasoning has been reinforced for a variety of reasons within the past few decades, not the least of which is the increase in life expectancy. With societal patterns changing the traditional family relationships, older retired couples seldom live out their lives with their children. In addition, pension funds and Social Security have raised the retired individual's ability to travel and acquire a second home.

Retirees are not as distance-conscious as active workers making the most of limited holiday weekends. They have, or expect soon to have, the time to travel, especially to places where the recreational or leisure season is extensive. Not only will they take the time to travel to desirable locations, but they also have the purchasing power to acquire the dwelling units that appeal to them. Most come from urban settings and seek the more relaxed and quieter life style which they associate with warm weather and a pleasant climate. Many do not seek excitement or major entertainment facilities.

Projects such as Sun City in Phoenix, Arizona, have created an environment which many retired individuals actively seek. There, land is inexpensive, the supporting facilities such as restaurants, senior citizens' clubs and health care services are more than adequate, and limited recreational facilities, such as golf courses, are offered. Potential residents are attracted through a series of complimentary fly-in visits and expense-free weekends, accompanied by a multitude of sales presentations by the sponsoring resorts. They acquire building sites, often by making a $1,000 to $2,000 down payment, with the balance paid off in expectation of retirement. Many own their primary residences and understand the value of real estate as a hedge against inflation.

How to Find the Ideal Retiree Location

Some of the most successful real estate projects have been geared exclusively toward retirees living on fixed moderate incomes. These developments are located in somewhat remote areas where land and building costs are relatively inexpensive, and offer limited supporting facilities. From time to time I have been associated with a major retirement community located some 15 miles from a southwestern city of approximately 400,000 people. With over 6,000 retired residents, this development only recently installed an 18-hole golf course and a major shopping center. As is often the case, the market was not demanding of these facilities initially, and the developer was able to channel his funds into more productive areas of promotion and lot development.

The attraction of the Sun Belt for retirees illustrates a truism about the resort and second-home market. People associate recreation with a change of environment, which is often as simple as a change in climate. In my past capacity as occasional consultant for a major resort project offering year-round recreation facilities including an intermediate ski lift, I have found that many long-weekend patrons were drawn from a radius exceeding 300 miles. With their primary residences located in an extremely hot and dry climate, they wished to escape to the cooler, greener mountains year-round, unconcerned about the exceptionally long drive. Without question, the full 5,000 plus acres of this project will eventually be developed.

Vast Opportunities in the Upper Income Markets

The most rapidly expanding market for second homes consists of professionals whose occupations generate considerably more income than they can spend on daily needs. Many have the stability to acquire resort holdings at values ranging into the hundreds of thousands of dollars. Disenchanted with such traditional forms of investment as savings accounts, stocks, or bonds during inflationary periods, they can shift these ample funds into assets with greater potential for appreciation. This market is expanding so rapidly that its actual size is neither completely known nor is it fully predictable.

Distance is not a critical factor in this particular market if air transportation is accessible, but year-round recreational facilities are essential. Especially attracted to these luxury resort areas are middle-aged individuals who are often accompanied by their teen-age children. A developer who offers separate entertainment for both age groups will attract premium prices. While the cost of developing a variety of supporting facilities needed to attract this particular group of investors is high, lenders are interested and reassured by the affluence of these individuals to the point of eagerly backing developers with proven track records for promoting these types of recreational complexes.

I recently visited a major ski resort in the Rocky Mountain area which caters exclusively to professional families, many with teen-age children. The prices that this development was obtaining for its condominium rentals were astounding in relation to the facilities provided and the length of time the resort had been in operation. Much of the land was being sold at values exceeding $500,000 per acre. I believe that the key to their success was their combination of night clubs, after-ski bars, shops, restaurants, and discothèques that catered to each specific age group, thereby permitting the parents and their children to socialize separately in a wide variety of ways.

How to Merchandise Developments Catering to Life Styles

The individual patronizing these luxury resort areas finds the life style offered to be the prime attraction. Compare him, for example, with the person of low income who is purchasing a second-home lot or a small cabin as a self-induced savings program. Still, for both, the potential appreciation is the basic motivation. The difference between the two lies in their ability to support the monthly carrying charges. The investor at the upper end of the market looks for the "in" place, whatever its distance from his primary residence, and will unquestioningly support its dining, entertainment and recreational facilities irrespective of their cost. Whether he is amply financed or simply prefers the vacation-now-and-save-for-retirement-later approach to life, the cost of his vacation becomes almost irrelevant.

Market stratification at this level is frequently defined by distance. A family-oriented resort area geared toward people in the moderate- to upper-income level should be located within 250 miles of the patrons' prime residences. The larger the family, the more important time and driving distance become. This market is by no means restricted to the moderate-income, weekend only families. Second homes located within this radius can be used several months out of the year, or even more extensively when the wage earner commutes and the rest of the family remains at the resort area.

One of my associates is involved in a resort complex combining skiing facilities with a year-round tennis facility. Many families occupy their units extensively during both seasons, while the wage earner commutes to and from his prime place of employment. I met one such owner who travels over 3,000 miles a week by plane in order to spend time with his family at this development.

The Importance of Supporting Amenities and Phasing

Traditionally, second-home developments have been sold to prospective buyers as potentially lucrative long-term investments. Most of these purchasers have no plans to construct residences in the immediate future, so developers often delay construction of the supporting facilities such as:

- golf courses and club houses;
- swimming pools and tennis courts;
- marina facilities;
- restaurants, night clubs; and
- extensive ski lifts.

The failure to do so has led in some cases to legal actions stipulating that the developer must make these substantial cash contributions to a development over a period of time to potentially increase the value of the investor's property. If future amenities are specified without completion dates, the developer becomes subject to having the sales of his lots rescinded by the federal government under provisions of the Interstate Land Sales regulations discussed in Chapter 10.

Many projects are designed for development in phases so that the extension of utilities, roads, and the construction of supporting recreational facilities will not consume large amounts of the developer's capital in the initial stages of the project. Lots in a phased development that lack near-term prospects for utilities should not be actively promoted or initially incorporated into the project, except on a long-term phased basis. This is a desirable situation for both you, as developer, and the potential purchaser, since the lots can be sold and prices based upon the time frame in which the individuals want to build. A buyer who plans to hold a lot until retirement sees no need to initially pay the price of a fully improved tract of land. By subdividing the lots gradually and selectively, the developer can project a viable feeling of construction activity at the rate necessary to stimulate sales.

I am currently trying to acquire several choice sites in a major resort located in the Southwest. The developers initially improved a large number of lots in relation to the sales that were to be eventually generated from the project. These large numbers of high-density sites were fully developed initially to the neglect of adjacent lower-density lots, and were provided with all utilities. The maturity of the project now dictates investing substantial sums in the areas that were passed over, due to the initial failure of the market to absorb the condominium lots.

Conserving Up-Front Funds by Utilizing Exchange-Into Provisions

Most respectable projects establish a program whereby a person who purchases a site in an area without utilities can exchange his property for a comparable parcel with utilities when he is ready to build. Alternatively, one who buys in an improved area with utilities and does not construct within a given period of time is often required to exchange his property for a parcel in a non-utility area. The exchange is normally accomplished on an appraisal basis reflecting the appreciation of the initial purchase price at the time the trade is effectuated, since land prices in most projects are uniformly marked up at periodic intervals.

A certain percentage of purchasers choose never to build for one reason or another, and the potential resalability of these lots constitutes the speculative element in second-home developments promoted for investment and appreciation purposes. The investor who attempts to resell his lot through an outside real estate agent must often compete with the company that initially developed it, a situation usually leading to complete frustration. Furthermore, many large second-home development companies have become involved in costly lawsuits because they failed to maintain a resale market for lots they initially merchandised.

This combination of possibilities makes it important for you, the developer, to maintain a staff for reselling these second-home lots, even if your efforts amount to little more than a token gesture. The downfall of many second-home projects has been a disappointed individual who made a sizable initial investment and subsequent, sometimes burdensome, payments over many years, only to find that his recreation or retirement plans changed or that he had to relocate in another geographic area. Nothing creates an atmosphere for a large class-action lawsuit more than the developer's failure to provide either the proposed recreational facilities or the means for reselling unimproved lots.

I recently witnessed the acquisition of a major resort development by a large New York Stock Exchange firm which instituted a program of offering available lots and homes in the development for resale. While the marketing vehicle was not totally successful, the program had an amazing effect on the sale of the newly developed lots. Potential buyers of this investment property apparently took great reassurance from the existence of a secondary resale market vehicle.

Establishing Density Requirements and Architectural Standards

Most second-home projects set minimum sizes and architectural standards, and also segregate the development areas. At one extreme may be a section catering exclusively to luxury homes of specified construction standards, while at the other may be an area for overnight campers or mobile homes. Typically, sections are exclusively designated for:

- high-density condominiums;
- detached single-family homes;
- rental units;
- commercial and retail;
- employee housing;
- hotels; and
- recreational vehicles.

This stratification is necessary in order to hold the value of each individual segment within itself, as many resort projects are located in counties where little or no formal zoning laws prevail. It also parallels the allocation of prime sites providing scenic views or accessiblity to shorelines or recreation facilities.

While all successful resort projects capitalize as fully as possible upon the natural resources, the choice of the salable amenities provides the developer with many difficult decisions. The most expensive improvements, and those which are potentially the most rewarding, are golf courses, convention facilities, and ski areas. Backup facilities, such as tennis courts and trails for hiking, horseback riding, and recreational vehicles, normally only serve to support the more expensive facilities, and are not considered to be in the make-or-break category for any second-home development.

As we have mentioned previously, urban withdrawal plays a large role in the selection of many second homes, even though some of the most successful projects have nothing more to offer than a view of the ocean or a private beach. I am currently associated with a group of individuals who are developing condominiums in a Mexican resort area. The simple, basic units being sold provide spectacular views along with miles of beach frontage and unlimited fishing and scuba diving. Constructed by Mexican laborers who are paid only a fraction of what their U.S. counterparts earn, the units are commanding a square-foot sales price far exceeding that of most resort developments in the continental United States.

The Economics of Theme Parks and Large Developments

Many developers are shifting away from the traditional land sales approach to recreational housing and aiming for a narrower market involving the creation of multi-million dollar man-made attractions. Major corporations are developing mammoth theme parks which serve as destination points where sizable investment funds are being committed for hotels, camp sites, and parks for recreational vehicles. The major facilities are owned by these corporations. Most of the traveling public lodge at these developments for extended periods, at considerable expense. Large initial investments are required to augment these attractions thereby extending the stay of their patrons, especially if the climate of the area limits or prohibits attendance during undesirable times of the year.

A lucrative type of resort activity is being generated at the outer fringe of these new destination points. Successful developers are converting from land sales operations to the development of condominium hotels, and time-sharing ventures, thus providing the finished product to the end user, a service that is not being offered by the major developer. These projects can often be presold after a model unit or two is constructed, without the speculative element typical of the large development operations. These projects permit an accurate prediction of the absorption rate and considerably limit your exposure on the basis of established presales.

Buying into a major resort without having to provide the infrastructure eliminates one of the major stumbling blocks found in resort development, that being where you must sell the improved lots to purchasers and carry the financing on the basis of limited down payments. In order to raise development funds, this often means that the purchase contract must be sold to a lending institution at a substantial discount and on a full recourse basis. Many seasoned firms with traditional land development orientation have found themselves in financial trouble because of their lot sales programs. Small down payments, combined with long amortizations and sizable upfront real estate commissions which are traditionally burdensome, often create a negative cash flow, at least during the initial period of development. I have seen many cases where the commissions paid to a salesman over the first 24 to 36 months exceeded the total funds paid in on the land contract. When condominiums, hotels, recreational vehicle parks, and time-sharing ventures are developed in conjunction with major resort projects, this cash-flow deficit can usually be eliminated to a large extent. Permanent financing, properly structured, usually permits you, as the developer, to receive 100% of the sales proceeds at closing on those improved portions of the development.

How to Successfully Buy into Major Resort Projects

In order to attract patrons who will pay premium prices, many major resort projects must commit sizable up-front funds for such things as ski areas, marina facilities, shopping centers, restaurants, night clubs, and related attractions. These supporting features can represent investments running into the tens of millions of dollars when spread out over the life of the development. These sophisticated amenities are often left to the managerial ability of the major developer, which normally is a sophisticated and well-financed corporation.

Herein lies a challenging opportunity for the small- to medium-sized developer. By purchasing a tract within the major development, you can participate in the action with a smaller, more manageable, self-contained and easily financeable project. Many of the larger resort development companies are content to absorb the up-front costs for the major facilities, selling off specific areas to local or regional developers for condominiums, recreation parks, or motels. If you acquire a tract early in the development of a resort project, you, as an aggressive developer, can often obtain favorable terms which permit you to phase a fairly large project with a minimal amount of up-front money.

I was recently offered an opportunity to acquire a sizable tract designated for condominiums in a relatively new major resort development, and as of this writing I am still considering the purchase. Like many of the newer resort areas, this particular development is not a sure bet, but the profits generated could be phenomenal in relation to the up-front equity if the projected sales for the condominiums are close to being accurate. The patronage generated by the successful development of a second-home project is potentially one of the most lucrative avenues for real estate investment, as these major development corporations are willing to option choice sites and provide the necessary leverage that accompanies successful development.

The Advantages and Drawbacks of Leverage

High-amenity resort development areas can often provide an interesting and leveraged financing vehicle to purchasers of block space. Because of the large initial commitments of the major developers, lending institutions will normally also fund to secondary developers if the prime company is seasoned, legitimate, and if they can be assured that facilities will be developed according to a predetermined plan. Many major development companies also make interim and permanent financing available to block purchasers in order to initially stimulate their sales. Additionally, the clamor to get in on the ground floor of a new project often attracts travel clubs, commercial airlines, and promoters of charter flights and package tours, all of which can also stimulate sales considerably.

However, all is not wine and roses in resort development. Beneath the glamour is the hard-nosed attitude of many of the traditional lending institutions, which surfaces particularly in times of tight money. A second home can be a dispensable luxury and therefore prone to foreclosure proceedings. When mortgage funds evaporate, single-family dwellings intended for use as primary residences are always considered safer investments. Even when mortgage funds are plentiful, second homes normally require larger down payments, carry higher interest rates, and have shorter amortization schedules than do primary residences.

I was recently approached by a savings and loan with a proposition to joint-venture a condominium project in a small, exclusive year-round resort area. Over the years, this lender had financed many second homes in this particular market, which provided excellent skiing and other year-round recreation facilities. As evidence of the soundness of their investments amassed, their faith in the area solidified. I am exploring several condominium sites in that particular resort area, optioning these tracts of land for this express purpose.

The Advantages of Selling Land Contracts to Accelerate Development

A major problem in developing resort subdivisions is initially obtaining and constantly maintaining the appropriate amount of financing to complete the preliminary construction and to carry or support further development of the project until the sales generate enough internal cash flow for the project to become self sufficient. To do this on a major tract usually requires structuring the purchase agreement in such a fashion that the immediately developable land is delivered unencumbered to either the lenders or the cash purchasers.

The high commissions often needed to attract qualified salespeople also can potentially erode your initial cash flow and detrimentally dictate your pricing. Initial pricing of resort properties must be high enough to establish a precedent for commanding even higher prices at a later date on the balance of the project. When commissions are high in relation to the sales price, as is the case in the initial phases where developer financing is prevalent, salespeople often trump up phony contracts in order to generate commissions. Once the commissions have been paid, these bogus buyers immediately forfeit on their obligations.

Because this practice is widespread, developers must often establish a rapport with the lending institutions that purchase these defaulted contracts, many of which are acquired at prices substantially discounted from their retail value. The purchasers of resort property normally execute non-recourse notes, leaving the developer with the improved land in the event of default. To successfully merchandise these contracts to lending institutions on the most favorable of terms, you normally have a recourse position on these notes, which can involve tying up a substantial line of credit on a major project.

On the other hand, reacquiring these properties is not complicated, as the mechanics for legally foreclosing and repossessing a land contract are quite simple. If the reacquired property has substantial value, you can take it back and normally resell it at a higher price. Several years ago I was associated with a major resort development in the Rocky Mountain region which had a controlling interest in a bank as a subsidiary company. In phasing their development, they periodically sold seasoned paper in this project to their subsidiary lending institution in order to raise the necessary construction funds. Through ownership of the lending institution, they rarely had to discount the land contracts substantially.

How to Analyze the Default Ratio on Sales Contracts

Because improved and desirable land has a tendency to appreciate with time, a multitude of lending institutions specialize in purchasing seasoned land contracts, especially in well-recognized locations. If a project is well-conceived and executed, selling off a portion of your inventory of contracts to lenders can generate the cash to continue improving the infrastructure, thus creating additional sales. In respectable projects where the proper amenities are provided on a timely basis, the default rate on these contracts averages around 5%.

This low default rate is by no means a universal average. When projects are merchandised through the use of direct mail, where the property is purchased sight unseen with a small down payment, the contract rescissions are often in excess of 25%. Lending institutions cease to acquire these contracts when the default rates are high, and begin to lose confidence in the developer as well. Contract rescissions also have a tendency to accelerate under these conditions. If individuals who have acquired lots in a development discover that the default rate is high and constantly accelerating, they tend to go into default themselves.

Four years ago, a major financial institution based in the Midwest approached me to acquire and complete the balance of a development of a small second-home subdivision in a fairly remote and mountainous area. This institution had purchased most of the land contracts from the initial developer and found, after a period of years, that they were holding an increasing amount of defaulted and worthless paper. After a long and detailed study of the project, I saw little or no possibility of turning the development around. To this day this lending institution holds millions of dollars worth of defaulted land contracts on this project.

How Modular Housing Eliminates Many Development Risks

A major concern of many lending institutions that actively finance second-home developments, is that loans on resort properties are not salable in the secondary money market. The FHA, the VA, and Fanny Mae, as a general rule, will not purchase these commitments. The loan portfolio liquidity factor is changing to some degree with larger developments where the collateral value is apparent, permitting mortgages to be sold in large pools when they are accumulated by the lending institutions. In practice, this happens only in major developments, where the resale values are well established.

In less recognized resort areas, modular homes can be beneficial to the potential developer. The more remote the location, the more difficult it is to obtain the appropriate contractor to complete a project in a given period of time at a realistic and predictable price. Taking this into account, several modular home manufacturers have structured an almost complete turnkey package for construction in resort areas, offering units that can be purchased, delivered, and assembled quickly. Not only does this practice minimize your exposure, but manufacturers of modular housing can often arrange for permanent financing for the end buyers. During the initial stages of development, they can often locate sources of interim financing for the developer as well. After the initial units are constructed and sold, the balance of the financing is somewhat simplified and easier to obtain.

Several years ago, I was associated with a manufacturer of modular homes who anticipated a major sales effort in a particular resort area. This firm made sizable deposits in one of the local banks and briefly discussed the possibility of opening a small subsidiary plant in the area in an attempt to get the financial community to fund the permanent loans on their homes. Even from my vantage point on the periphery of the activity, it became apparent that the financing for their modular units was made quite attractive. In fact, it was far more interesting than the units themselves. With less than an enthusiastic market acceptance, the modular manufacturer eventually abandoned the area altogether.

How to Budget for Advertising and Promotion

A traditionally successful method of promoting resort developments used in various cities throughout the United States is to invite select individuals to cocktail or dinner parties or other formal presentations. At these functions the most likely prospects are screened and complimentarily flown to the site of the resort. In the colder parts of the country these promotions take place during the winter months when second-home resorts in the warmer sections are particularly attractive. Celebrities are often used to attract prospective buyers, thus lending credibility to the project.

When this method of promotion is advanced, you can estimate that 30% to 35% of the total sales value of the project will go into an advertising and promotion budget. This traditionally breaks down into:

- 10% to 15% for direct sales commissions,
- 10% for institutional advertising and promotion, and
- 10% for overhead of the sales operation.

Overall allocation or distribution of the sales proceeds has historically been as follows:

- 1/3 of sales value for promotion,
- 1/3 of value for acquiring the land and improving it, and
- 1/3 of value for developer's profits.

FIGURE 15-2

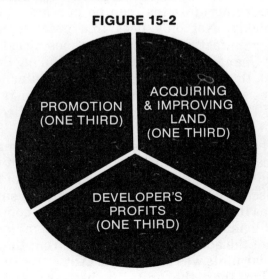

Large land sales operations function best when an organization has the funding to develop a project that creates a totally captive market. In Florida, for example, many new developments are not as successful as their predecessors which were put on the market when buyers lacked the ability to shop for comparable projects once they arrived at a given destination point on a sales promotion. In areas where these multiple resorts exist, developers no longer have the only game in town.

How to Use Newspapers, Television, and Direct Mail Advertising

Newspaper and television advertising, often combined with direct mail, is still the most effective and cost-efficient way to promote a second-home resort. Successful developers have singled out the appropriate markets and used weekly news magazines, various sporting periodicals, and Sunday supplements in newspapers, concentrating on the regional editions exclusively. Through these media they can usually reach a large potential market at a relatively low cost per subscriber.

An investor recently contacted me about acquiring an interest in a resort area promoted exclusively through the regional editions of a TV listings magazine. An attractive full-page ad with a detachable perforated self-addressed return postcard was the only vehicle used to generate the initial leads. The developer was quite successful, using a very limited budget for a project that was, in my estimation, second-rate at best.

Another form of project solicitation, direct telephone, has historically had a very low ratio of closings to initial contacts, but is also relatively inexpensive, as telephone bank solicitors are often paid on a partial commission basis. In addition to a small hourly draw, telephone solicitors are compensated on a percentage of the closings generated through their efforts. These solicitation groups scan the yellow pages of the telephone book for a given metropolitan area, contacting the potentially high-income groups, such as doctors, lawyers, and other professionals. They also have access to numerous mailing lists obtained from national organizations that specialize in providing names of individuals in the appropriate income brackets to purchase the product being offered for sale.

The advertising methods for selling resort developments that we have mentioned are basically employed in all aspects of the business.

For example, the Union Pacific Railroad promoted its Sun Valley development some forty years ago with movie tie-ins prior to the advent of television, yet they still relied heavily on direct mail contacts to the affluent individuals who rode their trains. The resort development business has traditionally depended upon sophisticated advertising to survive. The time-sharing projects which we will consider next are probably utilizing the greatest extremes of promotional ingenuity found in the business today.

New Opportunities in Time-Sharing

Time-sharing, or "interval ownership," is a new concept being applied to resort development. It offers a flexible, inexpensive package to an individual who desires to travel to one specific resort or a series of locations with a limited up-front equity investment. It is gaining popularity especially in vacation areas that are considered destination points, where it is being touted by the developers as the ultimate method to generate sizable profits.

Although the phrase "time-sharing" accurately describes the limitation of occupancy of these condominium projects in which a perpetual interest is not usually sold, the term is otherwise a misnomer. Individuals investing in these ventures are actually only prepaying their vacations. They purchase an interest in a unit for the specified period of years during which they expect to be utilizing their investment. The extreme limitations of ownership preclude much of the possibility for appreciation, which characterizes other forms of real estate holdings, and the promoters in the process become very well-compensated innkeepers.

The most successful time-share developments use existing facilities, such as hotels or condominiums, which have proven track records of occupancy at different periods of time during the desirable seasons. The average stay of the guests is easily predictable from past operating history, and can be converted readily into a salable time-sharing interval. A very talented appraiser with whom I have had many business dealings recently purchased an old established resort with limited recreational facilities, consisting of only a few dozen units. Patrons of this small resort kept returning year after year, and many were on a first-name basis. Offering a time-sharing plan to this tightly knit group of established guests was a relatively simple and risk-free venture.

How to Sell the Time-Share Unit

Time-sharing is promoted as an effective hedge against inflation. By participating, the purchasers obtain prepaid vacations over extended periods of time at a one-time fixed investment rate. Many are not limited to one location for the 15 or 20 years of their contractual agreement, since major time-share projects have reciprocal arrangements with their counterparts worldwide.

I am currently contemplating a time-share arrangement as a joint venture with an exclusive guest ranch. Over half of the people who have patronized this ranch have sufficient funds to purchase a time-shared unit. In this particular project there are 72 potentially time-shared units occupiable over nine months of the year. If the project is time-shared at one-week intervals, I will need 2,700 purchasers in order to successfully merchandise the project. I am currently analyzing the length of time previous guests have stayed, and the frequency with which they have returned, to confirm my suspicions that this particular resort constitutes a true destination point ideal for time-sharing.

How to Structure the Time-Share Period

Time-share programs are merchandised for use either at a fixed weekly or biweekly period during an open or floating period of occupancy. Prices vary both by the unit and the time contracted for, with the prime season commanding the highest prices.

Under the open or floating arrangement, advance reservations must be made for you to specifically occupy your unit during either the high or the low seasons. Currently, most projects operate under this concept, especially those that are tied into reciprocal arrangements with other resorts. Even though exchange privileges can complicate resort time-sharing, they do provide the management with considerable flexibility. Any individual developing a time-sharing project incorporating exchange privileges must be alert to the fact that occupants of less desirable vacation areas tend to gravitate toward the more attractive ones.

Having established a type and need for a project and an actual destination point, you, as a potential developer of a time-sharing program, must analyze the following salient factors:

- the type of potential purchaser;
- his ability to acquire;

- the normal length of his occupancy, and
- the desired amenities.

The choice between fixed and floating intervals will be determined by the normal patterns of occupancy for the area and the project. When potential purchasers have fixed periods of time when they must occupy their investment, a program of floating occupancy dates does not function well, particularly if the area is a popular one.

How to Retain a Lucrative Management Contract

The small resort hotel previously mentioned is an obvious candidate for fixed ownership periods which were, in reality, worked out over a decade or more by a basically congenial and harmonious group of guests. Educated and sometimes speculative estimations must be made with the newer projects, such as the previously mentioned condominium project at the Mexican resort with which I am associated. Where an existing and established pattern exists, the astute developer can analyze the trend and capitalize upon it.

Sizable profits can be generated by the individual who takes this long-term vacation lease approach to real estate development. Throughout the period of interval ownership, you retain the management contract and own the residual value of the property at the end of the time-shared period. One then has several interesting alternatives: selling to another developer, converting permanently to condominiums, or starting the process of time-sharing all over again.

The potential resale value is one of the factors I am seriously weighing in deciding whether or not to time-share the ranch property previously described. During the period of interval ownership I would be able to retain fee title to the units and thus fully depreciate them in a relatively short period of time. At the end of the time-shared period, I could offer this property for sale as a whole unit or sell my interest in the reversion with relatively minor tax consequences. The lack of dealer status and potential capital gains treatment add a whole new dimension to the investment outlook for time-shared developments.

Major Problems Found in Time-Sharing

Three obvious problems surface and are peculiar to time-shared projects as contrasted with whole-unit condominium sales:

- marketing and promotion costs,
- the cost of educating potential purchasers, and
- startup and other up-front costs.

Marketing costs can average between 30% and 40% of the gross sales price because each unit has multiple owners, often as many as 50 with year-round occupancy at one-week intervals. Educating buyers to the condominium rules, difficult at best in a primary residence development, is compounded by the sheer numbers and even made more complex with the floating interval ownership and operation. Purchasers must not only be educated to the ways of peaceful coexistence, but must also comprehend fully what they are acquiring so that the limitations inherent in their purchases are fully understood. Up-front development costs are high because the speculative element of such ventures and the managerial dexterity required prompts many lending institutions to place heavy financial requirements on their developers.

All of the above-mentioned complications are offset by the potential rewards derived from organizing a successful time-shared venture. Marketing costs are offset by the fact that time-shared units generate between two and four times the per-square-foot revenue obtained in whole-unit developments. Time-shared units sell with smaller down payments, making the market considerably larger. When an interval ownership project is completely sold out, permanent financing usually isn't needed, meaning that the development is not subject to interest rate fluctuations. You, as the developer, have a lucrative management contract during the interval ownership and retain control throughout this period, taking all of your profits up front. If you are able to acquire several sizable time-sharing ventures over a period of years, you probably will never need to look for other gainful employment during your lifetime.

The potential of time-sharing is exciting because its limitations have yet to be established. Like other forms of resort development, it is subject to predictable complications in the present economic and social climate, many of which will be projected in the next chapter, where we will take a broad look at the emerging investment trends to be found during the decade of the eighties.

16

An Overview for Investment Real Estate In the 1980's

The compounded effects of inflation, which has so dominated the economic picture from the time this book was first conceived, will persist through the 1980's. When and if the tide is stemmed, the necessity of living with the consequences of what has already taken place will remain. The foregoing chapters have called attention to the lessons of the past, tempering them with expectations of the future. Immediately obvious is the restructuring of the long-term debt markets that began some years ago. Few vestiges of the more comfortable practices of the past will remain throughout the decade of the 1980's.

Equally as obvious from the foregoing pages is the shifting of priorities for location of real estate ventures due to the energy shortages combined with the overextension of municipalities and their suburbs. The in-fill sites so largely passed over in the mad scramble of the 60's and 70's to develop the suburbs will constitute some of the most lucrative development areas of the 80's. Closely associated will be the reclamation of older buildings in the residential and commercial sectors, permitting creative individuals the opportunity to optimize existing structures, thereby cutting lead time, construction costs and exposure.

A Broad Overview for the 1980's

In the next decade, commerce and industry will continue to migrate to the South, Southwest and Southeast at the expense of the industrial Northeast and Midwest. Inexpensive labor, lower bases of taxation, and abundant supplies of energy will be even more of an attraction than they have been in the past.

Many of these factors, associated to a large degree with inflation, will substantially affect the public at large as well as you, the developer of real estate properties. An across-the-board stratification of housing markets is on the immediate horizon, as the average middle-income family will be priced out of owning an affordable home. Substantial profits will be made on the upper and lower ends of the market, ranging from mobile parks on the low spectrum to luxury condominium developments and secondary residences at the upper ranges.

This chapter begins with an overview of the residential, commercial and industrial sectors with emphasis on the important trends of the 1980's. From there it proceeds to a detailed analysis of changes in mortgage financing directly associated with and tied to the inflationary process. The balance of the chapter is devoted to a consideration of the various means by which an investor can maintain a realistic equity position during inflationary periods, stressing the relationship between inflated values, appreciation, predictable cash flow, and replacement costs.

Where the Action Will Be in the 1980's

The housing market will continue to be the most lucrative and challenging sector in the 1980's since it is ten times as large as any other aspect of the real estate market. However, the stratification which characterized it in the previous decade will be even more pronounced. The potential market for new housing will be in excess of $50 billion per year, and 75% to 80% of that market will be developed for the traditional single-family, detached, or condominium, for-sale dwelling unit.

During the latter part of the 1970's, the so-called Sun Belt accounted for more than three-quarters of all new residential construction. These areas of the country, the West, Southwest, the

South and Southeast, will continue to dominate the market for new housing at the expense of the industrial Northeast and Midwest. Whatever the area, new housing will be very much subject to floating and widely fluctuating mortgage rates tracking the economic cycles, showing, however, tremendous potential during periods of economic stability and strength.

The average developer will encounter difficulties during weak or slack periods in the housing cycle, as he will be denied the continuity of permanent and interim financing that permitted him to operate countercyclically in the past. Skillful timing will be essential to the successful continuity of your operation. The demand for new housing, after all, is continuous. What will be erratic is the supply of money to satisfy that ever-increasing market. The pent-up demand created at the bottom of the market can result in astronomical prices and profits in relation to your costs, when the cycle eventually peaks.

In the latter part of the 1970's, 85% of all new single-family residential units were purchased by people in the top 25% of income levels. This trend will continue, and needs careful and continuous monitoring. The upper ranges of the housing market have always been the strongest and most lucrative for the average developer. The middle range of new housing construction will inevitably dwindle, perhaps to the point of total evaporation, especially in the more stagnant economic areas. There will be periods of extremely tight money and high interest rates when conceivably no more than 5% to 10% of the population can afford new housing.

As long as creative vehicles for permanent financing are available, low-cost housing will constitute a strong and viable market. However, as the affordable financing deteriorates, which it must, so will the market. One thinks, of course, of mobile home parks at the lowest end of this range. Special problems may exist there for the average developer. Many of the manufacturers of mobile homes have become project developers. Not only do some possess the financial staying power needed to weather the cyclical extremes, but many also have the special advantages and abilities of merchandising. Few independent developers can expect to survive such competition where it exists or where it is contemplated.

The Outlook for Business Properties

Office complexes will probably account for about $10 billion annually in new construction and will continue to be one of the outstanding investments during the early part of the 1980's. They will show tremendous appreciation if the leases are of a relatively short duration and can cover increases in operating expenses fully through the use of additional rent escalation clauses. Even in the early stages, many of these projects show an after-tax return on equity of 20% to 25%. If they are held for a decade, many could yield as high as 100% to 200% on your initial investment.

In areas of relatively inexpensive labor and expanding markets for consumer products, such as those in the Southeast and Southwest, industrial parks will multiply during the early part of the 1980's, with about $5 billion being spent annually to construct them. Companies will continue to shift their manufacturing operations out of locations where the cost of living and housing of their middle management people is exorbitant.

Escalating energy costs and the almost complete maturity of the national interstate system will cause considerable change in the development patterns of new major shopping centers. Competition for these developments will intensify, driving distances will greatly affect patronage, and new construction will taper off dramatically during the first half of the decade to about $7 or $8 billion annually. Nonetheless, soundly conceived and well-located shopping centers will continue to provide an important leveraged investment hedge against continuing inflation. A shopping center acquired or developed at today's capitalization rates of 8% to 9% could very well show an overall return of 40% to 50% by the end of the decade with proper financing and carefully structured escalation clauses in the leases.

Travel and Recreation Facilities

Roadside operations will continue to be outstanding investments for the individual with the appropriate management capabilities. Motels and parks for recreational vehicles will show better than average returns during the 1980's. Their income can be adjusted on an almost daily or monthly basis to reflect the higher costs of operation, providing an advantage not found in properties subject to long-term leases. If they are located in well-traveled, rapidly expanding locations and properly managed, they can be expected to show tremendous returns. Like second homes in the resort areas, the most successful operations will be those which minimize driving distance and are close to desirable amenities.

The increasing and often exorbitant costs of taking large families on vacations, especially during peak seasons, will assure the continuation of a lucrative market for the development of second homes in resort areas and for time-shared, interval ownership projects. With an unstable, often unpredictable and inflationary investment market, many individuals with funds in excess of what they can use for their daily needs will be attracted by the potential appreciation found in these quality resort developments. Both wholly owned and time-shared second homes guarantee prepaid vacations at fixed prices, and those with the potential for year-round occupancy will continue to be the most attractive to developers and investors alike. Even today, luxury condominiums in Aspen, Palm Springs, and other "in" places are selling as fast as they can be constructed, at prices often in excess of $500,000. There are many smaller areas throughout the United States that offer the same year-round recreation potential where residential dwellings can be developed and sold at one-third of the square-foot price commanded at the "in" places.

Two possible limitations could surface in the development of recreational real estate. If inflation continues throughout the entire decade, the discretionary dollars currently used for recreation may evaporate altogether as the logical consequence of the continued erosion of the actual purchasing power. Second, environmentalists can conceivably block the development of many potential resort areas, especially if they are near metropolitan centers, in their attempts to preserve and extend orderly growth and open areas. Municipalities will probably support them in their efforts where deeded lots intended for second-home development remain virtually unimproved and could potentially block urban expansion and eventual annexation.

Major Shifts to Look for in the Financial Markets

Extensive and far-reaching changes are taking place in the long-term patterns of mortgage loan commitments. Real estate is no longer a vehicle characterized by localized lending. Loans for major developments are being made by major life insurance companies or lending institutions operating on a regional basis. Most residential loans are sold in the secondary mortgage market, through such vehicles as FNMA, Freddie Mac and the other traditional quasi-government agencies. In many instances, banks and savings and loan associations will be funding future mortgages with medium-term bonds secured by these mortgages. Ultimately, many lending sources may be subject to syndication through the traditional Wall Street fixed debt sources, with their interest rates and amortization subject to such things as:

- short-term bond interest rates;
- bank demand deposits;
- corporate commercial paper rates;
- medium- and long-term bond rates;
- currency exchange rates;
- movement of money through foreign financial markets; and
- fluctuations in gold and silver prices.

Many savings and loans will suffer acute liquidity problems, forcing them into a reorganization or merger status. Very few will continue to commit long-term fixed-rate mortgages in the coming decade.

How the Government Will Control the Financial Markets

With this increasing complexity, we will see a further centralization of financial power, with a high degree of governmental intervention in the long-term mortgage market financing. Traditional lending institutions will be controlled in their basic operations through the Federal Reserve, Federal Home Loan Bank, and the FNMA and GNMA pass-throughs sold in the secondary market. In addition to controlling interest rates, the Federal Reserve will attempt to restrict large outflows of foreign investment capital currently deposited in American financial institutions, by keeping interest rates high.

The Government's attempts to fine-tune the economy through intervention will be a constant source of uncertainty in the money markets, since politics and economics are inseparable. Under these circumstances, it is unlikely that the inflation rate will abate appreciably over the decade. Long-term financing will continue to detrimentally adjust to the trends already under way. Lending institutions will be able to justify higher interest rates, shorter amortizations, or equity kickers on their mortgage commitments.

Alternatively, some may choose a periodic "window" arrangement whereby they have the option of adjusting interest rates upwards to reflect their loss of real dollars as inflation continues to erode the outstanding principal balances of their long-term mortgage commitments.

The Era of Floating Interest Rates Has Arrived

Throughout the decade, the rate of inflation and the cost of money will move in tandem. My best estimate is that the average long-term rates on mortgage commitments will be a minimum of three to four percentage points over the rate of inflation at any given point in time. The basic interest rate on new mortgage commitments will be adjusted through "periodic windows" implemented in a variety of ways:

- Short-term commitments will be subjected to periodic adjustments so that they float with the bond market or treasury bill rates.
- Long-term commitments will be pegged to the secondary market rates such as the FNMA or Freddie Mac current auction prices.
- Residential loans, in order to have resale value in the secondary market, will adjust interest rates every three to five years.
- Commercial loans will be callable at shorter intervals. The average loan will be amortized on a 30-year basis with periodic calls each 5, 10, 15, or 20 years to adjust interest rates to reflect current market conditions.
- Long-term amortizations will still be achievable, but premium interest rates may be the price necessary for obtaining these commitments.

The New Look for Mortgage Vehicles

The newer vehicles, interest on deposits that fluctuates with current treasury bill rates, money-market funds, and bank-sponsored mortgage-secured bonds, will have the overall effect of eliminating the small local traditional lender from major real estate developments. These institutions will be replaced in the secondary resale market by large, quasi-governmental organizations such as FNMA and Freddie Mac or by the cash-abundant life insurance companies. New to the mortgage market will be the pension funds, which will take over where the insolvent real estate investment trusts capitulated. These institutions now have over $500 billion committed in real estate loans, and within the next two decades will be the largest lenders and owners of commercial real estate in the United States. Like many of the established life insurance companies, they have a predictable and stable source of income forthcoming, and reliable prognosticators predict that they will double their investments in real estate holdings in the next five years.

How the Lenders Will Attempt to Participate in Your Ventures

The massive entry of the pension funds into the mortgage market may be the one bright spot on the horizon for long-term interim and permanent financing in the 1980's. The decade of the 1960's and early 1970's was characterized by the bankruptcies created when too much money was chasing too few respectable properties. The REITs and many insurance companies often arbitrarily looked for sizable real estate investment sources to minimize the management of their funds. Large, well-managed companies such as Prudential Life Insurance now have over $15 billion worth of real estate mortgages and investments. Only rarely will they consider any commitment on properties with values under $25 million.

In the 1980's, many, if not a majority of lenders, will require some form of equity participation, floating interest rates, or loans callable at shorter intervals. Indications are that they will protect the constant value of the dollar on their mortgages in at least one of three ways:

- by requiring an equity kicker after the project is sold;
- by insisting on an option to convert their debt into equity; or
- by taking a percentage of the increased gross income during the term of the loan commitment.

They will use one or a combination of these methods to retain the purchasing power of the long-term, fixed dollars they commit to real estate mortgages. Developers will have no alternative but to adjust their thinking to lender participation when they desire realistic commitments in the future.

The bottom line is that the traditional extended-term, fixed rate, passive mortgage lender will become an equity partner in the 1980's. Developers will have to adjust to either short-term commitments, floating interest rates, or equity participation by lenders. As long as inflation persists, interest rates will remain high, particularly the rates for interim financing, and long term commitments will be extremely difficult to obtain. Banks and savings and loans are now offering certificates of deposit and "all savers certificates" in small denominations which are pegged to the price of such short-term funds as Treasury bills and corporate commercial paper. This vehicle has permitted depositors to shift their funds from low-yielding passbook savings accounts into these higher-yielding certificates of deposit. This additional cost of borrowing will become permanent and will be passed on directly to the real estate developer, and eventually the end consumer.

How to Achieve a Market Return on Equity During Inflationary Periods

During the early and middle part of the 1970's, most knowledgeable real estate investors could obtain a cash return on equity in the low double-digit range, with 12% to 15% not being uncommon. These yields were often achieved on quality properties, many with prime corporate leases at 100% locations. This began to change as the decade wore on, to the degree that some income-producing real estate was being merchandised showing little, or even in some cases a negative, cash return on equity. Seemingly contrary to all logic, these investments often involved fairly sizable equity positions and sophisticated investors. For instance, the Southern California apartment market during this period was attracting investors who often advanced a 30% equity contribution and correspondingly received a 5% or less return on those funds.

In order to explain this unique and puzzling situation, a historical perspective is necessary. In the past 15 years, apartment rents have increased by about 75%. During the same period, the consumer price index has more than doubled, and the cost of replacing most types of real estate has far exceeded the consumer price index. Even the layman in a single-family home is only too conscious of the inflated cost of replacing this asset. The investor acquiring the Southern California apartment building realizes that the increased cost of replacing commercial real estate falls somewhere over the doubling of the consumer price index and under the artificially inflated value of most newly constructed residential dwelling units.

The expenses relating to operating many types of investment properties have increased even faster than the cost of living indexes, especially in the important categories of

- energy;
- mortgage interest;
- real estate taxes;
- maintenance; and
- janitorial services.

The last two factors are, of course, very much affected by the recent Congressional increases in the minimum wage.

How Inflation Can Substantially Reduce the Cash Return on Equity

Rentals have not kept up with reproduction costs, and in many cases have not even stayed ahead of operational costs. The apartment rent multipliers of 5 to 7 times gross income traditionally used in the early to middle 1970's have been replaced by the 10 to 12 times gross income range in many growth-oriented areas of the United States. At the same time, return on equity is being reduced from the 10% to 12% which has been traditional, to the current 6% to 8% range.

So long as high interest rates and double-digit inflation prevail, there is basic and sound justification for the rapid decrease in the return on equity. When the inflationary rate was running at a 5% to 6% annual level in the early 1970's, investors could command double-digit returns on most income-producing property. Now the opposite appears to prevail. During periods of double-digit inflation, the investor seems to take more interest in preserving his basic equity in an asset through the inherent advantages achieved through leverage than he is in receiving an immediate cash return on the equity portion of that investment.

By the same token, an individual purchasing quality corporate bonds with a medium-length maturity will receive an annual yield approximately equal to the current inflationary rate. If you are in a reasonably high tax bracket, you will undoubtedly find that your net cash return is reduced to 7% or 8% after you satisfy your federal tax obligation. When you compare this after-tax return with the current double-digit inflation, you quickly realize that you are basically receiving no return after adjusting your yield for the deflated value of the dollar, and in the process are reducing your principal by some 5% to 6% a year. If your tax bracket is high enough, you can show a reduction of principal of almost 10% per year.

Why Investors Sacrifice Immediate Income for Potential Appreciation

Logically, a changing economic situation brings about a different psychological climate for investing. The higher interest rates obtained during inflationary periods are a tax-deductible expense. The rapid appreciation of the properties adds to their high replacement value, which is tax-deferred until the time of sale. These two factors combine during inflationary periods to create the effect of reducing the overall capitalization rates for prime properties. Furthermore, untaxed appreciation and sizable interest deductions can add up to a much more equitable after-tax return than an investor could achieve through the traditional fixed-income securities.

We have mentioned the inversionary effect that continued inflation has on one's overall equity return: a 10% to 12% return at a 4% to 5% inflation rate, and a 4% to 5% return during a 10% to 12% inflationary period. All things being equal, the lesser up-front cash return on real estate makes more sense on an after-tax basis when the time-deferred, after-tax value of money is considered. The major danger point of this psychology will surface when we reach an extended period of high interest rates combined with single-digit inflation.

What is happening during prolonged periods of inflation is that properties are rapidly approaching a negative leverage position where the overall return before debt service in some cases is less than the constant factor required for interest and amortization. On a project respectably leveraged in today's inflationary market, the cash yield before debt service can be two to three percentage points under the yield necessary for total amortization of the project. The tax-sheltered and appreciation-oriented deals purchased at a return on equity of 3% to 4% under the debt service requirement can conceivably find themselves in trouble, especially if increased operating expenses further erode the cash flow. Until such time as leases can be renewed at substantially higher rates, properties will show a potentially dangerous deficit in operating cash flow.

Will Real Estate Values Become Unrealistic?

Many investors have made large equity investments in properties whose quality or location will not justify rental increases sufficient to cover the increased operating expenses prevalent during prolonged periods of inflation. Such properties, as well as those subject to unsophisticated management, can be expected to provide a permanently low or negative return on the investor's equity.

Supply and demand are currently out of balance, especially in prime growth areas of the United States where investors have been paying exorbitant prices for properties whose values have soared since the 1973-74 real estate fiasco. Unrealistic returns are being assigned to many properties because of inflated reproduction costs, and due to the lackluster performance of the other traditional forms of investment during the same period of time. Ultimately, because of a combination of the many factors mentioned, substantial reductions in the values of some income-producing properties are quite probable.

When the stock market died some 15 years ago, a major American stock was selling at $110 per share. This bluest of blue chips is currently priced at 50% of its then market value. Oddly enough, this current price reflects the fact that this company's earnings have doubled within that same 15-year period. This and a multitude of similar situations lend credence to the current philosophy that the stock market is no longer a realistic place to preserve your equity during an inflationary period. Price-earnings ratios on the Dow Jones averages have dropped from about 15 times earnings during the early 60's to about 7 or 8 times earnings today. An investor who purchased that stock 15 years ago not only lost 50% of his actual cash investment, but he unknowingly sacrificed a tremendous amount in purchasing power with the erosion in the value of the dollar over that same period of time. Even the after-tax return on their increased dividend did not keep up with inflation.

Factors in Inflation That Will Affect Real Estate Investment

Four factors are paramount in analyzing a real estate investment during on inflationary period:

- the stabilized operating income after expenses;
- the amount of leverage or the loan-to-value ratio;
- the loan constant, or the amount of funds necessary to amortize the interest and principal on the loan; and
- the spread or differential between the cost of money and the rate of inflation.

At first analysis, it would appear that an income-producing property would tend to follow the same unattractive path as the stock market, since real estate rentals and expenses would parallel the income and operating expenses of a major corporation. During an inflationary period it would seem that the operating expenses of both would rise at a faster rate than the income. The exception might be found in growth-oriented areas where rental increases could be absorbed more quickly and would be paralleled by the elasticity of demand that a corporation might have which would permit it to increase its prices in order to keep up with or ahead of inflation. If we confine our analysis exclusively to the operating income and expense figures, including the steadily rising loan constants of the last decade, we should expect to find real estate values adjusted for inflation declining just as values have in the stock market.

FIGURE 16-1

| OPERATING INCOME AFTER EXPENSES | AMOUNT OF LEVERAGE OR THE LOAN-TO-VALUE RATIO | AMOUNT OF FUNDS NECESSARY TO AMORTIZE THE INTEREST AND PRINCIPAL OF THE LOAN |

INFLATION'S THREE KEY FACTORS THAT WILL AFFECT REAL ESTATE INVESTMENTS

How Inflation and Leverage Will Affect Your Yield

What has kept the values of investment real estate advancing upward is the fact that the detrimental effects of inflation have been largely offset by the high loan-to-value ratios achieved at relatively low interest rates in most real estate investments. Mortgage payments have traditionally been constant and have been repaid in deflated dollars. For instance, given an overall capitalization rate of 10% and an interest rate of 8%, with 75% loan to value, a typical real estate transaction through the middle or latter part of the 1970's would have been:

Mortgage lender's return, 8% × 75%	= .060
Investor's return on equity, X × 25%	= .25X
Overall capitalization rate	= .10

.25X + .060 = .10, 25 X = .04, X = .0016, or a 16% return on equity.

The current market situation can be summarized as follows, reflecting, say, 10% interest and 8% capitalization rates:

Mortgage lender's return, 10% × 75%   = .075
Investor's return on equity, X × 25%   = .25X
Overall capitalization rate   = .08

.25X + .075 = .08, 25X = .005, X = .0002, or a 2% return on equity.

What we are witnessing is an increased constant loan factor combined with a lower capitalization rate which can be accounted for by the hidden return reflected by the inflated future reproduction values of property. If inflation continues, capitalization rates will further decrease on newly acquired properties. In the event that income cannot be increased substantially over the operating expenses, the cash return to the investor purchasing a property with a low capitalization rate will be eliminated altogether.

How Increasing Rents Will Have a Compounding Effect on Property Values

Investors are currently speculating that they can, over a period of time, increase the net operating income on properties substantially and therefore resell them eventually showing an increased and distinctly positive cash flow. This is predicated on the fact that rents have not kept up with current replacement values and that new projects will not be developed until they do. This concept has proved itself, for instance, in areas of tight residential rental markets such as Southern California, Chicago and Denver. In such places, apartment complexes showing low or negative cash flows after debt service are being purchased and converted into condominiums. The consequent tightening of the rental market has to date produced rental increases far outdistancing the increased operating expenses.

In areas where rent control is in effect or will be implemented, many buildings showing marginal cash returns are being purchased for conversion. While the residential sector is primarily affected at this point, the same theory will eventually apply to office complexes, industrial buildings, and other investment property when the current economic rents do not justify the costs of developing new projects. This level is normally reached when reproduction costs are 25% or more above the current value as determined on an income basis.

At some point the investor must delineate between what is a respectable minimum cash flow under inflationary conditions and what the upside potential for appreciation will be in order to offset that limited cash flow. For the well-capitalized, sophisticated investor, purchasing real estate during a double-digit inflationary period can very well be the most respectable and rewarding long-run approach for protecting one's equity. Purchasing on a negative cash-flow basis is overly speculative to the point of being catastrophic in many instances. You,as an investor, should not consider less than a 5% cash return on equity on a property with a mortgage having a loan-to-value ratio in the 70% to 75% range. This minimum return should be considered only in substantial growth areas where vacancy factors are low and where long-term, non-recourse financing is available. Tax-deferred income will be the major incentive in such a purchase. With a cash return of less than 5%, you have to speculate that sizable appreciation will result through rapidly increased rental income.

Finding Desirable Real Estate Locations in the 1980's

The effect that the price of energy and the potential related energy shortage will have on the values of real estate should be closely monitored by investors and developers during the 1980's. Many in-fill sites in metropolitan areas were overlooked in the previous two decades as developers outdistanced each other in finding desirable suburban locations. The massive freeway systems constructed in the 1950's and 60's made it easy for the developer to find outlying areas where land was relatively inexpensive. Since the trend for the 1980's will be to conserve the time and energy required for commuting, particularly as gasoline prices continue to rise, the in-fill sites which were overlooked in extending urbanization will become increasingly important. Many such locations are relatively inexpensive and can be rezoned readily, as municipalities are becoming receptive to promoting these in-fill properties since, by doing so, they accomplish two things:

- they increase the existing tax base in the community, since in-fill development automatically stimulates local property tax revenues; and
- they increase this base and their revenues without having to make the traditionally large expenditures for extension of utilities and other municipal services.

The flight to the suburbs created an excess capacity in many underutilized metropolitan areas, just as the expansion to outlying areas strained many cities' capacities to extend their municipal facilities, school systems, and utility services. Real estate developments located at in-fill sites can be absorbed into the community with relative ease and provide direct benefits to both the developer and his community.

How the Federal Government Will Help Finance Metropolitan Development

During the decade of the 1980's, the federal government will provide many of the incentives for redeveloping downtown areas and in-fill sites as part of their programs for energy conservation. Among the proposed legislation will be major tax advantages found in the Economic Recovery Tax Act of 1981. Since concentrations of new residential activity will take place, shopping centers will certainly follow. Discontinuation of the urban sprawl will both affect the traffic generated in the most outlying of centers and stimulate the location of new ventures in neglected or passed-over in-fill sites.

The tracts of land needed to project the image of a major development as we have come to know it in the past decades are not as rare in inner city areas as you might initially expect. With a little ingenuity, many developers will find opportunities to lease valuable tracts of land that have been held for generations by the old established families or in trusts. With a properly structured land lease, you, as a developer, can readily conceive a major downtown real estate development with a minimum of up-front expenditures for land acquisition. A land lease with subordination rights permitting you to use the land as collateral for developing a project, presents an even more exciting possibility.

The inevitable return to the inner city will undoubtedly stimulate the use of leased land for real estate development. This concept has proved increasingly lucrative in the past, especially where it lends itself to varying degrees of subordinated leasehold financing. For generations, much of the prime land in the United States has been either underdeveloped or passed over by the urbanization movement. Negotiating long-term leases on such properties can and should be one of the more lucrative developmental activities of the 1980's.

How the Inflow of Foreign Capital Will Affect Real Estate Values

Selected areas of the United States real estate market have attracted an abundance of foreign capital. California has been a virtual haven for the Canadians, Texas for investors from the OPEC countries, and Florida for Central and South Americans. Much of the property acquired by these foreign investors has been sold at exorbitant prices during periods when prices were unrealistically inflated by this excessive and artificial foreign interest. Except for isolated regions, the influence of foreign investment money coming into the United States real estate market has been and will remain totally overestimated.

As previously mentioned, one of the major efforts of the Federal Reserve in the 1980's will be the preventing of large outflows of foreign capital. The basis for this premise and a major reason for stemming at least the Arab outflow can be directly related to the freezing of Iranian assets in U.S. banks. This catastrophic event had a major psychological effect on the long-term real estate investment in the United States by many of the OPEC countries. As a direct result, the majority of Arab investments will be confined to short-term Treasury bills, corporate bonds, or common stock of the major U.S. corporations. All of these investment vehicles can be shifted quickly to provide the necessary liquidity in the event of another OPEC domestic political disaster.

This is not to imply that all foreign investment was dampened or destroyed by the freeze of the Iranian assets. Canadians, in particular, will continue to shift capital without generating any particular publicity either in this country or at home. As the political unrest in Canada continues to accelerate, accompanied by the expansion of large, multinational companies, Canadian investors will continue to acquire sizable holdings, especially in the Sun Belt areas of the United States.

Finding Projects that Will Provide a Hedge Against Inflation

The long-term consequence of protracted inflation is potentially a factor for substantially reducing the standard of living, which some well-read economists and prognosticators believe is long overdue in the United States. This eventuality could have a tremendous impact and severe repercussions on real estate investments and development. In this concluding chapter we have primarily considered new development, which is the usual criterion by which the strength of the real estate industry is judged. In more challenging times, you may well have to think in terms of salvaging rather than demolishing the existing, a trend which is already apparent.

Condominium conversion will inevitably continue, at an increasing rate, as operating costs far outdistance the potential rentals and as rent controls accelerate. Residential properties will be particularly affected. Outpriced in the market for single-family detached homes, many individuals of middle income status will have little or no alternative but to invest in condominiums. This will continually represent an overall decrease in square footage of living space per family, accompanied by a corresponding reduction in the amount of energy consumed. The expanding market for residential condominiums will furthermore be affected by an increasingly precarious and unpredictable apartment market. With rising maintenance and operating costs, constantly threatened by rent control in many areas, the development of new apartment complexes might lose much of its charm as a long-term investment possibility.

In contrast with apartments, office buildings with well-protected, short-term leases, fully covered for inflation, will remain strong investment holdings. Relatively free from potential rent control, they will be less subject to condominium conversion. The tax incentives for renovating existing business property in the inner cities will continue to attract many developers into this investment category.

Summation of the Trends for the 1980's

As has always been prevalent in times of detrimental economic fluctuations, single-purpose structures have suffered and will continue to do so in the 1980's. Those locked into long-term leases allowing limited potential for raising rents will be marginal investments at best. General-purpose properties in exciting areas will continue to appreciate over this and future decades.

With the possibility of declining new construction, the investor seeking existing properties should be cognizant of pockets of undervalued investments which may surface in overdeveloped areas. This phenomenon will be fairly isolated and will be readily apparent under careful market analysis.

You, as an investor in the '80's, will need a hedge against the erosion of your purchasing power. The consequence of this will be the increased stratification at the expense of the middle-income consumer market and total market specialization among successful developers. In today's market, an investment which provides a fully expanded and leveraged hedge against inflation is viable, exciting, and totally worthwhile. One only needs to contemplate that a $100,000 cash return on a real estate investment in the early part of the '80's if not properly protected, might retain only one-third of this value in terms of purchasing power by the end of the decade.

Glossary

Accelerated depreciation – an artificial or accounting loss in the value of one's real estate holding, the benefits of which can be accelerated or increased for tax purposes during the early years of ownership. This differs from functional or economic depreciation in that it is a strictly tax-related concept. It is more commonly referred to as the accelerated cost recovery system under the Economic Recovery Tax Act of 1981.

Air rights – the right to use and acquire open space over and above vacant land or existing structures, usually for a fixed period of time.

At-risk provisions – a term relating to and measuring the equity and mortgage exposure an investor has in a highly leveraged situation. The total amount of the at-risk funds puts a ceiling on the investor's total tax deductions that can be taken over the life of an investment.

Balloon mortgage payment – a mortgage that provides for systematic payments that do not fully amortize the loan over the committed period. A final lump sum payment is called for prior to the full amortization.

Band of investment theory – a method of calculating the return on equity by balancing the given interest rate on any mortgage with the desired return on the equity position, as it relates to the percentage that both contributions make to the overall purchase price or value of an investment.

Book value – the value of a real estate investment as reflected in the accounting books of the owner, not necessarily the value it would bring in the open market. Book value reflects the cost of the asset less the accrued depreciation.

Capital gains – the profit realized from the sale of a capital asset, reflecting the differences between the sales price and the depreciated book value after the asset was held for a one-year period.

Capitalization method – a means of valuating investment real estate by analyzing the income, vacancy factor and operating expenses and then applying a recognized capitalization rate to determine the market value.

Capitalization rate – the desired rate of return found in the local marketplace after analyzing the quality and the predictability of the income stream.

Cash accounting – an accounting method in which the income and expenses are reported as they are received. This differs from the accrual method, where the expenses and income are reported when the obligations are due, and not when the cash is actually received or disbursed.

Component depreciation – a method of depreciation where the various components in a building are determined and depreciated separately. Such items as the shell, roof, mechanical, electrical, tenant improvements, landscaping and personal property all qualify.

Composite depreciation – a method of depreciation in which a useful life of a building is assigned to the entire structure and the depreciation schedule set accordingly. This is the only prevailing method since the Economic Recovery Tax Act of 1981.

Contract rent – the amount of income generated from a rental project by contractual agreement. This differs from economic rent, which is the amount of income that could be generated if the property were not subject to a long-term lease, and could be re-rented at current market rates.

Convertible debt – a mortgage vehicle in which the lender has the option to convert a portion or all of his outstanding mortgage obligation into an equity position at a predetermined point in time.

Cost-of-living indexes – a measurement of the average amount of money spent by consumers to acquire a predetermined list of goods and services. The index uses a base year as 100, as reflected by the indexes compiled by the U.S. Department of Labor.

Cost Recovery System – replaces the old system of depreciation according to useful building lives. The new system enacted under the Reagan administration's Economic Recovery Tax Act of 1981, known as Accelerated Cost Recovery System (ACRS), standardizes all building lives or cost recovery accounting to 15 years, irrespective of the age or type of use.

Dealer – an individual who acquires real estate holdings as a full-time profession, and therefore does not qualify for capital gains treatment on property used in the course of his business.

Demographics – various factors that have a material effect on the long-term viability of a given project. They include the community's economic base, per capita income, population, age distribution, and transportation, to mention a few.

Economic Recovery Tax Act of 1981 - the new Reagan administration's legislation that substantially affects depreciable building lives, the 10% investment tax credit, and the writeoffs obtained on older investment properties.

Encumbrance – a right, claim or lien against a real estate holding. It can take the form of either a first mortgage, a legal judgment, or unpaid taxes, to mention a few.

Equity redemption period – this is a statutory period in which the creditor has a period of time after being foreclosed on to reacquire the property by paying off the outstanding mortgage encumbrances.

Escalation clauses – standard clauses inserted in most commercial leases that provide for periodic rent increases, either based upon government cost-of-living indexes or reflecting actual increases in the tenant's operating expenses.

Exculpatory clause or non-recourse financing – this is a clause inserted in a mortgage document which relieves the debtor of any personal liability for repayment of the mortgage note.

Fanny Mae (FNMA) – an abbreviated name for the Federal National Mortgage Association, which is a lender that purchases mortgages in the secondary market.

Fee simple ownership – provides the owner with clear and marketable title to a property that is being conveyed to the individual by warranty deed. It means that one obtains ownership of a property without any unusual restrictions.

Gap financing – an additional loan obtained by a developer where the interim commitment is not sufficient to complete the project. This is normally a short-term loan which is repaid either from the permanent financing or from the sale of the asset.

GLOSSARY

Gross income – the total amount of funds received from an income property, calculated before operating expenses, depreciation and mortgage payments.

Industrial revenue bonds – a vehicle that can be applied to a limited number of real estate projects, in which highly leveraged non-recourse financing is obtained, where the interest paid on the bonds is exempt to the holders from federal taxation.

Joint tenancy – the method of holding title to real property between two or more individuals, which provides for the right of survivorship.

Land contract or deed of trust – this is a contractual arrangement to purchase real estate on an installment basis, deferring the payments over a predetermined agreed-upon time. The title or deed does not pass to the property under this arrangement until the financial obligation is fully repaid.

Leverage – a concept of using borrowed funds when acquiring investment or residential real estate, where one achieves the maximum return and tax benefits with the minimum amount of personal equity.

Limited partnership – an arrangement that provides limitation of exposure to the passive investors or limited partners, without the double taxation found in the case of corporations, giving the general partner the exposure and complete management authority and responsibility.

Loan-to-value ratio – a method of expressing the degree of financial leverage in which the outstanding mortgage amount is stated in terms of the appraised or market value of the property.

Mortgage amortization – the contractual period of time it takes to pay off the principal on a mortgage on an equal installment basis.

Mortgage constant – the amount of funds needed to repay the annual interest and principal on a mortgage. Normally this is expressed on a basis of constant dollars-per-thousand of mortgage obligation.

Performance and payment bond – a bond issued to a developer to guarantee that the contractor will satisfactorily complete the construction work and that the property will be delivered to the developer free and clear of all liens and encumbrances upon completion.

Present value tables – tables that are structured and show the investor the present value of the stream of the net income received over a predetermined period of time, discounted back to reflect the present value. These tables are figured at various interest rates.

Recapture tax provisions – the amount of sales proceeds that are subject to ordinary income tax upon the sale of a real estate asset, reflecting the difference between the amount of accelerated deductions taken over and above those allocated under the straight-line method of depreciation or cost recovery system.

Rental achievement clauses – these are provisions inserted in mortgages by lenders, requiring that a certain predetermined rental achievement be accomplished prior to permanent funding, both in terms of levels of occupancy and rental income.

Reversionary factor – the hypothetical market value that one utilizes when calculating the overall rate of return based upon the potential resale value and the corresponding effect that appreciation has on an investment's projected yield.

Sale-leaseback arrangement – an agreement where a seller of a property locates a purchaser who acquires his investment and the seller simultaneously enters into a long-term lease obligation providing a fixed return on the property being sold.

Stabilized cash flow – a means whereby the investor predicts over an extended period of time the amount of income any given investment property will generate after the corresponding expenses have been projected and deducted.

Tax-free exchange – a transaction in which two or more properties are traded or exchanged, either having equal value or adjusting the exchanged values by adding or subtracting mortgage obligations or cash equity.

Useful building lives – the periods of time that reflect the remaining economic lives that are allocated to various properties by the Internal Revenue Service. The economic longevity permits an investor to calculate the depreciation schedules. Under the Economic Recovery Tax Act of 1981, the economic life of a building is established at 15 years.

Warranty deed – a conveyance of interest in real property, in which the seller warrants or represents that he has merchantable title to pass on to the buyer.

Wraparound mortgage – a refinancing vehicle that permits the seller, or in some cases a lender, to increase the existing mortgage by adding a second or wraparound mortgage. This concept permits the seller or the lender to have complete control over both the first and second mortgages, and provides the buyer with additional leverage.

Yield – the expected or actual income received on an investment property, expressed as a percentage return on the overall investment or on the equity portion of a leveraged investment.

Index

A

Accelerated method, 84-87
Accounting, 107-108, 143
Amortization, 66-67
Analysis, investment, 21-41 (*see also* Investment analysis)
Annexation, 208-209
Annuities, 40
Apartment conversions:
  advantages, 178
  after-tax benefits, 180-181
  analyze competition, 181-182
  assessments, 190-191
  existing tenants, 192
  homeowners' associations, 190-191
  interim financing, 185-186
  leased land, 189-190
  limit your exposure, 186-187
  make best of older building, 188
  management team, 189
  metering utilities separately, 183-184
  neighborhood, 178-179
  owners' association dues, 184
  permanent financing, 185, 192-194
  potential, sizing up, 182-183
  pricing converted unit, 179-180
  professional expertise, 187-188
  warranties, 184
Apartments:
  accounting methods distort income, 143
  accurate cost analysis, 140-141
  building codes, 147
  construction costs, 147
  expenses affected by inflation, 152
  extreme vacancy, 142
  feasibility and unit size, 139-140
  lenders figure maximum mortgages, 154-155
  location, 138-139
  maintenance costs, 148-149
  mortgage financing, 153-154
  operating expenses and gross income, 149-150
  phony operating statements, 143-144

Apartments (*cont.*)
  predict market, 138
  pricing land as percentage of rents, 145-146
  property taxes, 144
  ratios of debt service to income, 150-152
  reserves for replacement, 152-153
  tenant profiles, 144
  underrented markets, 142
  unit composition, 147
  utilities, 146
  what developer determines, 141
Appraisal, 25-26, 75-76, 206-207
Appreciation, 31-32, 48-49, 319
Architects, 124, 125
Assessments, 190
Attorneys, 187

B

Bidding construction work, 127-128
Break-even point, 52-55
Building codes, 147-148
Building inspection departments, 187-188
Business properties, 311-312

C

Capital gains, 29-30
Capital gains taxes, 33-35
Capitalization rates, 26-27, 55-56
Carrying costs, hidden, 212
Cash flow:
  effect on yield, 30-31
  resale, 36
  stabilized, 26-27
  wraparound mortgages, 78-80
Commercial condominiums:
  after-tax advantages, 258-260
  highly leveraged situations, 260-261
  industrial, 266-267
  inflation, 257-258
  investment package, 268-270